The 4th Industrial Revolution

"Unprecedented and simultaneous advances in artificial intelligence (AI), robotics, the internet of things, autonomous vehicles, 3D printing, nanotechnology, biotechnology, materials science, energy storage, quantum computing and others are redefining industries, blurring traditional boundaries, and creating new opportunities. We have dubbed this the Fourth Industrial Revolution, and it is fundamentally changing the way we live, work and relate to one another."

—Professor Klaus Schwab, 2016

Mark Skilton · Felix Hovsepian

The 4th Industrial Revolution

Responding to the Impact of Artificial Intelligence on Business

Mark Skilton
Warwick Business School
Knowle, Solihull, UK

Felix Hovsepian
Meriden, UK

ISBN 978-3-319-62478-5   ISBN 978-3-319-62479-2   (eBook)
https://doi.org/10.1007/978-3-319-62479-2

Library of Congress Control Number: 2017948314

Cover credit : CatLane/iStock/Getty

Printed on acid-free paper

This Palgrave Macmillan imprint is published by Springer Nature
The registered company is Springer International Publishing AG
The registered company address is: Gewerbestrasse 11, 6330 Cham, Switzerland

Linda, Claire, Emma and David
Felix, to my brother Frederick and sister-in-law Frida

Foreword

It is rare for a week to pass without the press, digital media, radio, or television presenting an article or opinion on the future impact of new technology on society.

The adoption and acceleration of technology in the twentieth and now twenty-first centuries and the way in which it has altered our lives and environments is not a new phenomenon. It is instructive also to remember that many of the advances in biology, particle physics, quantum theory, electronics, computing, communications, and materials science are relatively recent. Decoding the human genome, discovering the Higgs boson, measuring gravitational waves, the micro manufacture of integrated circuits, the development of the Internet, and the mass adoption of personal computers and smart phones have mainly all occurred in the past 10 to 30 years.

Surely, robotics, artificial intelligence, machine learning, the Internet of Things, cyber-physical systems, and the blockchain are just examples of newer technologies that will advance civilizations development for the good? In effect, the so-called 4th Industrial Revolution will continue the progress made by the other three revolutions where steam, electricity, and then electronics took society from mechanical production to mass production and then automation. In the past, comfort has been drawn from the assertion that technology has always created more jobs than it has replaced. This has generally been true, although we should not forget that that job creation did not always land in the communities where employment had been lost.

Pertinently, Elon Musk, the CEO of TESLA, and Bill Gates, the founder of Microsoft, have, respectively, advocated a universal basic income and the taxation of robots. In fact, the majority of articles hitting our airwaves, screens, and papers are concerned more with the impact of technology than the technology itself. What is changing, and therefore generating debate, is the scale and number of new technologies, with all likely to mature in just a few years from now. Add to this the globalization of the workforce, and it is far from certain that businesses and governments will easily respond to very significant impacts on employment generated by the 4th Industrial Revolution.

For businesses, if everyone is out of work, where does the money come from to purchase their goods and products? For governments, how can economies be sustained for the benefit of society if no one is paying tax? These are of course extremes, but make no mistake they are real issues. In getting to grips with these issues, a prerequisite is deep understanding of what the technologies are, and what they might lead to. This book, "The 4th Industrial Revolution," is a well-structured and intelligent account of the myriad of sub-technologies that make up what will for certain be the 4th Revolution. It is based upon extensive research and presents the key concepts in an easy to read format.

For business leaders, the critical question of the moment is "what technologies are emerging, and how do I change my business model and strategy to exploit them, where relevant." This book will help bring color to this vital strategic debate. For policy makers and legislators, the likely scale and impact of mass adoption of fourth generation technology is easier to comprehend with this book to hand.

Warwick, UK   Simon Ricketts
May 2017   Former Group CIO Rolls Royce plc
                                   Senior Non-Executive Director HMRC
                                     Honorary Professor, Information
                                            Systems Management
                                      Warwick Business School, UK

Preface

While writing this, I am listening to music streaming over a cloud provider to my wireless headphones. The passage of connection is through multiple networks, Wi-fi to the local home network that passes through an internet gateway through the Internet service provider and to the music streaming service hosted on the subscribe service cloud datacenter. The return connection passed from the mobile phone to the Bluetooth headphones in milliseconds. If I move to another room or building, the connection automating switches to an available mobile cellular connection service provider and the music continues as I move around. The mobile application is making recommendations alongside each music track I play. It suggested music bands that I have never listened to or seen before. I click on the link and soon hear a similar sounding track. How is it doing this? Matching similar music could be done in several ways. Machine learning is a phrase used in this context that may operate by processing patterns of sound that follows similar characteristics processing the cloud streaming music library to match similar music. On the other hand, matching could be through human recommendations that seeks to crowd source the knowledge of hundreds or thousands or even millions of previously played tracks and preferences, their likes and dislikes, and comments. This could equally be manipulated by human curated tracks choreographed to provide recommendations or codified into the machine algorithms to promote preferences.

This machine intelligence could be used to combine both machine and human preferences to select music tracks that match my preferences. Algorithms play a role in everyday experience, the intelligence in the telecommunications network switching to optimize the service across distributed locations.

In background, the mobile phone device is also managing its battery energy through algorithms that make localized decisions to optimize the battery life and update GPS location tracking. At any given moment, this mobile device might be interacting with me in an active manner, or passively working in the background across many events and services of which I may be unaware. To a member of the public this behavior may appear as both magical and bewildering at the same time. This challenges the definition of what is "the self", freedom and individual choice, and the rapidly evolving role that human-to-machine, and machine-to-machine, interfaces play in our lives.

As human beings, we interact with machines and objects in our environment on a daily basis, and we are just beginning to appreciate the ever-increasing role that machine intelligence plays in that experience. But this story is only part of a much wider transformation in the nature of living, society, and the impact on personal enterprise strategic issues in the twenty-first century.

Warwick, UK   Mark Skilton
May 2017   Felix Hovsepian

Acknowledgements

The development of this book has involved many hours of research and interviews with professional practitioners and academics in the fields of artificial intelligence, computing and business sector expertize. We would like to give recognition and sincere thanks to the following people who gave their time in discussions, sharing thoughts and ideas that have helped us craft this book. Simon Ricketts, former Group CIO, Rolls Royce plc; Prof. Jon Crowcroft, Marconi Professor of Communications Systems, Computer Laboratory, University of Cambridge, UK, Associate Fellow of the Centre for Science and Policy and a Fellow of the Alan Turing Institute, UK.; Dr. Joanna Bryson, Reader/Associate Professor, Department of Computer Science at Bath University, UK, and Affiliate, Center for Information Technology Policy at Princeton University, North America; K.R. Satheesh Kumar, Chairman and Chief Executive Officer, Enzen Global Solutions Private Limited; Dr. Shweta Tripathi, Global Head Knowledge Studio, Enzen; Nikhil Kulkarni, Business Analyst, Enzen; Hayden Povey, Founder and Chief Technology Officer, Secure Thingz Inc; Jonathan Loretto, Global Partner, IBM Xi; Mark Burnett, Head of Innovation and R&D at BearingPoint; Michael Bradshaw, Professor of Global Energy, Warwick Business School, University of Warwick, UK; Sebastian Yuan, Consultant Pediatrician, George Eliot Hospital NHS Trust, UK; Prof. Tim Watson is the Director of the Cyber Security Centre at Warwick Manufacturing Group WMG, University of Warwick, UK; Prof. Abdulhusein Paliwala, Emeritus Professor of Law, School of Law, University of Warwick, Honorary Visiting Professor, Birkbeck University of London; Prof. Youngjin Yoo, is Elizabeth M.

and William C. Treuhaft Professor of Entrepreneurship and professor of information systems in the Department of Design & Innovation at the Weatherhead School of Management, Case Western Reserve University; Dr. Markos Zachariadis is Assistant Professor of Information Systems & Management at Warwick Business School and a FinTech Research Fellow at the Cambridge Centre for Digital Innovation (CDI), University of Cambridge. Dr. Nathan Griffiths Associated Professor in the Department of Computer Science at the University of Warwick and a Royal Society Industry Fellow and member of the machine learning work group.

Disclaimer

Contents

About the Authors

Mark Skilton is Professor of Practice in Information Systems and Management at Warwick Business School, the University of Warwick, UK. He has over 30 years' experience as a professional consultant with a track record in top 1000 Companies in over 20 countries and across multi public, private and start-up sectors. He is also currently a member of the senior executive team as global head of Digital Strategy at Enzen, a premium International Energy & Utility Consultancy based in UK, India, EU, Australia and North America. He has direct Industrial experience of commercial practice leadership, boardroom and investor strategy to program team and transformation management at scale. Mark has previously published two international practitioner books on building the digital enterprise and digital ecosystem architectures. He is a recognized International thought leader in Digital, IoT, automation and AI, cyber-physical systems, cyber security, company strategy, Telecoms, Digital markets and M&A strategies, CxO practices and technology governance. His work and views have been published in the FT, NYT, WSJ, Washington Post, Bloomberg, AP, Mail, NewScientist, Nature, Scientific American and many channels around the world, TV and Radio including BBC, Sky, ITV, Al Jazeera and many others. Mark has an M.B.A. and post graduate qualifications in production engineering, design management, and material sciences from Warwick University, Cambridge University and Sheffield University, UK respectively.

Felix Hovsepian holds a Doctor of Philosophy in Computer Science from University of Warwick, UK and Masters' Degrees in Information Systems Engineering and Mathematical Physics from London South Bank University and King's College, University of London respectively. He is a consulting CTO and a mentor, with over 30 years' experience ranging from software engineering, technology R&D to technology strategy within the education, legal and advanced engineering business sectors. At the start of his academic career, he spent 7+ years undertaking research in AI and Automated Reasoning, and held the position of Professor of Informatics at Western International University, Arizona, North America. In terms of software & systems development, he has designed and built enterprise-level imaging systems for multi-national engineering companies, x-ray imaging systems for dentists, a fingerprint recognition system, as well as BLDC electric controllers for electric vehicles, and AI-based eLearning systems.

Notes on Advisors

Dr. Joanna Bryson is Reader/Associate Professor, Department of Computer Science at Bath University, UK and Affiliate, Center for Information Technology Policy at Princeton University, North America.

Joanna's research focus is in AI ethics, and understanding human sociality more generally. She is working with computer science, politics, and psychology on several major research projects.

Primary research interest includes: Using artificial intelligence to understand natural intelligence. Secondary interests: agent-based modelling of animal societies & cultural evolution, modular models of individual intelligence, AI development methodologies, action selection and dynamic planning, intelligent and cognitive systems (e.g., intelligent environments, artificial companions, game characters), AI & Society. Hobbies include political science, neuroscience, and music.

Her natural science research interests concern distributed intelligence, interacting learning systems, how these come to evolve, and their benefits to both individuals & collectives. My original interest was modularity in individual intelligence—the differences between brain regions in architectural structure, memory and processing—also how animals regulate attention and expression across different goals and actions. This has extended to social learning, culture, and their role in individual behavior; the distribution and retention of intelligence (and other public goods) through a population; and the impacts of communication, social structures, and individual variation on cooperation and collective behavior.

She is also actively research Systems AI–methods for promoting the ease and safety of designing intelligent artefacts. My expertise includes intelligent system integration; action selection; and transparency for real-time AI. Real-time AI includes: robots, smart homes and offices, virtual reality, game characters, and some scientific simulations. Joanna's group is making advanced AI easier to build, understand, and control. Contributions include the Behavior Oriented Design development methodology, POSH action selection, and several systems of synthetic emotions.

Michael Bradshaw Professor of Global Energy, Warwick Business School, University of Warwick, UK. Prof. Bradshaw's academic background is in human geography. He competed his undergraduate training at the University of Birmingham (BSc) and he has an MA from the University of Calgary (Alberta) and he gained his Ph.D. at the University of British Columbia. He works at the interface between economic and political geography, energy studies and international relations. He is a Fellow of the Royal Geographical Society (and past Vice President) and an Academician of the Academy of Social Sciences. He is the author of several journal papers and books including Global Energy Dilemmas,-Energy security, globalization, and climate change, 2014, Polity Press.

Prof. Bradshaw's research has focused on the geopolitical economy of global energy. For almost 20 years he has studied the development of the Sakhalin oil and gas projects in Russia's Far East. This has led to research on energy security in northeast Asia. He is currently examining Russia's plans to develop its liquefied natural gas (LNG) industry. From 2008 to 2011 he was engaged in a program of research examining the relationship between energy security, globalization and climate change, funded by a Leverhulme Trust Major Research Fellowship. In October 2013 Polity Press published his book entitled Global Energy Dilemmas. He is currently completing a research project on Global Gas Security that is funded by the UK Energy Research Centre (UKERC). He plans to continue his research on the global geopolitical economy of the gas industry and is now working on the prospects for the development of shale gas in the UK and Europe (he is involved in a Pan European project on shale gas). He also plans to continue research on North American fossil fuel abundance and the global geopolitics of fossil fuels with further support from UKERC.

Mark Burnett is Head of Innovation and R&D at BearingPoint. Mark has over 20 years experience in technology and innovation. He has published articles on technology trends, innovation and problem solving techniques and spoken at and facilitated discussions at various conferences. His background is in solution design, enterprise architecture, strategy and innovation. He started his career in automotive working on data warehouses and analytics. He later became Chief Architect for a cloud services provider, a global aerospace firm and an international logistics firm before becoming Chief Innovation Officer for a global outsourcing firm. Mark is also an expert on Connected Car where he has provided consulting advice on services ranging from telematics to infotainment working across business, technology and cloud service providers. Mark champions the use of Artificial Intelligence and Machine Learning to augment our understanding of the world from big data and drive the next technical revolution toward more integrated human-machine partnerships. His work has won him a Management Consultant Association Award and he was highly commended in the category of digital consultant of the year 2015.

Jon Crowcroft is the Marconi Professor of Communications Systems, Computer Laboratory, University of Cambridge, UK. He is also Associate Fellow of the Centre for Science and Policy and a Fellow of the Alan Turing Institute, UK. Crowcroft joined the University of Cambridge in 2001, prior to which he was Professor of Networked Systems at University College London in the Computer Science Department.

He is a Fellow of the Royal Society, Fellow of the Association for Computing Machinery, a Chartered Fellow of the British Computer Society, a Fellow of the Institution of Electrical Engineers and a Fellow of the Royal Academy of Engineering, as well as a Fellow of the IEEE. He was a member of the IAB 96–02, and went to the first 50 IETF meetings; was general chair for the ACM SIGCOMM 95–99; is recipient of Sigcomm Award in 2009. He is the Principle Investigator in the Computer Lab for the EU Social Networks project, the EPSRC funded Horizon Digital Economy project, hubbed at Nottingham, the EPSRC funded project on federated sensor nets project FRESNEL, in collaboration with Oxford; and a new 5-year project toward a Carbon Neutral Internet with Leeds. Jon has had major contributions to a number of successful start-up projects, such as the Raspberry Pi and Xen. He has been a member of the Scientific Council of IMDEA Networks since 2007. He is also on advisory board of Max Planck Institute for Software Systems. Jon had written, edited and co-authored a number of books and publications which have been adopted internationally in academic courses, including TCP/IP & Linux Protocol Implementation: Systems Code for the Linux Internet, Internetworking Multimedia and Open Distributed Systems. Jon's research interests include Communications, Multimedia and Social Systems, especially Internet related.

Dr. Nathan Griffiths is a Professor in the Department of Computer Science at the University of Warwick and a Royal Society Industry Fellow and member of the machine learning work group. My primary research areas are multi-agent systems, trust and reputation, distributed systems, social network analysis, machine learning, peer-to-peer and ad-hoc networks, and biological systems. I am a member of the Systems and Software Group and my current research is focused around agent cooperation, self-organization and machine learning. Specifically, I am working on the areas of trust, reputation, coalition formation, motivation, social self-organization, norm emergence, and influence manipulation in social networks. I am also interested in the practical application of cooperative techniques to peer-to-peer (P2P) systems, ad-hoc networks (including MANETs and VANETs), service-oriented computing, and computational biology. Recent work has focused on trust in ad-hoc networks, the use of agents in modelling biology, and the use of social science and evolutionary biology techniques for establishing cooperation in agent-based systems.

Jonathan Loretto Global Partner, IBM Xi, Senior Global Business Intrapreneur, Strategy and Transformational Leader, Mentor, Plug and Play Tech Center. Jonathan is a Senior Business Executive with a solid reputation for delivering forward-thinking business programs that efficiently meet the full potential of new customer, market and technology impacts. He Excellent leadership and strategic planning capabilities that serves fast changing environments that are experiencing rapid changes through growth, acquisition, turnaround and customer transformation. Jonathan is characterized as a highly intelligent complex problem-solver with the ability to communicate clearly and concisely, as well as a talented people leader, motivator and mentor with the ability to nurture excellent relationships across the business at all levels. British born, Jonathan has professional experience working in Europe, Canada, USA, North Asia, South East Asia, India, Australia and New Zealand.

Simon Ricketts For the past 16 years Simon has been the CIO of 3 international FTSE 100 companies, collaborating at Board level and leading successful digital and process transformations in each. He has a reputation for delivering cultural change and performance improvement. He also has extensive experience in running large Information Technology and cyber security functions. In his earlier career, he held Director level roles in logistics, manufacturing and operations.

Simon also has an extensive non-executive career within the private sector and UK government. He was the senior non-executive director at ITNET PLC for 9 years, and at the Strategic Thought Group for 4 years. In government, he has spent 10 years advising on technology and digital transformation, this has included NS&I—7years, and currently HMRC. He is an honorary Professor at Warwick Business School, where he advises and helps develop their digital curriculum, also working closely with Deloitte developing and delivering their "future CIO" master class.

Prof. Tim Watson is the Director of the Cyber Security Centre at WMG within the University of Warwick. With more than twenty-five years' experience in the computing industry and in academia, he has been involved with a wide range of computer systems on several high-profile projects and has acted as a consultant for some of the largest telecoms, power and oil companies. He is an adviser to various parts of the UK government and to several professional and standards bodies. Tim's current research includes EU funded projects on combating cyber-crime, UK MoD research into automated defense, insider threat and secure remote working, and EPSRC funded research, focusing on the protection of critical national infrastructure against cyber-attack. Tim is a regular media commentator on digital forensics and cyber security.

Abbreviations and Acronyms

4IR	The 4th Industrial Revolution
5G	Fifth-generation mobile network and wireless systems
ACL	Agent communication language
Additive Manufacturing	A form of 3D printing
ADELEF	Agent methodology
AFR	Autonomous flying robot
AGI	Artificial general intelligence
AGU	Apollo guidance computer
AI	Artificial intelligence
AIDS	Anomaly-based IDS
AIS	Autonomous intelligent systems
AMOLA	Agent modeling language
AMS	Adjustable manufacturing system
ANN	Artificial neural network
AOSE	Agent-oriented software engineering methodology
API	Application program interface
AR	Augmented reality
ARPARNET	Advanced research projects agency network, originally funded by the IS department of defense built in the late 1960s
ASEME	Agent systems engineering methodology
AIS	Artificial superintelligence
ATM	Automatic teller machine
BDI	Belief-desire-intention
C4.5	Commonly adopted decision tree algorithm
CAD	Computer-aided design

CAM	Computer-aided manufacturing
CAPEX	Capital expenditure
CART	Decision tree inducing algorithm
CCS	Carbon capture and storage
CERN	The European Organization for Nuclear Research
CI	Computational intelligence
CIM	Computer-integrated manufacturing
C-IoT	Critical Internet of Things
CMOS	Complementary metal-oxide-semiconductor
CNN	Convolutional neural network
COP21	The Paris Climate Conference December 2015 is officially known as the 21st Conference of the Parties (or "COP") to the United Nations Framework Convention on Climate Change (UNFCCC)
CPS	Cyber-physical system
CPS-VO	Cyber-Physical System Virtual Organization
CovNet	Convolution network
CTF	Capture the flag
CX	Customer experience design
DarkNet	A UK hacker group
DARPA	U.S. Defense Advanced Research Projects Agency
DBM	Deep Boltzmann machine
DDOS	Distributed denial of service
DEF CON	World's longest running and largest underground hacking conference
DMS	Discrete manufacturing system
DNC	Differentiable neural computing
DNS	Domain network service
DoD	U.S. Department of Defense
DSKY	DiSplay&KeYboard
DT	Digital twin
EAD	Ethically aligned design
EV	Electric vehicle
Exa	1×10^{18}
FAO	Food and Agriculture Organizations of the United Nations
FIPA	Foundation for Intelligent Physical Agents
FMS	Flexible manufacturing system
FR	Flapping robot
Gaia	AN iterative, agent-oriented analysis and design methodology
GDP	Gross domestic product
GFLOP	Giga floating point operations per second

GFN	Global footprint network
GHG	Green house gases
GIS	Geospatial mapping system
Git repository	A version control system for a file management system
GLONASS	Globalnaya Navigazionnaya Sputnikovaya Sistema, or Global Navigation Satellite System, is Russia's version of GPS (global poositioning system)
GMO	Genetically modified crops
GPS	Global positioning satellite of US Government
GPU	Graphical processing unit
GUI	Graphical user interface
H21	Hydrogen UK Northern Gas Network initiative
H2H	Human to human interface
H2M	Human to machine interface
HAT	Hub-of-all-things
HCI	Human-computer interaction
HMD	Head Mounted Display
HPC	High-performance computing
HS2	Planned high-speed railway link UK
IDS	Intrusion detection system
IAE	International Energy Agency
IEEE	Institute of Electrical and Electronics Engineers
IFPRI	International Food Policy Research Institute
IMF	International Monetary Fund
IO	Input-output
IoE	Internet of everything
IoP	Internet of people
IoT	Internet of Things
IIoT	Industrial Internet of Things
I4.0	Industry 4.0, equivalent to II4
II4	Industrial Internet 4.0
IPCC	Intergovernmental Panel on Climate Change
IS	Information system
ISP	Internet service provide
IT	Information technology
JIT	Just-in-time
kNN	Nearest neighbor algorithm
LOQC	Linear optical quantum computer
LSTM	Long short-term memory
M-IoT	Massive Internet of Things
Mac	MIT algebraic computer
MaSE	Agent methodology
M2M	Machine to machine interface

M2H	Machine to human interface
MANET	Mobile ad-hoc network
MAS	Multi-agent system
MAVs	Micro aerial vehicles
MEM	Micro-electrical mechanical system
MITS	A US-based electronics company, Micro Instrumentation and Telemetry Systems
ML	Machine learning
MLaaS	Machine learning as a service
MLP	Multi layer perceptron
MMC	Mission control center
MOSFET	Metal oxide semiconductor field effect transistor
MOOC	Massive open online course
MR	Mixed reality
MR	Magneto-resistive
MVP	Minimum viable product
N-V	Nitrogen-vacancy
NASEM	National Academies of Sciences, Engineering, and Medicine
NEM	Nano-electro-mechanical
NSF	National Science Foundation
NMR	Nuclear magnetic resonance
OECD	Organization for Economic Co-operation and Development
OPEX	Operational expenditure
OMI	Oxford Martin Institute
OOD	Object-oriented design
OODA	Observe, Orient, Decide, Act
OWB	Objective well-being
Peta	1×10^{15}
PFLOP	Peta floating point operations per second
QC	Quantum computer
RBM	Restricted Boltzmann machine
RFID	Radio frequency identification
RMS	Reconfigurable manufacturing system
RNN	Recurrent neural network
RUP	Rational unified process software development process framework
SCADA	Supervisory control and data acquisition
Smart City	The use of digital technologies to enable citizen services in city living spaces and efficiencies
SPAD	Span protocol activity definition
SSL	Secure sockets layer encryption

SWB	Subjective-well-being
TCO LC	Total cost of operation through life cycle
TPU	Tensor processing unit
TFLOP	Tera floating point operations per second
ToC	Theory of constraints
TOTeX	Total expenditure
UAV	Unmanned and remote controlled drones
UEBA	User and entity behavior analytics
UGV	Unmanned guided vehicle
UKERC	UK Energy Research Center
UML	Unified modelling language
UN	United Nations
UNESCO	United Nations Educational, Scientific and Cultural Organization
UNFCCC	United Nations Framework Convention on Climate Change
UNP	United Nations Environment
UV	Under water vehicle
UX	User experience design
V2V	Vehicle to vehicle
VANET	Vehicular ad-hoc networks
VLSI	Very large-scale Integration
VO	Virtual Organization
VR	Virtual reality
WBS	Warwick Business School, University of Warwick, UK
WEF	World Economic Forum
Wi-Fi	Wireless network
Xenotta	1×10^{28}
Yotta	1×10^{24}
Zetta	1×10^{21}

List of Figures

List of Tables

Book Structure

This book explores the impact of recent technological changes that are moving beyond the PC, mobile and cloud computing and deeply transforming the physical, biological and social aspects of our everyday lives. The World Economic Forum has named this, the 4th Industrial era.

Inventions previously seen in science fiction such as virtual and augmented reality, artificial intelligence, 3D printing, robotics, blockchain, quantum computing, nanotechnology to bioengineering are now changing how materials, money, products, services are made, exchanged, and consumed. This is set against significant challenges in the next decades with growth in global population, diminishing global energy, water and rising emissions. The 4th Industrial revolution identifies these technologies and how they are changing industry processes, smart cities, connected homes, driverless cars, wearables to healthcare. But the 4th Industrial Revolution also highlights the paradox of these disruptive technologies and new skills which change productivity through automation. Increasing scarcity of resources to meet population growth demand that are affordable, secure and sustainable driven by that technology and connected society. The conjecture and evidence provided by this book exposes the need for a new kind of thinking and leadership, which recognizes the challenge of managing new kinds of automation that have occurred because of recent advances in artificial intelligence. In addition, these leaders need to contend with major transformation taking place in our society, as well as reconcile the paradoxes and other phenomenon that have arisen as a consequence of the 4th industrial revolution.

Today's popularization and technical description of AI has been polarized across significant alarms from superintelligence through to complex mathematical text books that focus on the details algorithms and mechanics of automation. Recent reports at a governmental level tend to be somewhere in-between, asking questions over the impact of automation on jobs, ethics and productivity of nations.

This book aims to provide a business practitioner viewpoint, of how advances in technology are forcing us to change the way we need to think about enterprise strategy, and necessity to embrace the impact artificial intelligence is likely to have on emerging practices.

In Part I: *The Era of Intelligent systems* introduces the 4th Industrial revolution themes from a practice viewpoint of technological changes that are reshaping business, personal experience and the rise of emerging intelligent systems. The aim is to orient the reader toward today's pragmatic considerations of AI and new technology disruption in their immediate organization and markets.

We provide a primer of the key terminology and emerging concepts in machine learning and artificial intelligence that is necessary in navigating this new era of intelligent systems. We include a historical context to example how computing science and cybernetics to help demystify the origins of artificial intelligence.

Part II: *Intelligent agents, machine learning and advanced neural networks* we explore the foundations of agents and intelligent agents and the multi-agent systems components. We then take machine learning a key component of agents and develop the foundations of machine learning life cycle in practice. The final chapter in this section then takes the reader into advanced neural networks which is the current prevailing tend in machine learning and a solid grounding in the theory.

Part III: *The Cross-cutting Concerns of Artificial Intelligence* explores the cross-cutting impacts of how artificial intelligence is how the internet works; the cyber security and privacy, to the issues of ethics impact on society and the essential issues of climate change, population growth, resources and global energy growth.

We conclude the book with real case studies of how artificial intelligence is being used in business and reflections of where the future of artificial intelligence may be heading. This includes a novel approach the *cognitive horizon* to describing how innovation and invention to aid practitioners in developing roadmaps for artificial intelligence adoption and exploitation as a new phenomenon in the 4th industrial revolution.

The book provides sources to references of several current leading academic and industrial publications and reports, notably in the field of the 4th Industrial revolution and artificial intelligence.

The book seeks to appeal to practicing professional and academic audiences seeking examples of how leading practitioners are observing the practical impact of artificial intelligence and the wider consequences to their industry and society. The focus of the text is to formulate current definitions of key terminology and identify key practical lessons learnt that can be applied to industrial and company strategy when planning and using automation concepts and solutions to achieve successful outcomes.

Part I

The Era of Intelligent Systems

1

The 4th Industrial Revolution Impact

Introduction

Technological advance through history predates the recent *digital era* and *computers* to previous centuries that saw radical change in political and social beliefs, as well as the spread of political power and material wealth through changing technological development in society.

Technology has traditionally been defined as the way in which scientific knowledge evolves in the production of goods and services or in achieving goals using tools and techniques to achieve outcomes. The term "technology" originates from the sixteenth century use of the Greek word tekhnologia "systematic treatment" and tekhnē "art, craft" and logia "-ology" [1]. The late renaissance period in Western Europe saw great progress in the arts and science, as well as social upheaval bridging the middle ages and modern history. Technology changed human skills-sets, we learnt how methods and processes were deployed to wield natural resources and gain advantages in competition and acquisition. The limitations of human mechanical strength and the discoveries of fire, metals, and enlightenment [2] brought the development of tools that assisted or substituted human effort.

Machines were constructed in order to provide a means for humans to operate and achieve certain tasks, or to replace the human effort in its entirety. Machinery consumed and converted energy provide by mechanical, chemical, thermal, electrical, or other means to convert work from one state to another. This evolved from personal and local use into a phenomenon that transformed society and the industrial economy.

© The Author(s) 2018
M. Skilton and F. Hovsepian, *The 4th Industrial Revolution*,
https://doi.org/10.1007/978-3-319-62479-2_1

The noun 'industry' stands for the production of goods or services through technology and commercial organizational advances, and 'industrialization' stands for the development of industries on a wide scale. The development of scientific knowledge and technology were essential for the emergence of industrialization, which in western cultures happened around the 1770s. The change from an agrarian society, based on agriculture and human social organization, to an industrial one based primarily around industry, has since become to be known as *"The Industrial Revolution"* [3].

The period from the late 1770s to the present day would witness a five-fold rise in global population, and a tenfold rise in GDP wealth, rates that were unheard of prior to the 18th century [4].

Most noticeable would be the shift in growth rates between the Western and Eastern economies; however, they are both converging in this information age and thereby helping to ignite the 4th Industrial Revolution, which we explore in the next section.

This chapter we shall discuss the following topics:

- The four Industrial Revolutions
- The transformations of energy and computation
- The foundations of Industrie 4.0 and cyber-physical systems

The Four Industrial Revolutions

The industrialization of the west and east of the global is a story of social and economic development that took divergent paths driven by geography and local regional power that grew with technological. It is generally accepted that the term "Industrial Revolution" refers to the period from the 1770s to the middle of the 1870s, where technological change enabled humanity to harness mechanical and electrical forces for its own endeavors. As a result, there were many changes in manufacturing and production methods, and working practices, which created new modes of transportation and provided a new kind of infrastructure for much of society. While its genesis in the west was in Great Britain, transforming it and its empire into the workshop of the world [5], within a century it had spread to the new world and through Asia and Pacific (see Fig. 1.1).

The term Industrial revolution first came into the lexicon of thought in 1799 [6]. By the end of nineteenth century, human society would witness world population double to 1.6 billion, a rapid rise in global GDP, and new inventions of electricity, mass production and globalization that we recognize today. The first few decades of the twentieth century saw the

West – East Dynamics of Industrial Revolution

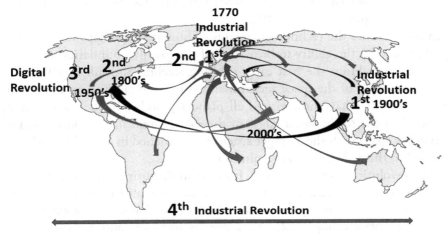

Fig. 1.1 West–East dynamics of Industrial Revolution

conflict of world war, and rapid changes in global power as west met east, the dawn of nuclear power and electronics. These transformations instigated the third revolution of information systems, and the automation of manufacturing and production. The geographical and time zone boundaries shrunk as telecommunications and new enlightenment in biology, miniaturization, transportation, media and engineering spread to consumerization and commercial acceleration through the twentieth century. The drivers for the latency with which the Asian markets, China and India in particular, arrived at industrialization were mainly due to geopolitics, proximity of a labor force and natural resources as well as colonization. In the case of India, it was a massive source of cotton and indigo that became a huge market resource for the products of the industrial revolution. The colonization of India provided huge capital funds to the British Empire, whose corporations and control of the shipping routes at that time prevented inward investment in India for its own industrial development [7]. Both India and China where affected by other factors including domestic political and military upheavals during the 1700s while Europe was going through scientific developments. China had other impacts of a large geographical country with a larger population of manual labor and relative isolation from trading marketing with other parts of the world. As recent as the 1960s, over sixty percent of the Chinese population worked in Agriculture [8]. It was not until the mid-twentieth century that industrialization at scale arrived in China to meet the needs of a rapidly growing domestic population and agricultural famine, driven by the Maoist Great Leap Forward plan in the cultural revolution of the People's Republic of China [9].

In recent times the technologic genius of humans is perhaps most visibility illustrated by the ability to break free of the earthly boundaries as seen in the space race. From the first earth orbiting satellite Sputnik in 1957 [10] during the dawn of the space age to manned mission landing on the moon. Robotic satellites have now visited all planetary bodies in the solar system, and reached out to the outer edges of the solar system in the Oort cloud of interstellar space with the Voyager space craft launched in 1977 [11]. All this achieved in the 3rd Industrial revolution.

This revolution, which started from manufacturing, will create more capital and enable humans to accumulate more wealth to drive economic growth, is perhaps moving from technology to one based on knowledge and accelerated social change [12]. No longer is technical automation a transformation from one energy to another at a faster rate as we saw in the steam and electrical revolutions of the eighteenth and nineteenth centuries. We can look back at the twentieth century as a kind of preparation, a prelude to a new era with the digital revolution laying the ground for electronics and computing that would spread knowledge and ideas built on the earlier industrial revolutions.

The Fig. 1.2 illustrates the major trends of change that are apparent in the transitions from the 1st Industrial revolution to the present day 4th industrial revolution and decades ahead. These can be summarized to include the movement of globalization through mechanical, electrification,

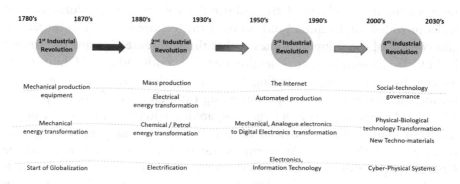

The 4th Industrial Revolution Impact

Fig. 1.2 The four Industrial Revolutions

petrochemical combustion and the internet digitization. A second trend is the harnessing of transformation of energy for work; the third, the rise of machinery automation that would enable mass production and the creation of mechanisms that exceed human limitations and the creation of new science and insights. There is a trend here, because the changes that we see through the eras have associated with them consequences for social interaction and societal values, which must evolve with the advent of new technology.

The 1st and 2nd Industrial Revolutions

Prior to mechanization, human endeavor was driven by hand and animal stock to build, work the land and travel. Mechanical action from water, wind and fire had been used for thousands of years, from the sales on a ship to the water wheel.

The first steam engine was built by Thomas Savery in 1698 in England, called the Savery engine, [13] it was used to pump accumulated water up from coal mines but had limited application, because it used atmospheric pressure and worked against the vacuum of condensed steam to draw water. It could not be more than 30 feet above the water level and therefore had to be installed down in the mine shaft itself. It was not until 1712 that Thomas Newcomen developed the first commercial steam engine based on a piston design. It could lift ten gallons of water from a depth of 156 feet that represented 5.5 horse power [14]. The jump from vacuum pressure, to mechanical kinetic energy, to continuous rotary movement did not occur until 1781 with the advent of James Watt's revolutionary design for his steam engine. This ten-horsepower engine enabled a wide range of manufacturing to production and agricultural machinery to be powered. This ushered in what is described as the 1st industrial revolution, because it enabled production of mechanical energy from thermal energy generated from combustion of chemical and oxygen, which could be applied to a range of movement and processing. It's revolution was the ability to harness mechanical energy on-demand without the use of human or livestock intervention. It enabled humans to work more effectively using mechanical energy that ranged from fixed stationary pumps, crane lifts and mills to locomotion in the form of trains and horseless cartridges; moreover, it signaled the beginning of mechanization.

By 1886, steam engines were capable of developing 10,000 horsepower, and were used to large scale ocean steam ships and long range industrial locomotive apparatus [15]. But around that time the 2nd Industrial revolution had already begun to arrive with the advent of industrial scale electrification and electric motors; the advent of petrochemical combustion engine and the early prototype for the modern gasoline engine enabled Gottlieb Daimler to build the first automobile in 1885 [16].

Beyond the Digital Revolution

The 3rd industrial revolution has been defined as the *digital revolution* that began with micro-electronics and semi-conductor developments in the mid 1950s through to the early 1970s, which saw the first very-large-scale integration (VLSI) processes create integrated circuits (IC) by combining thousands of transistors into a single chip [17]. The integrated circuit expedited the move from mechanical and analogue technology to digital electronics, and fundamentally changed (by orders of magnitude) the digitization of information and instigated pervasive computing. This ushered in the age of information technology at an industrial scale with enterprise computing from IBM, Hewlett Packard, Microsoft, Sun Microsystems and a plethora of others driving rapid expansion into automated services and production. Developments in telecommunications led to the inception of the Internet by the 1990s that in the following decade saw the ground work laid for global data centers and the emergence of search engines, online marketplaces, social media and mobile devices by Google, Amazon, Apple, Facebook, Twitter and a legion of others, that spread the digital revolution to all corners of the globe and industries.

The 3rd Industrial revolution connected people and industries on a unprecedented scale. This information technology scope included connected devices and industrial scaling of telecommunications infrastructure, and the phenomenon of massive computing both at the data center scale and micro-miniaturization and commoditization of mobile cell phones. The birth of the World Wide Web brought with it a new syntax and protocol that enable machinery to "talk" to each other and with humans. The rapid advances in spectrum and bandwidth investment provided links to business enterprises and cities, to the transportation, energy, and utility network infrastructures. Digital Marketplaces and digital workforces became possible, "hollowing out the internet", meaning that businesses and people could connect and exchange products and services. Scott McNealy, the chief executive of Sun Microsystems in 1999, famously remarked, "You have zero privacy anyway. Get over it [18]." This was a realization that internet enabled access (and personalization) would also collect your data and activities. The term "hollowing out" is now viewed with concern, the rise of automation and globalization has an impact on lower and middle-class jobs, creating what some observers describe as a "digital divide" in the inequity of internet access and monopolization of the large. These social issues are perhaps the real consequence of the rapid changes brought on by digitalization. Technical advances in materials science, new manufacturing techniques, machine intelligence, biological research, as well as changes in medical and healthcare have enabled developments within the 4th revolution that have the potential to change whole industries and human experience. We will explore some of these changes in the chapters that follow.

The 4th Industrial Revolution

The 4th Industrial Revolution (4IR) is described in the 2016 book by Klaus Schwab, Founder and Executive Chairman of the World Economic Forum [19], as a culmination of emerging technologies fusion into the physical and biological worlds the likes of which has not been seen before (See Table 1.1).

Industrie 4.0

The earlier version of this description with a similar namesake had been the Industrie 4.0 or Industrial 4.0 and the Industrial Internet of things (IIoT) developed four years earlier in 2010 by the German Government [20]. In 2006, Helen Gill at the American National Science Foundation (NSF) [21] coined the term Cyber-Physical Systems (CPS), which was born in the realm of machine-to-machine automation that lead to the Smart Factory. This is now viewed as part of the 4th Industrial Revolution and is part of a wider reshaping of all industries and a new genre of economic, social and societal change.

By 2014 the German federal government supported this idea by announcing that Industrie 4.0 will be an integral part of their "High-Tech Strategy

Table 1.1 Definition of the 4th industrial revolution

Definition: The 4th Industrial Revolution (4IR)
"The fourth industrial revolution, however, is not about smart and connected machines and systems. Its scope is much wider, Occurring simultaneously are waves of further breakthroughs in areas ranging from gene sequencing to nanotechnology, from renewables to quantum computing"
"It is the fusion of these technologies and their interaction across the physical, digital and biological domains that make the fourth industrial revolution fundamentally different from previous revolutions"

Table 1.2 Definition of Industrie 4.0

Definition: Industry 4.0 (I4.0)
The convergence of industrial production and information and communication technologies. Industrie 4.0 relates to the convergence of Internet of Things (IoT), the Internet of People (IoP), and the Internet of Everything (IoE) (22)

2020 for Germany" initiative, aiming at technological innovation leadership of the German economy. In 2016, research initiatives in this area were funded with 200 million euros from governmental bodies [23] (see Table 1.2).

Internet of Things

During the 1970s factory production systems began to adopt ideas from Computer Integrated Manufacturing (CIM), Just-in-Time (JIT) and Theory of Constraints (ToC). This evolved rapidly with various quality management fads as well as advances in computer processing, storage and Computer Graphics rendering in engineering CAD and CAM systems, together with the desire to connect with various enterprise and SCADA process control systems.

The *concept* of Internet of Things originated with the concept of "Ubiquitous Computing" at Palo Alto Research Center (PARC) by Mark Weiser [24], during the 1990s. Nearly ten years later, Kevin Ashton [25] coined the *term* "Internet of Things" (IoT), during the development of Radio Frequency ID (RFID) tagging and feedback loop optimization, for Proctor & Gamble's supply chain management.

By the early 21st century the fusion of these ideas enabled the customer to manage assets from the factory to their not just the production of goods, but also asset management from design, manufacturing through to delivery.

The term IoT subsequently evolved and by 2014, by which time it included a spectacular variety of sensors and devices, ranging from piezoelectric, solar panels, thermoelectric and a multitude of others, causing much confusion with the use of term "Internet of Things". For example, General Electric (GE) have challenged the current Consumer IoT focus, which is seen as populist notions of consumer home appliances and voice control services, as a limited view of the customer centric experience of connectivity and automation that use sensors and smart products [26]. GE further developed the discussion around the Industrial Internet where the focus is on the Industrial Internet of things (IIoT) that has given rise to a more effective minimum viable product (MVP). Moreover, this approach covers the whole life cycle [27] beginning with design, development, manufacturing through to delivery and services.

Table 1.3 Definitions of Internet of Things

Definitions: Internet of Things (IoT)
Industrial Internet (II), Industrial Internet of Things (IIoT)
The automation and communications network of smart embedded and external sensors and machines representing an intelligent industrial factory and supply chain lifecycle
Internet of People (IoP)
The personal data and human centric network of products and services. The focus is on privacy and personal-centric internet
Internet of Things (IOT)
Sensors and actuators embedded in physical objects, which are connected to the Internet
Critical – Internet of Things (C-IoT)
Sensor networks and systems relating to critical infrastructure at a corporate and national level. It refers to the control, security and robust design features of platforms that support mission-critical systems from on-board controls for automated vehicles; medical automation in surgery and cancer research to national energy and utility infrastructure
Massive-Internet of Things (M-IoT)
The huge growth of usage data and sensors at "the edge" of local, personal and internet network services. It refers to the scale and magnitude of large datasets generated and the unique characteristics of platforms able to handle and operate with hyperscale data generated by massive-IoT such as mobile, social media, wearables to municipal city and transport services

Recent classifications of IoT have been a key enabler in connecting trillions of assets, smart wearables for connected life-styles and health, to the future of smart cities and connected driverless transport. Concerns are growing over issues related to cyber-security and personal data collections. Table 1.3 provides some of the current definitions in use by Industrial, retail and telecommunications organizations in IoT.

The growth of IoT sensors, low power pervasive networks and advanced data collection techniques have accelerated the development of machine learning systems that use neural networks. This is mainly due to the widely available training data, such as text, images and spoken languages that have become available at sufficient volume and reasonable cost.

Cyber-Physical Systems

These concepts developed ideas in connected systems, and the role of organizations as complete system of systems [28, 29]. Within CPS, they evolved into the notion of CPS-VO (Cyber-Physical System Virtual Organization). CPS-VO recognizes the holistic nature of real-world systems and the need for physical and digital integration to work symbiotically with the organization itself, as well

Table 1.4 Definition of Cyber-Physical Systems (CPS)

Definition: Cyber-Physical System (CPS)
Is a system that integrate cyber components (namely, sensing, computation, and human users), connecting them to the Internet and to each other. It is the tight conjoining of and coordination between computational and physical resources called a digital twin (the physical assets, components, energy, materials, interfaces) and the cyber representation of the physical system (the software, digital data, usage, sensors that enables higher capability, adaptability, scalability, resiliency, safety, security, and usability [30]
"Such systems use computations and communication deeply embedded and inter-acting with physical processes to add new capabilities to the physical system. These CPS range from miniscule (Heart pace makers) to large-scale (the national power-grid)" (CPS-Summit 2008) [31]

as other systems and operations inside and outside the organization, in what could be considered to the connected supply chain networks (Table 1.4).

CPS embodies several key concepts to be found in Industrie 4.0:

Digital Twin Model tight integration: The creation of a digital model with sensor-feedback actions typically in, or near, real-time. The critical concept is that the physical asset, interaction and behavior, are digitally modelled and connected through external or embedded sensors with the physical system.

Outcome driven: Overall system properties that are cross-cutting concerns about the total CPS status within its organization or as a working subsystem (such as an onboard connected car platform for example) that has responsibilities for safety, efficiency, and secure operation of the overall system.

Automated machine to machine: A Level of automation that may include interaction with humans, but more typically involves autonomous operations between machine to machine.

Total Cost and Operational Lifecycle TCO LC: Integration of the life-cycle of the system and its various states of maintenance and connection to other systems and resources. Typically, both the capital expenditure (CAPEX), and operational costs of running and support operational costs (OPEX), which together combine to a complete total cost of operational expenditure (TOTeX) model of operation is considered the scope of the CPS.

CPS systems have grown most rapidly in the Digital Manufacturing and Smart factory concepts within Industry 4.0. It is predominately about connected factory automation and self-management of the subsystems and the overall automation of the factory and its operations. Similar initiatives with the Future of Manufacturing in the European Union and Manufacturing 2.0. [32] (around 2007) had similar initiatives, but originated from Demand-

Table 1.5 Definition of Human Computing Interaction HCI and Machine to Machine M2M

Definition: Human-Computer Interaction (HCI)
researches the design and use of computer technology, focused on the interfaces between people (users) and computers. Researchers in the field of HCI both observe the ways in which humans interact with computers and design technologies that let humans interact with computers in novel ways
Definition: Machine to Machine M2M
The direct communication between devices using any communications channel, including wired and wireless. This includes machine sensors to collect and provide data on machine performance and software that can use this data to modulate itself and/or other machines automatically to achieve some goal. A key feature of M2 M is automation that excludes human intervention but may be part of a process for HCI

Driven Value Networks (DDVN), concepts that perpetuated as recently as 2014, and were from the Web 2.0 era of web services messaging across a supply chain network [33].

The concept of CPS has grown to include new human-computing Interactions (HCI) and the combination of Internet of Things embedded technologies of sensors and devices, into machine to machine (M2M) automation and embedded systems into product-service systems (see Table 1.5).

The concept of CPS, of tight digital twining of technology and the physical and biological domains, has evolved from its origins in manufacturing into many other industries at the small and large scale.

Micro-and Nano Scale Technology

New technologies have developed at the micro-scale and nano-scale physical materials in nanotechnology and miniaturization. 3D printing, also known as additive manufacturing [34] is a key example of digital control systems that manipulate molecular level composites.

Nanotechnology [35] is a field that is concerned with the manipulation of atomic and molecular levels through the use of advances in electron microscopes (scanning tunneling Microscope) and nanoparticles, such as Buckminsterfullerene's (buckyballs) or Fullerenes carbon molecules [36]. The development of several new fields of science, engineering and medical engineering became possible through direct control of matter at the atomic and molecular level, such new surface materials, nanotubes materials, semiconductor design, microfabrication and molecular engineering.

This field is closely associated with bioengineering [37] and genetic engineering [38] that involves the creation and manipulation of genes to biomedical engineering of organs, prosthetics and many neuro, immune, cellular, pharma and biochemistry manipulation and applications. Developments in gene therapy, genetically modified crops (GMO) using biotechnology to manufacture and control biological processes.

Macro Scale Technology

At the macro scale, new technologies can be found as a development of connected systems across many industries. These include a plethora of growing use cases in embedded sensor controlled components found in mobile cell phone devices, connected home appliances, connected automobiles to human wearables, bioimplants for pacemakers, patient care monitoring to crowd surveillance in cities, airports and sports grounds.

The wider landscape of cooperating Internet of Things, people and places through devices and systems will include next-generation power grids, new retail delivery supply chains, new open banking systems, future defense systems, next generation automobiles and intelligent highways, flexible robotic manufacturing, next-generation air vehicles and airspace management, and other areas, many of which are as yet untapped.

The New Fusion of Physical, Digital and Biological Domains in the 4th Industrial Revolution

These new technologies have generated new kinds of interaction from the macro, the micro and nano levels (see Fig. 1.3).

Fusion is the key, in which the digitization and information coupled to feedback loops have enabled new kinds of IoT machine and Human generated data.

The phenomenon of the 4th Industrial Revolution sees both human and machine intelligence as becoming increasingly intertwined.

In the next chapter, we will explore the types of technologies that are integrating physical materials, locations and machines with biological processes, human physiology and psychology. The fusion of physical, digital and

The fusion of the 4th Industrial Revolution

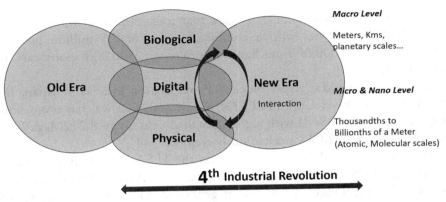

Fig. 1.3   The new fusion of the 4th industrial revolution

biological domains with various new kinds of technologies are now able to interact in an intelligent manner, and thereby generate new forms of intelligence. This is the key concept that makes this an industrial revolution – the 4th Industrial Revolution.

Harnessing the Transformation of Energy

1st Industrial Revolution

The term "horsepower" is defined as a description of energy needed to lift an average body weight of 75 kg by 1 meter in 1 second. The first commercial steam engine, the Newcomen steam engine in 1712 could produce 5.5 mechanical horse power. The James Watts steam engine (around 1765) introduced the first rotary piston that became a key design moment in the industrial revolution and produced 10 horse power [39].

James Watt used the term horsepower to demonstrate the efficiency that resulted from artefacts engineered using steam. The term horsepower and Watts as units of power, illustrate a feature that we see time and again in the translation of one era to another, that have a cultural overhang from the vocabulary and mindset of the early generation, in the first case the horse. Even today the term Watt hearkens back to an earlier progenitor of Steam.

3rd Industrial Revolution

In 1969, the Saturn V Launch Rocket that took NASA astronauts to the Moon had five engines with a combined thrust of 7.5 million pounds, equivalent to 160,000,000 mechanical horsepower, 500,000 sports cars, or 543 jet fighters [40].

The current world's largest Nuclear Power station located in Japan, the Tokyo Electric Power Co.'s (TEPCO) Kashiwazaki-Kariwa, has seven boiling water reactors (BWR) with a gross installed capacity of 8,212 MegaWatts equivalent to 11,012,000 mechanical horsepower [41].

The most powerful Nuclear bomb was the U.S.S.R.'s Big Ivan Bomb—a multistage RDS-220 hydrogen. On Oct. 30, 1961, Mityushikha Bay Nuclear Testing Range, Arctic Sea, it generated and average power of 5.4 yottawatts, approximately 1.4% of the power output of the sun. The blast was 10 times greater than all the munitions set off during World War II and destroyed everything within a 40-mile radius of epicenter. This is equivalent to 5.4×1024 watts or 39.1×1028 xenotta mechanical horsepower [42].

The 4th Industrial revolution will harness a range of energy sources that will become critical for enabling the connected digital society, addressing the massive growth in population and their demand on resources, as well as having to deal with the increases in climate change threats.

In "Part III Cross-cutting Concerns", we shall discuss the paradoxes and challenges that ensue from the 4th industrial revolution.

Harnessing the Transformation of Computation

The game of chess has long been held as an example of intelligence and in the 20th century became the first great public test for artificial intelligence versus the human.

The history of chess can be traced back nearly 1500 years. The earliest origins are believed to have originated in Eastern India, c. 280–550 [43] in the Gupta Empire [44]. By the 6th Century was known as chaturaṅga (Sanskrit: चतुरङ्ग), literally four divisions [of the military]—infantry, cavalry, elephants, and chariotry, represented by the pieces that would evolve into the modern pawn, knight, bishop, and rook, respectively. The game reached Western Europe and Russia by at least three routes, the earliest being in the 9th century. By the year 1000, it had spread throughout Europe [45]. The old form of chess that originated in this period was known by the Arabic work Shatranj, in Middle Persian Sanskrit chaturanga چترنگ) meaning catuḥ: "four"; anga: "arm". Western culture through the Persians, Greeks and India via the Persian Empire. Around 1200, the rules of shatranj started to be modified in southern Europe, and around 1475, several major changes made the game essentially as it is known today [46].

The game indirectly led to the rise of wisdom and the documentation of Knowledge. A famous example of this is the Libro de los Juegos, ("Book of games"), or Libro de axedrez, dados e tablas, ("Book of chess, dice and tables", in Old Spanish) was commissioned by Alfonso X of Castile, Galicia and León and completed in his scriptorium in Toledo in 1283, is an exemplary piece of Alfonso's medieval literary legacy. This was part of the search for wisdom by the Spanish King Alfonso X, also called Alfonso the Wise [47]. Alfonso was instrumental in the formation of an academy where learned Jews, Muslims, and "Christians" could collaborate. To facilitate their work, the king created and financed one of the world's first State libraries.

In 1947, the world's first chess computer programs were developed by the British World War II codebreakers at Bletchley Park. Members of that team, Shaun Wylie along with Donald Michie designed an early form of computer program called "Machiavelli" which competed against a program designed by Alan Turing called "Turbochamp". Both were paper based programs as there was no software or hardware available at that time that could run the programs [48].

In 1996, IBM developed Deep Blue, a super computer of it's time, that became famous for the first computer chess playing system to win both a chess game and a chess match against a reigning world champion, Gary Kasparov, under regular time controls.

After initially defeating Deep Blue in 1996, Kasparov issued a rematch challenge for the following year. To prepare, the team tested the machine against several Grandmasters, and doubled the performance of the hardware.

A six-game rematch took place in New York in May 1997. Kasparov won the first game but missed an opportunity in the second game and lost. Kasparov never recovered his composure and played defensively for the remainder of the match. In the last game, he made a simple mistake and lost, marking May 11, 1997, as the date on which a World Chess Champion lost a match to a computer [49].

Technical specification of Deep Blue at that time in 1996 was an IBM RS/6000 SP parallel supercomputer Thin P2SC-based system with 30 nodes, with each node containing a 120 MHz P2SC microprocessor, enhanced with 480 special purpose VLSI chess chips. Its chess playing program was written in C and ran under the AIX operating system. In June 1997, Deep Blue was the 259th most powerful supercomputer according to the TOP500 list, achieving 11.38 GFLOPS on the High-Performance LINPACK benchmark [50]. By joining special purpose hardware and software with general purpose parallel computing, the team developed a system with a brute force computing speed capable of examining 200 million moves per second – or 50 billion positions – in the three minutes allocated for a single move in a chess game, with a typical search to a depth of between six and eight moves to a maximum of twenty or even more moves in some situations [51].

Deep Blue was the fastest computer that ever faced a world chess champion. Today, in computer chess research and matches of world class players against computers, the focus of play has often shifted to software chess programs, rather than using dedicated chess hardware. Modern chess programs like Houdini, Rybka, Deep Fritz, or Deep Junior are more efficient than the programs during Deep Blue's era. In a November 2006 match between Deep Fritz and world chess champion Vladimir Kramnik, the program ran on a personal computer containing two Intel Core 2 Duo CPUs, capable of evaluating only 8 million positions per second, but searching to an average depth of 17 to 18 plies in the middlegame thanks to heuristics; it won 4-2. [52].

Successors to Deep Blue have added more processors and decreased power requirements. Blue Gene, a more recent product of IBM research improves performance by a factor of 100 over Deep Blue. In March 2005, Blue Gene had reached peak performance of more than 100 teraflops, capable of doing simulations that used to take hours in nanoseconds. But Blue Gene, for all its computational skill, occupied up to 20 refrigerator-sized racks and continued to consume massive amounts of power, although considerably less than Deep Blue.

The fastest Super computer in the world in 2017 is currently the Sunway TaihuLight in the National Supercomputing Center in Wuxi, China. It has 10,649,600 Cores and been measured with a peak processing speed of 125,435.9 TFLOPS and 15,371 KW Power consumption [53].

IBM have recently been reported to be developing the next generation Supercomputer with a peak performance speed of 200 PFLOPS by 2018 [54].

By comparison, an Apple iPhone7 plus with a A10 quad core System on a Chip (SoC) has been reported to rate at between 47GFLOPS and greater than 1 TFLOP performance, or something like having four Deep Blue super computers in your hand depending on how you benchmark it [55].

Our human brain runs on no more than 20 watts of power equal to the refrigerator bulb. The Average Human Adult consumes 100 Watts of energy by the brain only covert 20% of that, 20 Watts [56].

The 4th industrial revolution will be a scale of computational power leading to astonishing possibilities of data and intelligent processing scale. We are as the cusp of what some call the "post Moore's Law" revolution that representing the doubling of processing chips using silicon coming to an end. We explore this phenomena in later chapter as the new technology of the 4th industrial revolution.

After the Apollo Moon Landing Era

In W. David Woods 2011 book, "How Apollo Flew to the Moon" he presents details of NASA's planning and engineering rocket science; eloquently explained the climax of an era that was at the cusp of the 3rd industrial revolution. "The 12-year Apollo lunar exploration program (1961 through 1972) occurred during the second half of a transformational period between the end of W-W-II (1945) and the demise of the Soviet Union in 1991, a period of major technological, political, economic, and cultural dynamics. Technologically, the digital computer was in its infancy, yet automation and robotics were clearly imminent. The Apollo astronauts were required to bridge this gap, as humans capable of using a computer to assist in manually operating the vast array of systems, techniques, and procedures necessary to leave the earth, fly to the Moon and explore the surface of the Moon, and safely return. The crew had to operate the hardware manually because computers did not yet have the reliability or capability necessary to operate autonomously and by the nature of the design strategy, Mission Control Center (MCC) did not really "control" the spacecraft either. At any point in the mission, the crew had to be prepared to operate on their own without any contact from Earth, using only the equipment and computers on board, together with pre-calculated maneuver data" [57].

Achieving such goals was driven by the belief that technology innovation would be able to reach such heights, whereas the ability to solve the real-world challenges of complex problems would require the human as interpreter and go between. The idea of the automatic machines that could perform such tasks was well advanced, yet the reality in practice fell to the ingenuity, bravery and the ability to organize humans and activities effectively [58].

The 3rd Industrial revolution of digital computation and the rise of knowledge in materials, physics and biological processes was racing ahead, opening up new frontiers of possibility but presenting new challenges and skills to learn. Over 400,000 people worked on the Apollo program and ranks as one of the great engineering achievements in human history [59].

The Shuttle, international space station and the grand tour of the planets by robotic satellites demonstrated our ability to orchestrate a multitude of interdependent tasks, involving technology and other resources to achieve such ambiguous goals. However, it was reaching the moon that marks our crowning achievement of what is possible, when we adopt new thinking, ways of working, and the utilization of connected technology to solve problems thought impossible. Moreover, it clearly showed that such skills would be essential in the future to meet other grand challenges and overcome them.

"Apollo was the combination of technologies, none of which was particularly dramatic. Combining it was the achievement. This was a bunch of people who didn't know how to fail. Apollo was a triumph of management, not engineering" [60].

It is important to remember just little computational power the computers of the "Apollo era" had when compared to today's laptops and mobile computing devices. It has been often cited that the total onboard computing power was less than a washing machine of present day standards [61]. The Saturn V for example, had two Apollo Guidance Computers (AGU), one mounted on the control panel of the Command Module Capsule and another in the Lunar Landing Module (See Fig. 15). The AGC was one of the first integrated circuit-based digital computer designed by the MIT Confidential Instrument Development Laboratory (later named the Charles Stark Draper Laboratory in honor of the American scientist and engineer who pioneered the inertial navigation and the AGC).

The AGC ran programs for guidance, navigation and control of the spacecraft and approximately 64k of memory made up of 16-but word length, 2048 words RAM (magnetic core memory read-write) and 36,864 words ROM made from wires weaved through magnetic iron cores. Astronauts communicated with the AGC using a numerical display and keyboard called the DSKY. Instructions could be entered using verbs and nouns by the astronaut as machine code and the unit ran a program called Luminary, written in a language called Mac (MIT Algebraic Compiler). The AGC is regarded as the world's first embedded computers [62].

In passing from the 3rd industrial era to the 4th industrial era we have encountered many such challenges, although many of the goals were not as lofty as reaching the moon. The "spin-offs" that went into industry and society from the Apollo program included examples such as fuel cells, inertial guidance systems, fire-retardants and cooling garments for firefighters, freeze-dried foods for military and survival use. It was perhaps the microelectronics of electric circuits that was the most significant contributor to many innovations after the Apollo program. These included the video, lasers, the Personal Computer, the Graphical User Interface and mouse controller to the mobile cell phone.

The World in 2050

In a 184-page report by the National Academies of Sciences, Engineering, and Medicine (NASEM) was produced in 2017, which was co-chaired by Professors Erik Brynjolfsson, an economist at the Massachusetts Institute of Technology's Sloan School of Management, and Tom Mitchell, a computer scientist at Carnegie Mellon University. The report described the issues faced by the job market and the impact on employment, as a result of advances made in A.I. during recent years. The key findings of the study concluded that "advances in information technology (IT) are far from over, and some of the biggest improvements in areas like artificial intelligence (AI) are likely still to come. Improvements are expected in some areas and entirely new capabilities may emerge in others." [63] Brynjolfsson and Mitchell discussed the finding of the report that describe new forms of business on-demand models from Uber, Lyft to Etsy, eBay and a myriad of other types of human "contract by internet" services. More notable was the rise of Artificial intelligence as a new force of change in the way jobs and tasks could be automated and transformed in new ways. Machine algorithms and deep neural nets where being used across various industry sectors, from retail recommendations, medical research in image recognition to driverless cars, robotics and many others. Their report concluded a lack of data on the consequences of this new technological revolution meant governments where "flying blind" in being able to assess and plan ahead for the impact of predominately artificial intelligence on the workforce, workplace and wider economy.

The report recommendations included the need for improvements in track how technology is changing work by introducing measuring systems to provide an "index of technology displacement" the impact of technology is and will have on the creation or replacement of jobs [64].

Over the past 30 years information technology has moved from the 3rd Industrial revolution. This digital revolution originally saw huge analogue and digital machinery, specialist computing systems that used to fill large air conditioned rooms that run basic operations, finance, administration and planning tasks. Then the PC together with the Internet broke down various barriers and introduced an extended interconnected world, which in a short space of ten years in the new millennium, underwent a second shift as mobile devices, tablets fuelled by massive social networks and multi-media digital services. This shift exploded the volume of collective information about people, products, places and workspaces on a planetary scale. So entered the scaling of the digital revolution into the physical and social domains of the 4th Industrial Revolution.

New physical and virtual connections have created new kinds of social and machine innovation, and interconnected supply chains that work across many country borders. Together with advances in computing power, speed, storage, and falling costs have given rise to machine learning techniques that have transformed the threshold of computing and changed the job skills arena [65].

The information era created by various information technologies, has brought with it an exponential scale of inter-connections and exabytes of information. Moreover, it has introduced a new level of on-demand computing power that fits within the palm of your hand. This empowers many task that previously required educated learning and skills in order to navigate, interpret and make complex decisions. Tasks, which in 2017 remain difficult, may not be such an obstacle by 2050. (See Table 1.6).

These examples are just the tip of the technological enabled innovation curve that may be possible sooner or later in the oncoming drive for move advanced and effective technology. But what does this also mean for the jobs of brown collar and white collar worker, the middle classes maybe under threat?

Table 1.6   The world 2050

Computing tasks in 2017	Computing tasks in 2050
• Optical face recognition • Voice translation • Location awareness • Transport simulation • Basic robotic movement • Biological wellbeing • 3D Printing (Digital to physical object - basic)	• Emotional interpretation built-in by default • Natural language subject expert advice by default • Location sensing and context advise—protect, promote and coordinate unconnected or connected participants • Real time integrated transport systems • Natural physical movement in situ of other objects and humans • Integrated body implants/augments and health services • 3D assembly and fabrication manipulation of complex objects

In 2013 there was a report on the impact of automation on jobs by the Oxford Martin Institute (OMI) and the Department of Engineering Science, Oxford University by Carl Benedikt Frey, Co-Director Oxford Martin Programme on Technology and Employment Citi Fellow, and Michael A. Osborne, Dyson Associate Professor in Machine Learning Oxford University and Co-Director of the Oxford Martin Programme on Technology and Employment. The Report had conducted an early assessment of 702 occupations from the impact of computerization and famously concluded that up to 47% of U.S. jobs in the next twenty years could be replaced by automation.

Among many recommendations of such reports, include suggestions of new links between data analytics monitoring worker jobs at risk from automation with new online eLearning platforms. These new systems will alert, and enable, the workforce to plan and retrain as existing jobs are automated, and the workers will need to acquire new skills in order to move onto new jobs. Ironically both data analytics and eLearning are new forms of 4th Industrial revolution technologies that blend digital and human needs but seem to be part of the new era that creates new business and social transformation. Many more studies will become necessary for governments and enterprises seeking to understand impacts of the 4th Industrial Revolution.

It is not an exaggeration that these converged physical, digital and biological domains will redefine the living and workspaces by becoming automated with artificial intelligence that the world of 2050 will see changing whole groups of jobs and activities into automated services.

Summary

The definition of technology we started with was the application of scientific knowledge for practical purposes, especially in industry, perhaps does not adequately describe the many boundaries that technology has connected and is changing.

Neither is just technological change the only area of change that is an adequate definition of 4th industrial scale transformation. This is also being driven by increased world populations and migrations, rising climate change, emissions and weather pattern changes; stresses on food supply security as well as energy security to support populations in these changes. These transforming forces are not just in business transformation. The are also in the social and political transformation of society to finite and renewable resources, food and energy. These are pervasive systemic changes brought on through automation, rising consumption affecting the balance of power in demand and supply. They are deep structural changes at the ecosystem trans-formation at macro and micro technological, economic, biological, social, societal, ethical, legal, political and personal levels.

The twenty first century is the first century that will really feel the impact of these convergences in the lifetime of many of the readers of this book. This new era will require new skills and a new language to describe the impact, to harness the power of these technologies and to understand the consequences.

In the next chapter, we explore the combinations of physical, digital and biological domains, the rise of the intelligent systems and the central role of Artificial Intelligence within the 4th Industrial Revolution.

Notes and References

1. Oxford English Dictionary, Technology, https://en.oxforddictionaries.com/definition/technology.
2. Age of Enlightenment, Age of Reason, Zafirovski, Milan, The Enlightenment and Its Effects on Modern Society, Springer 2010.
3. Baten, Jörg (2016). A History of the Global Economy. From 1500 to the Present. Cambridge University Press. p. 13–16. ISBN 9781107507180.
4. By El T - originally uploaded to en.wikipedia as Population curve.svg. The data is from the "lower" estimates at census.gov (archive.org mirror)., Public Domain, https://commons.wikimedia.org/w/index.php?curid=1355720.
5. Share of Global GDP, 1000 years, Data table in Maddison A (2007), Contours of the World Economy I-2030AD, Oxford University Press, ISBN 978-0199227204. By M Tracy Hunter - Own work, CC BY-SA 4.0, https://commons.wikimedia.org/w/index.php?curid=34088589.
6. Industrial Revolution and the Standard of Living, Clark Nardinelli, 2nd Edition, www.econlib.org, Concise Encyclopedia of Economics http://www.econlib.org/library/Enc/IndustrialRevolutionandtheStandardofLiving.html.
7. Economic History: Why did Asia miss the Industrial Revolution that began in the 18th century?https://www.quora.com/Economic-History-Why-did-Asia-miss-the-Industrial-Revolution-that-began-in-the-18th-century.
8. Why Did The Industrial Revolution Take Place In Europe And Not Asia? Daniel Venn January 23 2005 https://blogs.warwick.ac.uk/danielvenn/entry/why_did_the/.
9. Peng Xizhe (1987). Demographic Consequences of the Great Leap Forward in China's Provinces. Population and Development Review Volume 13 Number 4 (Dec 1987). pp. 648–649.
10. Russian Space Web - Spunik Development history http://www.russianspaceweb.com/sputnik.html.

11. NASA confirms that the Voyageur 1 probe has entered interstellar space (again), The Independent July 11 2014, http://www.independent.co.uk/life-style/gadgets-and-tech/nasa-confirms-voyager-1-has-entered-interstellar-space-9599916.html.
12. Crouzet, François (1996). "France". In Teich, Mikuláš; Porter, Roy. The industrial revolution in national context: Europe and the USA. Cambridge University Press. p. 45. ISBN 978-0-521-40940-7. LCCN 95025377.
13. Savery, Thomas (1827). The Miner's Friend: Or, an Engine to Raise Water by Fire. S. Crouch.
14. bbc history Thomas Newcomen http://www.bbc.co.uk/history/historic_figures/newcomen_thomas.shtml.
15. Baten, Jörg (2016). A History of the Global Economy. From 1500 to the Present. Cambridge University Press. p. 13–16. ISBN 9781107507180.
16. Gottlieb Daimler's First Automobile (March 8, 1886), http://germanhistory-docs.ghi-dc.org/sub_image.cfm?image_id=1261.
17. The History of Integrated Circuits, Nobleprize.org http://www.nobelprize.org/educational/physics/integrated_circuit/history/.
18. The Tragedy of the Internet Commons, May 18, 2012, The Atlantic, Bill Davidow, https://www.theatlantic.com/technology/archive/2012/05/the-tragedy-of-the-internet-commons/257290/.
19. Klaus Schwab, The Fourth Industrial Revolution. January 2016, World Economic Forum. ISBN 1944835008.
20. Jürgen Jasperneite: Was hinter Begriffen wie Industrie 4.0 steckt in Computer & Automation. http://www.computer-automation.de/steuerungsebene/steuern-regeln/artikel/93559/0/.
21. Helen Gill, A continuing Vision, Cyber-Physical Systems, March 10–11, 2008. Annual Carnegie Mellon Conference on Electricity Industry. Energy Systems: Efficiency, Security, Control. https://www.ece.cmu.edu/~electriconf/2008/PDFs/Gill%20CMU%20Electrical%20Power%202008%20-%20%20Cyber-Physical%20Systems%20-%20A%20Progress%20Report.pdf.
22. Design Principles of Industrie 4.0 Scenarios, January 2016 16th Hawaii International Conference on System Sciences, iEEE DOI:10.1109/HICSS.2016.488.
23. R. Drath, and A. Horch, "Industrie 4.0: Hit or Hype?", IEEE Industrial Electronics Magazine, 8(2), 2014, pp. 56–58.
24. "Computer for the 21st Century, Mark Weiser, PARC, ACM SIGMOBILE Mobile Computing and Communications Review Vol 3 Issue 3, July 1999 Pages 3–11 http://dl.acm.org/citation.cfm?id=329126.
25. Harnessing the power of feedback loops, Wired June 2011 https://www.wired.com/2011/06/ff_feedbackloop/all/1.
26. Forget The Consumer Internet Of Things: IIoT Is Where It's Really At, GE Reports, Oct 13, 2016, http://www.gereports.com/forget-consumer-internet-things-iiot-really/.

27. Everything you need to know about the Industrial Internet of Things, GE Digital, https://www.ge.com/digital/blog/everything-you-need-know-about-industrial-internet-things.

28. System of Systems Interoperability – (SOSI): Final Report – News. U.S. Department of Defense May 2003 https://resources.sei.cmu.edu/asset_files/TechnicalReport/2004_005_001_14375.pdf.

29. System-of-Systems. Carnegie-Mellon University, Software Engineering Institute, http://www.sei.cmu.edu/sos/.

30. Cyber-Physical Systems: Foundations, Principles and Applications, Edited by Houbing Song, Danda B. Rawat, Sabina Jeschke, and Christian Brecher, Series Editor Fatos Xhafa. Intelligent Data Centric Systes, Elsevier AP. 2017.

31. Cyber-Physical Systems Summit, "Holistic Approaches to Cyber-Physical Integration", April 24–25, 2008| St. Louis, Missouri http://cps-vo.org/cps-summit/2008.

32. Manufacturing 2.0. Industry Week June 8 2007 http://www.industryweek.com/companies-executives/manufacturing-20.

33. Demand-Driven Value Network (DDVN) - Gartner IT Glossary http://www.gartner.com/it-glossary/demand-driven-value-network-ddvn.

34. The rise of additive manufacturing, The Engineer, 2010, May 24 https://www.theengineer.co.uk/issues/24-may-2010/the-rise-of-additive-manufacturing/.

35. Buckminsterfullerene and Buckyballs – Definition, Discovery, Structure, Production, Properties and Applications. AZO Materials, July 15, 2006 http://www.azom.com/article.aspx?ArticleID=3499.

36. Richard P. Feynman (December 1959). "There's Plenty of Room at the Bottom". A 1959 lecture by Richard Feynman has become an important document in the history of nanotechnology. Nature: Nanotechnology 4, 783–784 (2009) DOI: 10.1038/nnano.2009.357 http://www.nature.com/nnano/journal/v4/n12/full/nnano.2009.357.html.

37. Definition of Bioengineering, University of California, Berkley. http://bioeng.berkeley.edu/about-us/what-is-bioengineering.

38. Definition of Genetic Engineering, United States Environmental Protection Agency, EPA https://iaspub.epa.gov/sor_internet/registry/termreg/searchandretrieve/termsandacronyms/search.do?search=&term=genetic%20engineering&matchCriteria=Contains&checkedAcronym=true&checkedTerm=true&hasDefinitions=false.

Harnessing the Transformation of Energy

39. bbc history Thomas Newcomen http://www.bbc.co.uk/history/historic_figures/newcomen_thomas.shtml.

40. Re: How much thrust does a Saturn 5 Rocket send out a minute? Nov 26 2001 David Ellis, Researcher, NASA Lewis Research Center. http://www.madsci.org/posts/archives/2001-11/1006882182.Eg.r.html.
41. Top 10 nuclear power plants by capacity, Sept 27 2013 http://www.power-technology.com/features/feature-largest-nuclear-power-plants-world/.
42. By The Numbers: The World's Most Powerful Things, Jan 28 2009 https://www.forbes.com/2009/01/28/most-powerful-things-business-power08_0128_powerful_slide_2.html?thisspeed=25000.

Harnessing the Transformation of Computation

43. A king's Search for Wisdom Awake! – 2007 http://wol.jw.org/en/wol/d/r1/lp-e/102007004?q=king&p=doc.
44. "Hindi and the origins of chess". chessbase.com. 5 March 2014.
45. Bird, H. E. Chess History and Reminiscences (London: Dean, 1893).
46. Shatranj, the medieval Arabian Chess, http://history.chess.free.fr/shatranj.htm.
47. The Oxford Companion to Chess by David Hooper, Kenneth Whyld, Oxford University Press; 2nd Revised edition (Oct. 1992).
48. Chess Programming Wiki Shaun Wylie. https://chessprogramming.wikispaces.com/Shaun+Wylie.
49. Endgame, Defeating the World Chess champion, http://www.computerhistory.org/chess/main.php?sec=thm-42f15cec6680f&sel=thm-42f15d3399c41.
50. TOP500 Super Computer List – June 1997 (201–300) https://www.top500.org/.
51. Press release, May 1, 1997: Ancient game, modern masters IBM Deep Blue, Kasparov to engage in historical chess match crossing the technology threshold into the 21st century https://www.research.ibm.com/deepblue/press/html/g.1.2.html.
52. "The last match man vs machine?". English translation of Spiegel Article. ChessBase. 23 Nov 2006.
53. A look inside China's chart toping supercomputer, June 20, 2016 Nicole Hemsoth, https://www.nextplatform.com/2016/06/20/look-inside-chinas-chart-topping-new-supercomputer/.
54. IBM's 200 petaflop Summit supercomputer to crush China's Sunway TaihuLight 27 June 2016, Graeme Burton. https://www.theinquirer.net/inquirer/news/2462885/ibms-200-petaflop-summit-supercomputer-to-crush-chinas-sunway-taihulight.
55. iPhone 7 and 7 + Will Allow "Console-Level Gaming" with New A10 Fusion Chip, Sept 7 2016, Sharon Coone, http://twinfinite.net/2016/09/iphone-7-will-allow-console-level-gaming-with-new-a10-fusion-chip/.
56. Drubach, Daniel. The Brain Explained. New Jersey: Prentice-Hall, 2000.

After Apollo

57. How Apollo Flew to the Moon, W. David Woods, Springer Praxis Books, 2nd Revised & enlarged edition 1 Jan 2011.
58. Apollo's Army, Airspace Magazine, June 17, 2009 http://www.airspacemag.com/space/apollos-army-31725477/.
59. The Apollo Missions, IBM http://www-03.ibm.com/ibm/history/ibm100/us/en/icons/apollo/.
60. With less computing power than a washing machine, The Guardian, David Adam, 2 July 2009 https://www.theguardian.com/science/2009/jul/02/apollo-11-moon-technology-engineering.
61. Apollo 11: The computers that put man on the moon, Computer Weekly, Cliff Saran. http://www.computerweekly.com/feature/Apollo-11-The-computers-that-put-man-on-the-moon.
62. The Apollo Guidance Computer: Architecture and Operation, Frank O'Brian, 2010 edition Springer Praxis Books.

The World in 2050

63. Information Technology and the U.S. Workforce: Where Are We and Where Do We Go from Here? (2017) April 2017 https://www.nap.edu/catalog/24649/information-technology-and-the-us-workforce-where-are-we-and.
64. Track how technology is transforming work, Tom Mitchell & Erik Brynjolfsson 13 April 2017, Nature http://www.nature.com/news/track-how-technology-is-transforming-work-1.21837.
65. The future of employment: How susceptible are jobs to computerization?, Carl Benedikt, and Michael A. Osborne, September 17, 2103, Oxford Martin Institute, Oxford University, UK http://www.oxfordmartin.ox.ac.uk/downloads/academic/The_Future_of_Employment.pdf.

2

The Technology of the 4th Industrial Revolution

Introduction

This observation of a shift to pervasive machine automation has been made by many observers, driven by artificial intelligence into products and services; in living experiences; in design and manufacturing capabilities; to utilities and transport infrastructure and changing social and work boundaries. This topic was raised in the recent Davos 2017 Summit in a public discussion lead by Klaus Schwab, Founder and Chairman of the World Economic Forum, with Sergey Brin, Co-Founder of Google, Alphabet [1]. During the conversation, Klaus Schwab reflected that since the publication of his original book on the 4th Industrial Revolution just 12 months prior (in 2016), that much had changed. New technologies had appeared, including commercial drone deliveries, 1 Terabyte SD memory cards, carbon nanotube transistors, dust-sized sensors that can be implanted within the human body, SpaceX and Blue Origin reusable rocket landings, while Google's Artificial Intelligence beat the world-class Go player, Lee Se-dol, 4-1 [2]. But the most notable change they both agreed had been in artificial intelligence. Sergey Brin pointed out that "When I was heading up GoogleX a few years back we had one project which is now called "Google brain" (a deep learning research project at Google). I did not pay attention to it at all. Myself had been trained as a Computer Scientist in the 90s and everybody knew AI didn't work. People had tried neural nets but none of them had worked out. But Jeff Dean, one of our top computer scientists, (Google Senior Fellow in the Systems and Infrastructure Group) would periodically show examples (of machine

© The Author(s) 2018
M. Skilton and F. Hovsepian, *The 4th Industrial Revolution*,
https://doi.org/10.1007/978-3-319-62479-2_2

learning) in development but that was a few years ago. Now Google Brain touches every single one of our main projects, ranging from search, photos, adverts, to everything we do at Google. There is a revolution in deep neural nets has been very profound and surprised me, even though I was sitting right there and could throw paper clips at it! This is an incredible time and very hard to forecast what these things do, we don't really know the limits" [3].

Driven by such rapid change is polarizing opinions across the spectrum of legal, technical, academic and government practitioners. This includes the dangers of social order from changes in jobs automation to new ways of doing things with technologies, which challenge the traditional economics view that new technology will replace the old and create new jobs from new technology. The 4th Industrial Revolution has this time raised the question whether this technological revolution might result in an overall reduction in human jobs, in the near term and decades ahead. But it also has the potential to revolutionize knowledge, science, and human potential, via robotics and augmented intelligence. This is set against the larger global issues of population growth and wellbeing, greenhouse gases, resource scarcity and sociopolitical change.

Sergey Brin and Klaus Schwab elaborated that the consequences of these technological changes deserve a lot of thought and that you cannot stop it, but you can try to channel it. There is a combination of the biological and digital revolution seen in examples such as CRISPR-Cas9 gene-editing [4] to genomics. On the other hand, machine learning has enabled advances in many fields impacting the economy, electronics to astronomy. Investing in these new kinds of intelligence creates a multiplier effect in many industries. We now have the ability to change our genes, to embed sensors into our body to connect and integrate into the social fabric of society. It seems to challenge what it means to be human in the future, what is individuality, and what kind of society do we want.

Technology is moving beyond the analytical to predictive and prescriptive powers with the rise of artificial intelligence. These technologies change how humans need to look at the values and norms of society. The agrarian revolution mechanized farming in the 1st industrial revolution, changing the availability of food and working practices, leading to cities and the infrastructure to industry and urbanization. Nevertheless, with the advent of 4th Industrial revolution we are beginning to see different concerns, which may have both good and bad consequences.

Klaus Schwab postulated that "we are looking at technology as threatening our present thinking and interpretation of how the world evolves, we need new thinking to define meaning, new concepts to define what humanity is, and what is the purpose of our lives?" [3].

This chapter provides a brief primer of the emerging technologies that are part of the 4th Industrial revolution, and considers how they are combining physical, digital and biological contexts that are radically altered by automation. In addition, we look at the rise of intelligent systems via advances made in artificial intelligence.

- The new technologies of the 4th Industrial Revolution
- The impact of physical, digital and biological systems
- The rise of Intelligent Systems

The New Technologies of the 4th Industrial Revolution

The digital revolution developed from the 1960s to the 1990s, during which time we saw the rise of digital electronics and its miniaturization, video, lasers to the personal computer and the mobile cell phone. The birth of the internet, together with advances in material and biological sciences instigated a fusion of these technologies, moving them into industries underpinned by telecommunications and computing. The 4th industrial revolution brought forward new breakthroughs in science, commerce, engineering but also and most significantly, cross-cutting issues in governance of society and social impact from these pervasive technologies.

It is perhaps surprising that historically many of these breakthrough technologies have origins well before the present decades and began in the middle to early part of the last century.

Technologies including digitization advances in Internet of Things (IoT), Virtual Reality (VR), Augmented Reality (AR), quantum computing and artificial intelligence (AI); to new physical manipulation in materials science in nanotechnology and 3D printing; to biological manipulation in bioengineering of genes, robotic surgery, prosthetics and wearables all have origins that can be traced back through several evolutionary steps (see Fig. 2.1). It is only when certain materials, physics, computational and commercial cost considerations are available, and properly aligned that ideas become a reality and move into the mainstream of use.

Origins of 4th Industrial Revolution Transitions

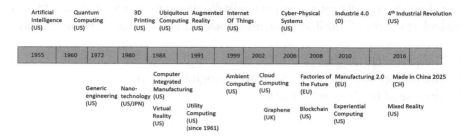

Fig. 2.1 Origins of the 4th industrial revolution transitions

Cloud Computing Multisided Platforms

Before we examine these technologies, it is important to remember that the genesis of on-demand computing happened during the digital revolution when the Internet was created. The protocols and networks established during that period saw the rapid rise of utility computing and functional architectures, which enabled the on-demand computing that we see today. Utility computing originated around 1991 but can be traced back to the early 1960s. John McCarthy, American Computer Scientist pioneer, speaking at the MIT Centennial as far back as 1961 said "Each subscriber needs to pay only for the capacity he actually uses, but he has access to all programming languages characteristic of a very large system. Certain subscribers might offer service to other subscribers. The computer utility could become the basis of a new and important industry. If computers of the kind I have advocated become the computers of the future, then computing may someday be organized as a public utility just as the telephone system is a public utility" [5].

While this story is now decades old it is also an important aspect of enterprise computing that enabled provisioning of computational resources, accelerating digitization across all industries and company sizes. Current debate and academic research, places great emphasis on digital platforming strategies, such as the multi-sided platforms (MSP) that can service multiple markets and customer sizes, as well as facility sharing and co-selling of the platform as-a-service [6]. We are surrounded by a multitude of examples from etsy and eBay, uber and Lyft, PayPal and Stripe, to amazon and Alibaba, google, Facebook and twitter. This is the shift to the "gig economy", "uberization" and massive networked marketplace infrastructures for exchange, collaboration and trading. MSPs and other forms of digital platforms are significant in the 4th industrial revolution, because they establish the utility infrastructure on top of the internet that enables, at scale, various kinds of enterprise and social computing architectures and solutions. Just looking at the current Amazon Web services platform, demonstrates a huge variety of computing resources that include, processing, storage, databases, network and content delivery, analytics, artificial intelligence, security, identity and compliance, mobile, Internet of Things and messaging. Together with a polymorphic range of development tools and software, and access to a skills marketplace, make this a readily available platform for on-demand with pay-as-you-go services. This transition has catapulted utility computing into a global market size for cloud computing in 2017, estimated by Gartner at $246.8 billion with the fastest growth in cloud infrastructure services (IaaS) at 36.8% [7], from a total global Software and IT services spending in the IT industry of $3.5 Trillion for 2017 [8]. All this in a mere ten years that saw the first Amazon EC2 Elastic Compute Cloud service launched (2006) and the first Apple iPhone in 2007, quite astonishing.

Machine Learning and Artificial Intelligence

The first use of artificial intelligence in mainstream research was in 1956, at the Dartmouth conference organized by John McCarthy, Marvin Minsky, Nathaniel Rochester and Claude Shannon, and is commonly cited as the birth of AI as a professional field of study [9]. The concepts of Artificial intelligence developed with other computational fields in database and programming languages, hardware developments and Graphical Unser interfaces and the invention of Very Large Scale Integration micro-electronics and semi-conductors in the 1970s. The 1980s saw new foundations laid in neural networks theories as well as the introduction of intelligent agents. The emergence of powerful computing resources, and the availability of vast amounts of information during the 1990s, enabled researches to develop more powerful models of computer learning, such as "deep neural networks", that we see today.

The concepts of the thinking machine, brain theories and neural nets and the first programmable Digital Computer were ideas that had been born in and not long after the WWII years by Alan Turing [10] and many others together with parallel processing theory by Richard Feynman the connection machine [11] in the 1950s. Foundations of Computational algebra originated form the work of John Von Neumann self-self-reproducing automata [12], Kurt Gödel incompleteness theorems [13] and Solomon Lefschetz work on algebraic topology [14] in the 1920s and 1930s. The concepts of cybernetic and formalization of the notion of feedback was instigated from the work of Norbert Weiner, Professor of mathematics at MIT [15] in the same period.

One approach to estimating the size of today's machine learning and artificial intelligence global market is to consider the chipset computing markets that specialize in machine automation, as well as the more general range of specialist machine learning functionality; termed machine learning as a service (MLaaS), which is emerging in a many specific industry sectors. Machine learning chipsets by Technology are predicted by marketsandmarkets.com to be a market worth $16.06 Billion and a CAGR of 62.9% from 2016 to 2022 [16]. These include deep learning chips set such as Graphical Processing units GPU, Google's Tensor Processing Units (TPU), for example, which are specialized for neural network computation acceleration. Software personal assistants that are algorithms for querying methods to Natural Language Processing (NLP) are other examples of a huge number of applications of AI. The fields of robotics and context aware processing, such as image recognition and sensor-actuator automation, are also increasing the range and scope of the AI market. The Machine learning as a service (MLaaS) is a rapidly growing new market with examples from Amazon Artificial Intelligence, Google AI and IBM Watson. Market size forecast by marketsandmarkets.com is a nacient $613.4 million expected to grow to 3.75 Billion at CAGR of 43.7% from 2016 to 2021 [17]. Featured services of MLaaS include software tools and environments for enterprise to build machine learning algorithms and neural networks, and an increasing library of commercially available algorithms covering examples such as marketing, risk analytics & fraud detection, predictive maintenance, to network Analytics.

The surveys report wide range of industry adoption of AI technologies in several industries such as manufacturing, media and advertising, healthcare, BFSI, and transportation and automotive as the key factor supporting the growth of the AI market in the North American region.

For the remainder of this chapter, as well as subsequent chapters, we will explore how Artificial Intelligence has become a critical technological change for the 4th Industrial Revolution.

Internet of Things, Micro-Electro-Mechanics and Bio Sensor Tech

The Internet of things (IoT) as described in the previous chapter originated as a term during the late 1990s with advent (and industrial usage) of Radio Frequency ID (RFID) tagging technology. This was the outcome of research and development efforts by organizations such as Proctor & Gamble [18].

IoT has long ago moved past RFID technology to embrace many types of sensors and telemetry to become a cornerstone of integrated and embedded systems feedback and control.

IoT in physical fusion is now common place in advanced engineering assets from jet engine turbines to automobile condition monitoring systems and nuclear power plants. Instrumentation connected to programmable controllers that integrate with supervisory control systems are found in supply chains automation and robotics, to metrology devices for measurement and calibration. Drones, be they manned or unmanned, semi or fully autonomous vehicles, work through sensor technologies to provide accurate and timely information on contextual situations; this information is used by the on-board computer and for the remote control of the vehicle. Drones are commonly used for location and remote operation of assets.

In Biological fusion, miniaturized IoT sensors may be attached to the human body (epidermis), ingested or integrated with organs, thereby enabling biological monitoring and augmentation of the host organism. These kinds of devices perform a vital role in mHealth and eHealth, such as mobile monitoring and measurement of medical and well-being status, as well as remote diagnostics and response. Wearable technologies use a variety of sensors that measure psychological and physiological states through sensory data collection, aggregation and analytics. Biological fusion also includes plant, animal and biosphere monitoring and integration as seen in automated agriculture and hydroponics.

Estimating the market size of IoT has proven difficult due to its many sub-segments with a wide range of variance in estimate from many analysts, consultancies and vendors. Examples include Gartner estimating 8.4 Billion connected things by 2017 [19] growing to 50 billion objects by 2020 in earlier forecast by Cisco and others [20]. Current estimated market valuation vary from examples of $8.6 trillion and 212 billion connected things by 2020 forecast by IDC in 2012 [21] revised in 2015 to $1.7 trillion [22] to BCG predicting the market will reach $276 Billion by 2020 [23]. Gartner forecast by 2020, more than half of major new business processes and systems will incorporate some element of the internet of things and a rise in IoT Security will become a key sub-segment of the market [24].

IoT and concerns centered around cyber security have become a major cross-cutting feature of the 4th Industrial era technology that we discuss in detail in a later chapter of Part III. This topic was again in a recent lecture at the November 2016 ReWork NewScientist Reinventing Energy Summit in London. Mustafa Suleyman, co-founder of Google DeepMind, reminded the audience that with recent IoT attacks publicized in the media, such as remote hacking into cars and changing traffic lights remotely, highlight the fact that connected systems are particularly vulnerable to such security breaches. Hooking up everything to machine intelligence so that it can regulate and solve problems for us such as saving energy, reducing greenhouse emissions, enabling home appliances and the interconnected city infrastructure is very attractive because it's convenient. Optimizing these may require controlling people's habits and behavior when they don't really want to be told what to do, so working in background may be more practical. But at the same time, it makes us a bit more vulnerable because if you connect everything IoT, it will increase the surface of attack. While we have many conventional methods to harden and take action to secure those systems, it is one of those trade-offs we need to make, in order to benefit from these new automated intelligence enabled systems. We need to pursue the utility and powerful agency these systems can deliver, but only to the extent to which we can do that safely and with all of the guarantees of security that we would like [25].

Robotics

While artificial intelligence in the form of software algorithms could be described as the "soft" side of machine intelligence, it is the physical manifestation of machinery acting on the physical world, using sensors from IoT integrated into robotics that present a new form of automation. This field is a great example of the 4th industrial revolution fusion of potentially all digital and biological concepts in automata related to remote and unmanned activity, as well as human augmentation and human mimicry.

This can be seen on the wide range of robotics systems born from the earlier era of cybernetics that involved the study of complex control systems pioneered by Norbert Wiener in the 1930s. In recent years the classifications made, for example, by the International Society of Intelligent Unmanned Systems (ISIUS) of the robotics field for unmanned and automated systems [26] include:

- Unmanned systems

  - Unmanned aerial vehicle controlled remotely or by onboard computers (UAV)s, Micro aerial vehicles (MAVs) that are a miniaturized class of UAVs and can be 15 centimeters or less to insect size. Unmanned marine vehicles (UMVs), under water vehicles (UVs).
  - Multi-agent systems used in network load balancing, traffic management to perimeter security defense systems (MAS). Unmanned guided Vehicles (UGVs), blimps, swarm intelligence, autonomous flying robots (AFRs), and flapping robots (FRs).

- Robotics and biometrics

  - Smart sensors, design and application of Micro-Electro-Mechanical systems (MEMs) and Nano-Elecro-Mechanical (NEMs) that use. These fields develop micro and nanosystems technology and micro and nanomachine technologies and nano materials science such as nanowires that are nanostructures of $10-^9$ meters.
  - Intelligent robotic systems, evolutionary algorithms, control of biological systems, biological learning control systems, neural networks, and bioinformatics.

- Context Aware Computing

  - Software computing also referred to as computational intelligence (CI) that focus on use of inexact solutions to computationally hard tasks, ubiquitous computing, distributed intelligence, distributed/ decentralized intelligent control.

- Control and computation

  - Distributed and embedded systems, embedded intelligent control, complex systems, pervasive computing, discrete event systems, hybrid systems, network control systems, delay systems, identification and estimation, nonlinear systems, precision monitoring control, control applications, computer architecture and very-large-scale integration (chip design) VSLI, signal/ image and multimedia processing. Software-enabled control, real-time operating systems, architecture for autonomous systems, software engineering for real-time systems and real-time data communications.

Todays forecast for the market for unmanned and remote controlled Drones (UAVs) ranges from a predicted $21.23 Billion by 2022 by marketsandmarkets.com [27] to $127 Billion by 2020 forecast by PwC [28].

The growth area of Industrial Robotics in manufacturing and assembly processes has seen more mainstream development with Asian markets, China being the biggest robot market since 2013. This is followed by Europe leading the development and implementation of robotic automation in electronics, metals, chemical, plastics and rubber and automotive sectors. The current market size is forecast to grow to $79.58 Billion by 2022 [29] with 160,600 units sold in Asian markets a rise of 19% followed by Europe at 10% growth to 50,100 units and 38,100 industrial robots shipped to Americas, 17% more than 2014 [30].

Virtual Reality, Augmented Reality and Mixed Reality

Creating a virtual model of the real world from data from the physical and biological inputs and events have been around since the early Victorian days when the magic lantern image projector was introduced. The earliest known sound recording device, the Phonautograph by French inventor Édouard-Léon Scott de Martinville was developed between 1853 and 1861. The world's first digital camera was created by Steve Sasson an Engineer at Eastman Kodak in 1975. The 8 pound camera recorded 0.01 megapixel black and white photos to a cassette tape. The first photograph took 23 seconds to create [31]. Seeking ways to blend real world and imaginary images was seen in examples such as stop-motion capture of Ray Harryhausen in the Science Fiction movies of the 1950s, including the Oscar winning special effects in the 7th Voyage of Sinbad in 1958, and the famous skeleton sword fight in the 1963 film, Jason and the Argonauts [32]. This form of 3D motion capture was seen as recent as Clash of the Titans movie of 1981 but has since been superseded by full digital motion capture of objects and human body and complete digital image design and digital motion animation by the 1990s.

In 1968, Ivan Sutherland with the help of his student, Bob Sproull, created the world's first virtual reality and augmented reality head-mounted display system (HMD), which he affectionately named the "Sword of Damocles" after an ode to the threat of power everywhere [33].

The notion of virtual worlds modelled by software as three dimensional representations can be seen within the ideas of virtual reality (VR) that aim to immerse the human user in images, sounds and other data that represents the real physical environment or an imaginary setting. By the 1980s the ideas of VR were becoming mainstream by pioneers such as the company VPL Research in 1984 by Jaron Lanier, a futurist who popularized Virtual Reality impact on Society and introduce early VR technology concepts [34]. The 1990s saw the first commercial VR headsets including Sega-VR [35], and Nintendo stereoscope 3D projection game "virtual boy" in the video gaming market [36]. Full PC powered VR gaming and industrial usages followed in the 2000s and 2010s from medical imaging, advanced engineering design and simulation; digital building architecture and geospatial mapping systems (GIS). Today, VR technology provides complete immersive headsets, or stereoscopic glasses, for use in systems that can include fully render wall, floor, ceiling to complete 360-degree room with 4K photorealistic environments. Compare this to the visual resolution of a human eye is about 1 arc minute, which a viewing distance of 20″ that is about 170 dots per inch or pixels per inch PPI. A 30″ monitor to achieve 170 dpi would need 4400 × 2600 pixels. An Apple MacBook Retina display is 2880 × 1880, a 5K screen is 5120 × 2880 and 8K is 7680 × 4320 pixels but varies with distance, the human eye's own visual acuity quality based on the Snellen chart (20/20) [37]. VR is now combined with motion sensors, wearable feedback groves and sensors offering six of more degrees of freedom movement capture, it is possible to interact with the VR objects in real-time.

Consumer products in VR, such as Google's glass entered the market in 2012 providing flat screen projection in line of eyesight, but was later discontinued in January 2015 [38]. Other developments include, Microsoft HoloLens that focused on augmented and mixed reality started in March 2016 [39] and included computer vision and object-recognition to enable the spatial positioning of real objects.

Real world spatial contextual awareness is where overlaid virtual objects and physical objects can be seen together in the same physical location. This requires physical positional data from GPS/GLONASS geolocation that is accurate to a few meters, or from physical symbols such as QR code (or other propriety barcode), which is able to link the physical location of specific digital data relative to a physical location. Techniques such as 360 degree photography, laser light detection and range scanning called LiDAR 3D scanner, are able to generate and collect a geographic "point cloud" of x, y and z coordinates of objects and their positions. These are commonly used in LiDAR Aerial Surveying (LAS) and in 3D modelling of buildings and objects such as AutoCAD Map 3D [40].

Mixed reality (MR) has now become the latest mainstream idea of blending physical and digital objects co-existing and interacting in real-time. This requires "digital twinning" as a concept from Cyber-Physical Systems (CPS) that was first defined as a term by Paul Milgram, Haruo Takemura, Akira Utsumi and Fumio Kishino from ATR Communications Systems Research Laboratories, Japan in 1994 as "Virtuality continuum" of combined physical and virtual reality [41].

The current market size of Virtual Reality is positioned as a niche market from $3.7 Billion in 2016 to $40.4 Billion by 2020 by Statista.com [42]. The Augmented reality market is estimated to be $162 Billion market disrupting mobile by 2020 forecast by IDC [43].

3D Printing, Additive Manufacturing and Near Net Shape Manufacturing

The development of digital information for physical design and materials manufacturing in computer-aided design (CAD) originated in 1961 with Ivan Sutherland who, then at MIT, described a computerized sketchpad, while under the supervision of his PhD by Claude Shannon [44]. This representation of digital information has become common place with integration into Computer aided Manufacturing (CAM and CADCAM) creating a flow of digital design, testing into manufacturing and production. This led to the rise of new forms of integrated design, manufacturing, assembly and production including Discrete manufacturing systems (DMS), adjustable manufacturing systems (AMS), and the rise of flexible manufacturing systems (FMS) and reconfigurable manufacturing systems (RMS). These paradigms have been enabled by the use of machine learning, robotics and advanced materials manipulation that have changed design, fabrication, assembly machines and configurations into more configurable and responsive systems for higher efficiencies through modularity and adaptability [45].

3D printing, also sometimes termed "Additive Manufacturing" represents a new digital to physical fusion of technology, printing and materials design and fabrication that originated from stereolithography back in 1986 by Charles Hull [46]. The speed and choice of materials are today rapidly increasing to a stage where additive manufacturing is seeing 3D printing machinery embedded into mainstream flexible and reconfigurable manufacturing in examples of printing jet engine parts by GE [47] to and in medical breakthroughs for human tissues [48]. "Near net shape" manufacturing is another related technique within additive manufacturing that aims for the initial production to be physically made near the completed final product as possible, to reduce additional completion stages. This technique has advanced due to recent developments in ceramics, plastics, metals and composition molding and forming technologies.

The 3D printing market is forecast by marketsandmarkets.com to be $30.19 Billion by 2022 [49] with expectations to become further integrated inline into smart flexible manufacturing process and customer centric systems as seen in the Adidas 3D printed soles of sports shoe wear [50].

Quantum Computing, Nanotechnology and Biochips

High performance computing (HPC) and more generally described by the term "supercommputing", were developed in the early 1960s by Tom Kilburn at University of Manchester, UK [51], and Seymour Cray at Control Data Corporate who went on to found Cray computers [52]. The technology was built using germanium and silicon based semiconductors or what is often classified as complementary metal-oxide-semiconductor (CMOS) technologies, and its design features in metal oxide semiconductor field effect transistors (MOSFETs) for logic functions. Supercomputing is the specialist field of computation tasks widely used in complex modelling from weather forecasting, advanced physics research to biomolecular simulation. Supercomputers of this type use the method of "parallelism" involving multiple computation at bit, instruction, data and task levels simultaneously, using techniques of multi-threading and hardware configurations, including multi-core, multi-processor, clustering and other methods to accelerate specific computational tasks.

The speedup of the overall task by splitting it into sub-tasks increases latency with more sub tasks [53], and is known as Amdahl's law, which was introduced in 1967 to describe the upper limits for these kinds of parallelism techniques. While this law only fits and restricts certain types of tasks, there are other considerations on the limits of current computing architecture models that include limits of Moore's Law and number of transistors in a dense integrated circuit doubles approximately every two years [54].

Present chip technology transistor component density is 22 nanometers (nm) in 2012, 14 nm in 2016 and 10 nm is predicted by late 2017 with a revised deceleration of Moore's law scaling to two and a half years [55]. While 7 and 5 nm (sub 30 atoms scale) technologies are envisaged by Brian Krzanich, Intel CEO [56], the costs and time scales to innovate this level of design is increasing each year, driving exploration for alternative methods and new technologies beyond silicon.

Apart from atomic scale limits, increasing energy consumption is the main issue for high-performance computing physical limits as well as increasing effects of quantum physics at this nano scale with atoms used in silicon chip fabrication around 0.2 nm.

Other current research fields are looking into alternative computing architectures [57]. The IEEE international Roadmap for devices and systems in 2016 looked beyond CMOS to emerging ideas, highlighted conventional and novel new approaches to computing architectures [58]. These included moving towards non-Von Neumann non-procedural, less-than-reliable computing models and data centric approaches that use machine learning techniques including neural network as new computing architectures that we discuss in more detail in later chapters of this book. The field of nanotechnology development for these reasons discussed here are reaching a critical point in the next decades when we are moving from evolutionary CMOS to revolutionary CMOS in the 22 nm to beyond sub 10 nm that is the level of molecular and atom manipulation manufacturing that has been aptly described in the IEEE roadmaps as "exotic science" and "really different" [58].

Quantum Computing

Quantum computing represents an alternative computing model that was founded on principles developed by Richard Feynman in the 1960s and in the 1980s [59]. David Deutsch demonstrated in 1985 the ability to use quantum properties that interfere constructively and destructively to perform complex calculations, infeasible by classical computing. Quantum computing techniques were shown to enable processing such as factoring very large prime numbers [60]. The key principles of quantum computing based on "superposition" and "entanglement" to perform calculations.

A "qubit" is a term used to define a quantum computing (QC) unit of information. There are several techniques to manufacture a qubit at atomic scale that seeks to hold the qubit in a stable state called "coherence time" that has been shown to last from seconds to hours, or minutes at cryogenic and room temperatures respectively [61].

Superposition is a quantum mechanical property that exists in sub-atomic scales enabling the use of a quantum bit to hold both 0 and 1 state simultaneously. While a quantum computer is running, the qubit can also be in any one of an infinite number of superposition between 0 and 1, so the qubit has a probability that it is in state 0 and a probability that it is in state 1. Nevertheless, superpositions are very fragile, and if we attempt to measure the value of a qubit the wave collapses into one of the basic states, 0 or 1.

Technically speaking, 2 qubits can be in any one of four basic states, $|00>$, $|01>$, $|10>$ and $|11>$, which are the states that 2 classical bits can assume, however, there are infinitely many states formed by superposition (or linear combinations) of these basic states.

In order to understand this a little better, let us return to the case where we have just one qubit, that has two states, $|0>$ and $|1>$. Let us consider a superposition, which might look something like

$$\sqrt{2/3} \cdot |0\rangle + \sqrt{1/3} \cdot |1\rangle$$

What does this mean? It means the following: if you attempt to observe, or measure, this qubit, 66% of the time you will find it in state $|0>$ and 33% of the time you will find it in state $|1>$ (Fig. 2.2).

One can represent the qubits as points on the unit circle, and in such a case the horizontal distance from the origin represents the probability of the qubit being observed in state $|0>$ and the vertical distance from the origin represents the probability of the qubit being observed in state $|1>$. Note, that in this representation a classical bit would appear as two distinct points on the unit circle, one at (0, 1) and one at (1, 0).

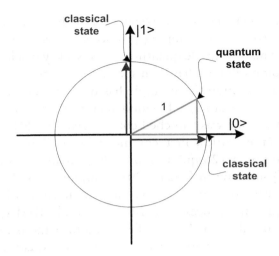

Fig. 2.2 Quantum and classical states

Quantum calculations involve the movement of this coherent transfer of a superposition spin state. The nuclear spin and electron split for "processing and "memory". An electron spin is suitable for a qubit in quantum processor, because an electron spin can be manipulated and can be coupled to other electron spins with a much shorter time scale than a nuclear spin. A nuclear spin is suitable for a qubit in quantum memory, because a nuclear spin has a much longer coherence time than an electron spin [62, 63].

Qubits can be currently manufactured using a range of evolving techniques. These include silicon QC to lithographically place atoms, nuclear magnetic resonance (NMR) QC, Superconducting QC, Ion Trap QC, Linear Optical QC (LOQC), Nitrogen-vacancy (N-V) center in diamond, electrostatically defined quantum dot, and several other competing technologies, many of which are still in the research stage [64].

Entanglement is a second physical property when pairs, or groups of particles, are generated in ways such that the quantum state cannot be described independently of the others, even when separated by large physical distance they remain the same and the quantum state. In quantum computing, calculations are made in quantum circuits using quantum gates and a n-qubit register performing several types of quantum algorithms. When processing the entangled states use quantum mathematics that can be manipulated and on termination of the algorithm the states fall out of quantum entanglement become decoherent and the result can be read off as a classical probability. Developing protocols to detect and quantify the entanglement of many-particle quantum states is a key challenge for present day quantum computing but has been successfully commercialized recently.

The most famous enterprise example has been the D-Wave corporation that demonstrated a prototype 16-qubit quantum annealing processor in 2007. The D-Wave one was launched commercially in 2011 and described by D-Wave as "the world's first commercially available quantum computer", operating on a 128-qubit chipset [65]. quantum computer model D-Wave 2000Q shipping in January 2017 [66] and IBM launching a new quantum computing division "IBM Q" in March 2017 using IBM's publicly available quantum processor. IBM aim to build IBM Q systems with approximately 50 qubits in the next few years to demonstrate capabilities beyond today's classical computers [67]. Googles quantum computing partnership with NASA in 2015 used D-Wave 2X quantum computing machine [68].

Quantum computers can solve specific types of problems that classical computing cannot do because of limitations in digital computing speed previous discussed. The term qubit was in fact indirectly defined by Stephen Wiesner in 1983 from seeking to develop "quantum banking" that aimed to prevent bank notes from being forged using a technique called conjugate coding [69]. Quantum computers are described as quantum Turing machine (QTM) also known as a universal quantum computer that is a model of the concepts of the quantum computer that Alan Turing described between 1936 and 1937 and seen as the foundations of modern procedural computers [70].

Quantum computing processing power by comparison has been described, for example, as 10^8 more powerful than a classical digital computer but this is for specific tasks that benefit from quantum parallelism typically in applications include complex mathematical calculations in fundamental research, machine learning with the potential to undermine cyber security through integer factorization, which underpins the security of public key cryptographic systems. Quantum computing can factor two 300 digital primes quickly that would be infeasible computationally for digital computers. Quantum cryptography is where quantum speedup properties have been successfully used in security systems using quantum entangled keys to prevent correction of the security keys. Recent examples of quantum encryption has been achieved by Chinese researchers in June 2017 sending quantum encryption between earth and orbiting satellites as "spooky action" at a record distance of entanglement of 1200 km.

Today's market size for quantum computing is still nascent with market-sandmarkets.com forecasting the High-performance computing and super-computing market to grow from $28.08 billion in 2015 to $36.62 Billion by 2020 [71]. The Quantum computing market forecast by marketsandmar-kets.com to reach $5 Billion by 2022 [72].

Neuromorphic Computing

Carver Mead along with Nobel laureate Richard Feynman, the distinguish professor John Hopfield established three new fields of study, namely: Neural Networks, Neuromorphic Systems and Physics of Computation. The trio attempted to understand the morphology of individual neurons, the circuits they form, and the behavior that results as a consequence of these particular kinds of biological elements. Moreover, they attempt to understand the computational aspects of such systems, namely its ability to store (or represent) information and how to process this information in a manner that is robust to damage, yet able to learn and adapt to various environmental influences. Neuromorphic Engineering focuses on producing devices specifically aimed at modelling and implementing devices within the realm of human perception, such as vision, touch, auditory and olfactory systems.

In a very interesting interview, Carver Mead [73] has this to say about computing hardware suitable for processing biological perception type problems:

> … it's also true that [digital] isn't the only paradigm for doing that kind of computation, and that the digital machines that do discrete symbol manipulation are not exactly matched to this very soft kind of fuzzy computation, that goes on in perception systems. The neural technology that's coming along on silicon also, it's piggybacking on the same base technology that the digital stuff is driving, are evolving to where we're starting to be able to do really very competent things for ten thousand times less energy than you can do them with the same [digital] technology

The current trend is to utilize what are called mixed-signal techniques to design these artificial neural systems, which function in a manner analogous to the spiking of the natural biological neurons, but constructed out of a different material (silicon rather than a carbon-based material that is commonly found in mammals). Carver Mead was initially inspired by Max Delbruck, and the observations of synaptic transmissions in the retina, which motivated Mead to consider the transistor as an analog device rather than a digital one.

Not only did Carver Mead instigate this entire field of research, but also collaborated with others (including some former students) in order to establish start-up companies that developed and sold some of these inventions, which are in everyday use today. Some of these inventions include cochlea implants, the touchpad found on most modern computers and silicon retina, not to mention some of the first noise cancelling microphonic chips that were used in early smart phones.

Nevertheless, given the significant results shown by these mixed-signal chips, especially their ability to operate at very low power, has attracted the attention of giants within the world of microelectronics, such as IBM who have a massive effort in place to create neuromorphic computing devices of their own [74, 75], as well as efforts by Qualcomm [76], which are in the form of a software SDK for their popular Snapdragon platform. In addition, one should mention the effort underway by the group of ten organizations that make up the European Human Brain Project, including the effort by Manchester University's Prof. Steve Furber who is building a vast neural device called SpiNNaker [77] using chips from ARM.

According to Karlheinz Meier, a physicist who is a computing pioneer working within the realm of neuromorphic computing and currently the leader of the European Brain Project [78]:

Moving to neuromorphic computing architectures, he believes, will make emulating the brain function not only more effective and efficient, but also eventually accelerate computational learning and processing significantly beyond the speed of biological systems.

Technically, traditional kinds of processors (CPUs) operate using a global clock, a kind of metronome that dictates when instructions are to be moved and when they are processed. However, by distributing the neuromorphic equivalent of cores in a manner that allows them to operate in parallel—using an event-driven model, means these kinds of distributed processors operate without the need of a global clock, using a spiking behavior. This architecture not only reduces the huge power overhead, but also operates thousands of time faster than conventional systems.

Why is this a big deal? First reason relates to the long-awaited end of Moore's Law, which now seems ever more imminent, therefore researchers around the world are evaluating different models of large-scale computing that is often inspired by nature. Second, AI systems typically require lots of processing power, processing power in the past meant computers needed huge power sources, making them impractical where mobility was concerned. The typical power consumption of a neuromorphic chip made by IBM, which contains five times as many transistors as a standard Intel processor, yet consumes only 70 milliwatts of power, whereas the comparable Intel processor would use approximately 70 watts of power, almost a thousand times more.

So where are the challenges? Modern neuromorphic chips act like a general processor, similar to the way that our own cortex does. While this may sound like the kind of thing we all would like to have, we have to remember that such processors are only useful if they have some kind of algorithm, or program, specifically designed for them—hence the challenge for these kinds of chips.

There are some groups working on solutions that will aid the development of such algorithms and simulations. One such group is lead by Chris Eliasmith at University of Waterloo, who together with his team have created Nengo: a python tool for building large-scale functional brain models [79]. The point about Nengo is that not only is it able to run on conventional hardware, but also more specialized neuromorphic hardware such as SpinNaker.

Nengo is built on the Neural Engineering Framework (NEF) [80], which is a framework for constructing neural simulations.

Market segment for neuromorphic processors is looking very bright, according to recent reports

> Future Market Insights' report, titled "Neuromorphic Chips Market: Global Industry Analysis & Opportunity Assessment, 2016-2026," projects that the global neuromorphic chips market, which is currently valued at an estimated US\$ 1.6 billion, will rake in revenues worth US\$ 10,814.9 million by 2026 end. According to the report, the size of global neuromorphic chips market will expand exponentially – at 20.7% CAGR. [81]

The global neuromorphic computing market size was valued at USD 1490.8 million in 2016, and expected to reach USD 6480.1 million by 2024 according to a new study by Grand View Research, Inc. [82]

Biochips

Other research outside of CMOS and quantum computing has been in the fields of biological computing and examples including Nanomorphic cells and the use of DNA as a storage medium that seek to learn approaches from biology and nature. This field combines both nano-engineering and biotechnology, and is another great example of the 4th industrial revolution's fusion of physical, digital and biological, as the limits of the digital revolution are reached in the micro and nano scales. Research into bacteria cells as computers describe single-cell living organisms as having Turing Machine [70] features they exhibit behavior following Von Neumann concepts of information processing [83] as building blocks of the cell itself. In addition, the cell also exhibit the ability to learn, communicate with each other and to self-repair and reproduce. Research has shown that human designed and developed, nano scale semiconductors could not match biological living cell processing capabilities that include: 1000 times more memory capacity, Logic greater than 10 times, 1 million times more power efficient and algorithmic efficiently 1000 times greater [84]. A research collaboration between Harvard Medical University, Wyss Institute and John Hopkins University in 2012 saw researchers demonstrate storing an entire genetics textbook in less than a picogram of DNA—one trillionth of a gram—an advance that could our ability to save data. 5.27×10^6 bits [85].

These ideas of fusing biological and technologies systems have ramifications for the future of energy management and new biotechnological systems based on natural systems.

The need for increasingly faster computing have been grounded on the wider planetary scale problems of increasing population, global warming, water and other resource scarcity. These complex, often seemingly intractable factors, require more complex models of processing to resolve these impacts. There is a race between the latency of time to research in order to bring these technologies to mainstream use and the costs of getting this wrong, and the potential existential risks to humanity is a core feature of the 4th industrial revolution [86].

The basic equation of computing efficiency as a function of algorithmic logic speed, memory storage capacity and inputs and outputs interaction within a given volume of space, heat dissipation and energy consumption requirement is challenging the ideas of silicon. Research measurements made comparing the human brain computational power has established this as 10^{19} bits per second binary information throughput [87] and 10^8 MIPS instructions per second [88]. And the human brain does all this computation consuming less than 30 Watts of power. Biological cell processes work at extraordinary scales at exa (10^{18}) speeds and memory speeds that far exceed todays silicon based computing technology. We experience this every moment with an almost instant response of brain-eye object recognition, hand-eye-movement coordination, language, deliberate movements, controlling body organs and hormones and many others. This all happens continuously and real-time in fractions of a second. This suggests basic algorithms need to work in very few steps and on tiny energy consumption, heat generation and spatial resources at the molecular and nano scale [89].

An argument for the importance in pursuing alternative technologies was put forward by John Schmitz in 2009 IEEE International Integrated Reliability Workshop suggested the need for new chip design that went beyond "Moore's law" that combined measuring logic processing speed and memory capacity to what he called "intelligent systems". These would include power management, communications and sensor-actuator functionality. These would be the hybrid devices that are already emerging today and include MEMS devices, Biosensors, magnetoresistive (MR) sensors, RFID sensors, e-Pill, security and Secure Sockets Layer encryption SSL, Hybrid car power and battery management and in vehicle networked devices that represent the fusion of next technologies of the 4th industrial revolution [90].

Blockchain

Satoshi Nakamoto, is a name reference to an unknown person or group of people, who in 2008 created the first reference implementation specification that theorized the design of a distributed database made of records called "blocks" or "blockchains", each block of which contains a timestamp and is linked to previous block. A key feature is that data is distributed across the whole network of blocks making its almost impossible to attack, as a there is no central point that hackers might exploit, therefore the data stored in the blockchain is regarded to be incorruptible. Blockchain security includes the use of a public key cryptography that is an address held on that blockchain. It can be generally summarized that every node or miner in the decentralized distributed ledger owns a copy of the blockchain that is propagated by massive data replication and computational trust. No centralized copy exists and all users are equally trusted.

When a blockchain technology is used to execute a transaction, the digitally signed transaction is sent to the node miner to verify the transaction, which is then broadcast to all connected nodes as a block. The network validates the data using a consensus algorithm of a certain time duration and o successful validation, a time stamp as proof of the transaction by all the blocks is made and the receiver receives the transaction [91].

Blockchain was originally created as a form of cryptofinance payments that are made directly between payer and payee (P2P), which removes the need for a central authority but can be used for many other transactions requiring transaction exchange and verification.

Blockchain technology is generally ran and developed as public open source protocols and algorithms to create transparency and network effects. There are several types of blockchain that have evolving including permissionless that uses blockchain as a transport layer to private and permissioned blockchains that can restrict to some degree participants but can lack transparency. Groups of users can do what is termed software forks, or hard forks, which create different descendant blockchains with separate histories from that point forward. Soft forks are backward compatible with older blocks while hard fork are not. Types of blockchains include transactional blockchains and logic optimized blockchains, which can embed additional code and state information which can be used to create online markets and programmable transactions known as "smart contracts" [92]. Smart contracts have additional properties that can facilitate the execution of contracts with complicated outcomes. They can also be used to create auctions. A smart contract, for example, can be coded to sell an item at a predefined price. Buyers will bid and transfer their payments, yet the smart contract will only pick up the maximum offer and transfer back the remaining amount of money to the bidders [93].

Blockchain has also been described as a threat to national government currencies as it creates an unregulated currency denomination that is not overseen by any central bank. The nature of the blockchain does away with intermediaries, in the case of financial services industry Iris Grewe, a Partner at the UBS Innovation Forum in December 2016, described the blockchain innovation as having the "internet of information" today as one's and zero's transporting content, but not the ownership level or the payment level. With blockchain you separate this so you essentially create an "internet of value" in one step, which has the potential to be very disruptive to many kinds of business models. Before blockchain technologies, companies have information flows on one level, and then payments and ownership levels being organized and involving several parties at another level. We also currently have mediators and brokers that organize all this such as the financial stock exchange, banks and clearing houses. With blockchain technology we do not necessarily need these anymore. But there are areas that have not yet been addressed by the blockchain communities that include examples such as credit finance, large infrastructure finance and investment management syndication. This is still areas where the existing banking organizations could setup their own blockchain environment for these services [94].

There are today many examples of open-source, public, blockchain-based distributed computing platform including public chains where anyone can access, read and transact. For example consortium blockchains that use consensus processes controlled by a pre-selected set of nodes such as a group of financial institutes. Another example is private blockchains were permissions are kept centralized to one organization and may allow public or restricted read access [95].

The early rate of adoption of blockchain had reported problems but is now following the technology adoption path that some observers describe as similar to TCP/IP as a foundational technology with great potential [96]. Today's cryptocurrency market capitalizations value bitcoin BTC at $19,361,633,948, followed by ethereum ETH $4405,266,360, Ripple XRP $1255,129,952, Litecoin LTC $559,794,449 and Dash DASH, Monero XMR and others [97]. Cryptocurrency usage is in alternatives to credit card and PayPal transactions and in software based purchases in online retailer and selected business starting to adopt it as an alternative currency with minimal transaction overhead.

Blockchain is not just a system for financial transactions but as a system for assurance of potentially any transactions that require 'smart contracts" of exchange. Examples include

- Utilities

  - Blockchain technology is used to develop smart digital grids that include consumers being able to buy and sell solar energy peer-to-peer P2P trading. Trials are already underway in business-to-business B2B energy trading using blockchain technology between Utility conglomerates and other utilities. Blockchain can also be used to authenticate and manage utility billing processes for Electric Vehicle charging stations. This together with smart contracts to manage cost savings across the utility industry [98].

- Healthcare

  - Blockchain could transform electronic patient records enabling interoperability between different providers and the patient and carer parties more efficiently. It could also drive personal data management to enable personal records to be accessed and managed securely by the public [99].

- Land Registry

  - Land registry control could be automated through blockchain technology simplifying the processes of registration and governance.

- Taxation

  - Blockchain technology could be used to create new taxation mechanisms that are built into the blockchain itself such as small transaction tax enabling the potential for real-time taxation.

- Real estate

  - Properties and exchange of sale could be managed through blockchain technology.

- Legal

  - Law firms that utilize the blockchain technology and deal with law suits related to cryptocurrencies, which are also known as crypto-law enterprises, can convert content of various documents into hashes to deposit onto a blockchain. Given the fact that hashes stored on the blockchain can never be altered, the documents' validity can be universally confirmed in front of any court of law. Storing legal documents on the blockchain promotes the credibility and integrity of court data and legal evidence and renders tampering with such sensitive data an impossible task to achieve.

- IoT Security

  - Blockchain could support remote device and edge sensor security. Blockchain technology can be utilized to investigate the history of various devices connected to the IoT. Furthermore, it can be utilized to execute and confirm transactions taking place between various devices connected across the IoT. This can help in taking IoT to a whole new level of maturing independence via using the public ledger technology to record all data exchange operations among devices, human users and services connected via the IoT [100].

- Pharmaceutical Supply chain security

  - Block chain can be used to manage subscriptions for drugs, drug product serialization of drug categories that could help stem the flow of counterfeit drugs. Blockchain could enable blockchain registered supply chain pharmaceutical packaging. One such branded solution Cryptoseals uses provides tamper-evident seals with a Near Field Communication (NFC) chip embedded with unique identity information which is immutably registered and verified on a blockchain. In addition to an object's identity, the seal also records the identity of its registrant and packaging or asset metadata to the blockchain [101].

An interesting aspect of Blockchain is that it is based on distributed consistency protocol. This concept in general uses nodes (also sometimes call "miners") to validate and authorize transactions collectively to a consensus written into the "blocks". While digital currencies are typically held by individual's digital wallet that is updated with the blockchain "virtual ledger". Several examples of problems have been highlighted and hackers have exploited these and other weaknesses. Overall the benefits of the distribute ledger and that these types of attack are very rare, and difficult to achieve, which makes blockchain a reliable and significant technology, though technically no system is ever totally secure in reality but work within limits of trust and validation. Some of the famous examples of blockchain problems are listed here.

- Double spending problem

    - Occurs if an individual can spend the digital currency balance more than once. Protection against this can be through a confirmation process verifying each transaction has not been previously spent. While extremely difficult with the nature of the distributed consistency of blockchain, it is possible to double spend leaving a node miner not receiving digital currency payment, this is regarded as accounting fraud [102].

- Two Generals problem

    - Related to getting consensus between two nodes where either node may be at error due to incorrect information sent or received, or deliberately fraudulent. It is so known as the coordinated attack problem and illustrates communications between two or more nodes over an unreliable communications link that may arbitrarily fail [103]. Each tries to confirm a message to the other over a constantly unreliable link and this can perpetuate indefinitely. Mathematically this has been proven to be unsolvable because it is impossible to get consensus when its uncertain either party may be erroneous [104].

- Byzantine Generals problem

    - Is a generalized case of the unsolvable two generals problem that applied to the problem of coordinating common consensus across multiple distributed nodes, is sometimes also called the byzantine failure or the byzantine fault tolerance (BFT) [105, 106].

The Fusion Impact of Physical, Digital and Biological Domains

We can see that the 4th Industrial revolution described by Klaus Schwab as a fusion of physical, digital and biological domains is really a recognition of new technological structures that are radically transformational. This is the "post Moore's law" world that in a sense looks beyond what defined the silicon semi-conductor and digital era, while by no means over, has reached the

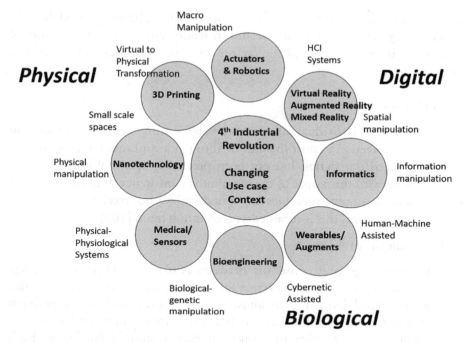

Fig. 2.3 The fusion into changing context of experience

exotic limit stage of sub 10 nano meters. This is a world of atoms and molecular engineering, evident in the silicon world but in the 4th era is also seeing this spread to bioengineering and physical materials manipulation. This is what the underlying themes of the 4th Industrial revolution meant by the *fusion* of these technology across boundaries, as well as moving into advanced new ways to build, and change, the context in which they are used.

This is the fusion of new technologies that are becoming increasingly interconnected with each other. The rank and scale is enormous, just consider medical sensors in wearables can take continuous body temperatures readiness, many other parameters that are transmitted through an Internet of Things IoT network to a range of services we have only just begun to explore (Fig. 2.3).

New kinds of interactive experience will be possible as the immersive world of social media and new forms of virtual media and augmented devices increasingly blend the physical world and the overlay of virtual and augmented experiences as seen in emerging VR and AR technologies.

But these will not only change how physical, biological and enabling digital information processing can be connected, it will change the nature of living in those domains as well as forms of non-human agents, such as robots that can move and manipulated manufacturing, services and transportation processes. The development of connected homes and work environments are just one of the things that will radically evolve as they become augmented with data and intelligence about activities, work and collaborative activities.

The Rise of Intelligent Systems

The physical state of materials, objects and information on their energy, rate of use and performance are becoming integrated back into themselves. Social and societal interactions have equally become integrated into social media and telecommunications connected domains that can reach, and at times divide the social and economic communities that have access (or lack access) to these modern physical and virtual architectures and infrastructure edifices the 4th industrial era.

Massive data and informatics generation from digital, physical and biological domains are giving rise to new forms of information and *intelligence* about those macro and micro environments at unprecedented rates.

This is a key difference that the 4th industrial era has from the previous eras of energy and material transformations, which saw material wealth and geographical globalization. This time it involves changes to the nature of control and feedback that we are now able to exert on our planet, down to the local effects of crowd and material manipulation right down to the micro and nano scales.

Therefore our human relationship to these changes of context of social, material and digital manipulation are transformational in the level of insight and automation, which is now possible and what may come in the near future.

The fusion of physical and digital control is creating intelligence about those materials and energy requirements. Consumption of power, commodities to advanced engineering and transactional capabilities from machine integration into these processes and physical artifacts.

Complex systems relationships are forming when these physical, biological and digital domains entangle and converge. Information is now shared and disseminated through the internet and collective awareness of groups. What kind of planned directed and emergent behavior can result creating new experience and social interaction?

In what the World Economic Forum described as the technological tipping points and societal impact [96], are changes that will matter to individuals, enterprises governments and society as a whole.

The impact of the 4th industrial revolution as we saw in the industrie 4.0 of cyber-physical systems CPS, have the capacity to transform interaction

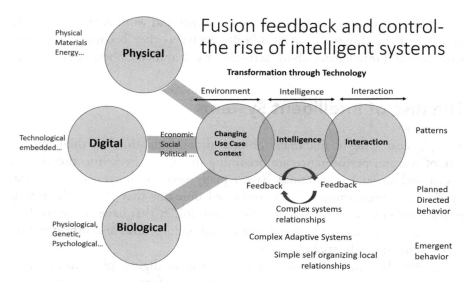

Fig. 2.4   Fusion feedback and control—the rise of intelligent systems

4th Industrial revolution impact on interaction

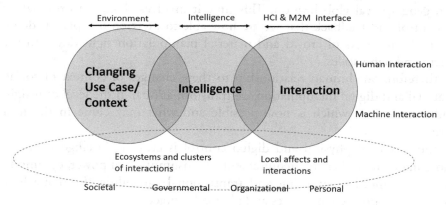

Fig. 2.5   4th industrial revolution interaction impact

between humans and machines, and in machine to machine automation (see Figs. 2.4 and 2.5).

This experience augmented by such technologies is crossing the boundaries of personal data liberties, biological insights and new forms of responsive care and lifestyles. This can transform practitioners, consumers, partnerships and collaboration crowd sourcing information sharing and insights. But on the other hand requiring new governance over personal data privacy, ethics and cyber security controls and broader governmental regulation and policy making for this future.

We see this everywhere we look with these technologies becoming increasing embedded into contextual experience across all industries.

It is this transformative impact on the spatial, temporal experience in these contexts, the rise of machine intelligence and new immersive and embedded technology which will shape the next era.

How will ecosystems, clusters of organizations and supply chain networks, work in this ever expanding and connected world? What will be the affects and interactions in the way services and products are created, manufactured, delivered and consumed?

These and many others changes as described by Klaus Schwab as a fusion of physical, digital and biological domains is really a recognition of new technological structures that are radically transformational [96].

Paradoxes of the 4th Industrial Revolution

In this book we seek to explore several interconnected consequences of this transformation as we begin to see the effects to the fusion of new technologies (see Fig. 2.6).

The Changing Human-Machine and Machine-Machine Interaction Space

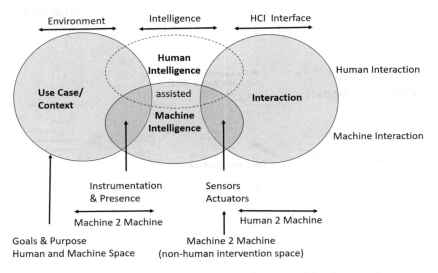

Fig. 2.6 The changing human-machine and machine-machine interaction space

4th Industrial Revolution Technologies

4th industrial revolution Technologies represent ways to develop new industries and to disrupt and change existing industries. Examples of these include driverless cars, smart factories, smart utility grids, digital banking and many others.

4th Era Transformation of Skills, Jobs, Work and Things

This leads to the consequences of planned change or the result leading to unintended disruption to skills, employment and everyday objects and items that may become connected or as-a-service.

Degree of Automated Interconnected Industries

These transitions of machines, work and objects will have transformational impact on interconnected industries. Examples of these include integrated connected transport, automated supply chains, digital finance and banking mediation, connected health, digital government and many others.

Cross-Cutting Concerns

The paradoxes of change are seen as new technologies change patterns of jobs and employment, and the resulting changes impacting industry, mar-

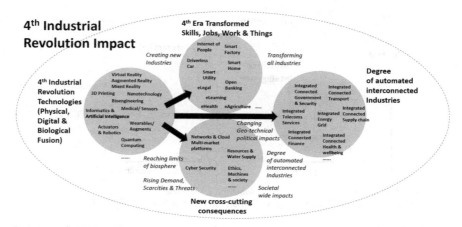

Fig. 2.7 Paradoxes of the 4th industrial revolution impacts

kets and enterprise level organizations. The 4th industrial revolution will drive cross-cutting concerns that will have an impact on the nature of work, security, transparency, trust and privacy for human kind [96]. It will also change economic activity, ways for government to protect its citizens, and the concept of national identity that must bridge between physical and connected worlds. The definition of what is an organization or a community and the very essence of what it is to be an individual, will also change as information and shifting ownership of assets occur, wealth and society values will be challenged by these intelligence systems (see Fig. 2.7).

Summary

We have examined the technological impacts on the larger scale of society and industry, however, at the human level there is the expectation that these changes will go beyond disruptive digital transformation of work and industrial operations. What is clearly different is the rise of automation and machine intelligence or Artificial Intelligence (see Fig. 2.8).

The ramifications are only just becoming apparent and is a key issue for governments and enterprise, as the speed and changes brought on by the 4th Industrial revolution technologies starts to impact. How will economic

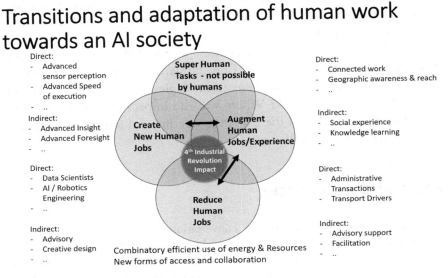

Fig. 2.8 Towards an AI society

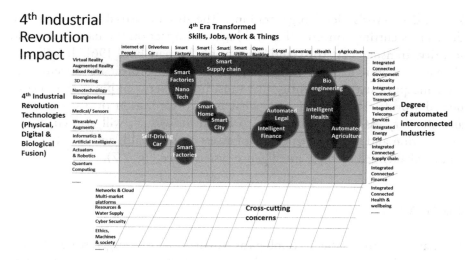

Fig. 2.9 The 4th industrial revolution impact

growth be generated and competitive industry function with these changes in light of recent developments in intelligent systems?

The near to longer term impact of Artificial Intelligence and the fusion of intelligent systems into industries, individuals and societies will have profound impact on the role of the human at work and human experience [107, 108].

A central theme of this book is to explore these impacts for the practitioner who is faced with the challenges of learning what these technologies are, and what they are capable of, so they may prepare for the impact of these changes on their organization.

How will these technologies create new forms of skills and employment, or will it reduce and remove tasks from humans through automation? Will there be a augmentation of these technologies to support and enhance human experience and work? Where will the impact of intelligent systems be? and what concerns will there be in navigating and responding to the rise of this AI society? (Fig. 2.9).

Notes and References

1. Klaus Schwab and Sergey Brin in conversation, Davos 2017, World Economic Forum. https://www.youtube.com/watch?v=30rx3dBPbIs.
2. The 10 Best Technology Advances of 2016, Luke Larsen, Paste magazine, December 23, 2016, https://www.pastemagazine.com/articles/2016/12/the-10-best-technology-advances-of-2016.html.

3. Davos 2017—An Insight, An Idea with Klaus Schwab and Sergey Brin in conversation, World Economic Forum. https://www.youtube.com/watch?v=ffvu6 Mr1SVc&t=732s.

4. CRISPR/Cas9 and Targeted Genome Editing: A New Era in Molecular Biology, https://www.neb.com/tools-and-resources/feature-articles/crispr-cas9-and-targeted-genome-editing-a-new-era-in-molecular-biology.

5. The Cloud Imperative, Business Report, MIT Technology Review. Simson Garfinkel, October 3, 2011, https://www.technologyreview.com/s/425623/the-cloud-imperative/.

6. Platform Revolution: How networked markets are transforming the economy and how to make them work for you. Geoffrey G. Parker, Marshall W. Van Alstyne, Sangeet Paul Choudary, W.W. Norton & Company. 2016.

7. Gartner Says Worldwide Public Cloud Services Market to Grow 18 Percent in 2017, February 22, 2017, http://www.gartner.com/newsroom/id/3616417.

8. Gartner Says Global IT Spending to Reach $3.5 Trillion in 2017, October 19, 2016 http://www.gartner.com/newsroom/id/3482917.

9. A proposal for the Dartmouth Summer Research Project on Artificial Intelligence, August 31, 1955, Hannover, New Hampshire, http://www-formal.stanford.edu/jmc/history/dartmouth/dartmouth.html.

10. Computing machinery and Intelligence, Alan Turing, MIND, A quarterly Review, October 1950.

11. Richard Feynman and The Connection Machine, W. Daniel Hillis for Physics Today, http://longnow.org/essays/richard-feynman-connection-machine/.

12. Theory of Self-Reproducing Automata, John Von Neuman, edited and completed by Arthur W. Burks, University of Illinois Press, Urbana and London 1966. http://cba.mit.edu/events/03.11.ASE/docs/VonNeumann.pdf.

13. Gödel's Incompleteness Theorems Jan 20, 2015, https://plato.stanford.edu/entries/goedel-incompleteness/.

14. Algebraic Topology, Solomon Lefschetz, American Mathematical Soc., 31 Dec 1942—Mathematics—389 pages.

15. Norbert Wiener Invents Cybernetics, livinginternet.com http://www.livinginternet.com/i/ii_wiener.htm.

16. Artificial Intelligence (Chipsets) Market worth 16.06 Billion USD by 2022, maeketsandmarkets.com, http://www.marketsandmarkets.com/PressReleases/artificial-intelligence.asp%20.asp.

17. Machine Learning as a Service (MLaaS) Market by Component (Software Tools, Services), Organization Size, Application (Marketing, Risk Analytics & Fraud Detection, Predictive Maintenance, Network Analytics), Service and Region—Global Forecast to 2021, http://www.marketsandmarkets.com/Market-Reports/machine-learning-as-a-service-market-183667795.html.

18. Harnessing the power of feedback loops, Wired, June 2011, https://www.wired.com/2011/06/ff_feedbackloop/all/1.

19. Gartner Says 8.4 Billion Connected "Things" Will Be in Use in 2017, Up 31 Percent From 2016, Gartner, February 7, 2017, http://www.gartner.com/newsroom/id/3598917.

20. The Internet of Things: How the Next Evolution of the Internet is changing Everythings, Dave Evans April 2011, Cisco Internet Busness Solutions Group (IBSG), www.cisco.com/c/dam/en_us/about/ac79/docs/innov/IoT_IBSG_0411FINAL.pdf.

21. The Internet of Things Is Poised to Change Everything, Says IDC, Business Wire, October 3, 2013 http://www.businesswire.com/news/home/20131003005687/en/Internet-Poised-Change-IDC.

22. Internet of Things Market to Reach $1.7 Trillion by 2020: IDC, June 2, 2015 https://blogs.wsj.com/cio/2015/06/02/internet-of-things-market-to-reach-1-7-trillion-by-2020-idc/.

23. Winning in IoT: It's All About the Business ProcessesJANUARY 05, 2017 by Nicolas Hunke, Zia Yusuf, Michael Rüßmann, Florian Schmieg, Akash Bhatia, and Nipun Kalra, https://www.bcgperspectives.com/content/articles/hardware-software-energy-environment-winning-in-iot-all-about-winning-processes/.

24. Gartner Says By 2020, More Than Half of Major New Business Processes and Systems Will Incorporate Some Element of the Internet of Things, Gartner Newsroom, Jan 14, 2016. http://www.gartner.com/newsroom/id/3185623.

25. Reinventing Energy Summit, Nov 25, 2016, London 2016 https://www.re-work.co/events/reinventing-energy-summit-london-2016.

26. International Society of Intelligent Unmanned Systems ISIUS http://www.isi-usys.org/.

27. Drones Market worth 21.23 Billion USD by 2022, marketsandmarkets.com http://www.marketsandmarkets.com/PressReleases/commercial-drones.asp.

28. World Drone Market Seen Nearing $127 Billion in 2020, PwC Says, Bloomberg.com Wojciech Moskwa, May 9, 2016, https://www.bloomberg.com/news/articles/2016-05-09/world-drone-market-seen-nearing-127-billion-in-2020-pwc-says.

29. Industrial Robotics Market by Type (Articulated, Cartesian, SCARA, Cylindrical, Parallel, Collaborative Robots), Component (Controller, Robotic Arm, End Effector, Sensors, Drive), Vertical and Geography—Analysis & Forecast to 2022, marketsandmarkets.com http://www.marketsandmarkets.com/Market-Reports/Industrial-Robotics-Market-643.html?gclid=CjwKEAjwrMzHBRDW3saA88aT80MSJACbvo1TvbSlz-JI8wGWSES9_W37E2EAIcgMzI3f4vnUq41kYRoCYIrw_wcB.

30. Executive summary World Robotics 2016 Industry Robots, https://ifr.org/img/uploads/Executive_Summary_WR_Industrial_Robots_20161.pdf.

31. The World's First Digital Camera by Kodak and Steve Sasson, Michael Zhang, Aug 05, 2010, PetaPixel. https://petapixel.com/2010/08/05/the-worlds-first-digital-camera-by-kodak-and-steve-sasson/.

32. The Ray & Diana Harryhausen Foundation, http://www.rayharryhausen.com/.
33. Ivan Sutherland A.M.Turing Award 1988, http://amturing.acm.org/award_winners/sutherland_3467412.cfm.
34. Virtual Reality Society VPL Research Jaron Lanier, https://www.vrs.org.uk/virtual-reality-profiles/vpl-research.html.
35. Sega-VR headset 1991, http://segaretro.org/Sega_VR.
36. Virtual Boy Nintendo 1995, http://nintendo.wikia.com/wiki/Virtual_Boy.
37. What is the highest resolution humans can distinguish? Eyewear April 21 2013, http://blog.eyewire.org/what-is-the-highest-resolution-humans-can-distinguish/.
38. The history of Google Glass, http://glassalmanac.com/history-google-glass/.
39. "With HoloLens, Microsoft aims to avoid Google's mistakes". Reuters. May 2016, Sarah McBride, San Francisco, http://www.reuters.com/article/us-microsoft-hololens-idUSKCN0YE1LZ.
40. About Point Clouds and LiDAR Data, Feb 8, 2016, Autodesk, AutoCAD Map 3D, https://knowledge.autodesk.com/support/autocad-map-3d/learn-explore/caas/CloudHelp/cloudhelp/2016/ENU/MAP3D-Use/files/GUID-7C7DD8A7-B561-45B0-A803-852E0A667F3C-htm.html.
41. Augmented Reality: A class of displays on the reality-virtuality continuum: Paul Milgram, Haruo Takemura, Akira Utsumi and Fumio Kishino from ATR Communications Systems research Laboratories, Japan SPIE Vol. 2351, Telemanipulator and Telepresence Technologies (1994), http://etclab.mie.utoronto.ca/publication/1994/Milgram_Takemura_SPIE1994.pdf.
42. Virtual reality software and hardware market size worldwide from 2016 to 2020 (in billion U.S. dollars), https://www.statista.com/statistics/528779/virtual-reality-market-size-worldwide/.
43. The virtual and augmented reality market will reach $162 billion by 2020, BI Intelligence IDC, August 2016, http://uk.businessinsider.com/virtual-and-augmented-reality-markets-will-reach-162-billion-by-2020-2016-8.
44. Sketchpad: A man-machine graphical communcations systems, Ivan Edward Sutherland, Technical Report, Number 574, University of Cambridge, computer Laboratory, UK, UCAM-CL-TR-574, ISSN 1476-2986, Sept 2003, https://www.cl.cam.ac.uk/techreports/UCAM-CL-TR-574.pdf.
45. Assessment of reconfiguration schemes for Reconfigurable Manufacturing Systems based on resources and lead time, Erik Puik, Daniel Telgen Leo van Moergestel, Darek Ceglarek, Robotics and Computer-Integrated Manufacturing 43 (2017) 30–38.
46. History of 3D printing, https://3dprintingindustry.com/3d-printing-basics-free-beginners-guide/history/.
47. Additive Manufacturing, GE, the world's largest manufacturer, is on the verge of using 3-D printing to make jet parts. MIT Technology Review Martin LaMonica, https://www.technologyreview.com/s/513716/additive-manufacturing/.

48. A 3D bioprinting system to produce human-scale tissue constructs with structural integrity, Hyun-Wook Kang, Sang Jin Lee, In Kap Ko, Carlos Kengla, James J Yoo,& Anthony Atala, Nature, Biotechnology, 34, 312–319 (2016) http://www.nature.com/nbt/journal/v34/n3/full/nbt.3413.html.
49. D Printing Market worth 30.19 Billion USD by 2022, http://www.marketsandmarkets.com/PressReleases/3d-printing.asp.
50. Adidas is going to sell 100,000 sneakers with 3-D printed soles, cnbc, April 7, 2017, http://www.cnbc.com/2017/04/07/adidas-3d-printed-trainers-futurecraft-4d.html.
51. Memories of the Ferranti Atlas computer, http://curation.cs.manchester.ac.uk/atlas/elearn.cs.man.ac.uk/_atlas/.
52. Seymore Cray, Cray.com, http://www.cray.com/company/history/seymour-cray.
53. "Validity of the Single Processor Approach to Achieving Large-Scale Computing Capabilities" Amdahl, Gene M. (1967). AFIPS computer conference. http://dl.acm.org/citation.cfm?id=327215.
54. Cramming more components onto integrated circuits. Gordon Moore, Electronics, Volume 38, Number 8, April 19, 1965, http://www.monolithic3d.com/uploads/6/0/5/5/6055488/gordon_moore_1965_article.pdf.
55. Intel pushes 10 nm chip-making process to 2017, slowing Moore's Law, Infowrold, James Niccolai, Jul 16, 2015, http://www.infoworld.com/article/2949153/hardware/intel-pushes-10nm-chipmaking-process-to-2017-slowing-moores-law.html.
56. Intel CEO Says Reports of the Death of Moore's Law Have Been Greatly Exaggerated abc news, Alyssa Newcomb, April 27, 2016, http://abcnews.go.com/Technology/intel-ceo-reports-death-moores-law-greatly-exaggerated/story?id=38703042.
57. Beyond Moor's Law: SRC Views on Nanoelectronics, Victor V. Zhinov, Ralph K. Cavin,, Nano-tec Workshop, Barcelona, Spain, Nov 6–7, 2012, SRC Semiconductor Research Corporation is a consortium of companies including IBM, AMD, Intel, and others.
58. Roadmap for devices and systems, 2016 that looks beyond CMOS to emerging devices. IEEE 2016, http://irds.ieee.org/images/files/pdf/2016_BC.pdf.
59. Simulating Physics with Computers, Richard P. Feynman, International Journal of Theoretical Physics, Vol 21, Nos. 6/7, 1982, https://people.eecs.berkeley.edu/~christos/classics/Feynman.pdf.
60. Deutsch, David (1985). "Quantum Theory, the Church-Turing Principle and the Universal Quantum Computer". Proceedings of the Royal Society of London A. 400 (1818): 97–117. http://rspa.royalsocietypublishing.org/content/400/1818/97.
61. Kamyar Saeedi et al. (2013). "Room-Temperature Quantum Bit Storage Exceeding 39 Minutes Using Ionized Donors in Silicon-28". Science.

342 (6160): 830–833. Bibcode:2013Sci...342..830S. doi: 10.1126/science.1239584. PMID 24233718.

62. Chapter 14, Spin Qubits for Quantum information Processing, http://www.nii.ac.jp/qis/first-quantum/forStudents/lecture/pdf/noise/chapter14.pdf.

63. Vladimir Privman, Dima Mozyrsky, Israel D. Vagner, Quantum computing with spin qubits in semiconductor structures. Computer Physics Communications 146 (2002) 331–338, https://arxiv.org/abs/cond-mat/0102308.

64. T. D. Ladd, F. Jelezko, R. Laflamme, Y. Nakamura, C. Monroe, & J. L. O'Brien, Quantum Computers, Nature Vol 464 / 4 March 2010 / doi: 10.1038/nature08812 http://qeg.mit.edu/images/QuantumComputing.pdf.

65. D-Wave Announces Commercially Available Quantum Computer, Forbes Alex Knapp, May 17, 2011, https://www.forbes.com/sites/alexknapp/2011/05/17/d-wave-announces-commerically-available-quantum-computer/#20bd6e1b3707.

66. D-Wave Announces D-Wave 2000Q Quantum Computer and First System Order, Jan 24, 2017, https://www.dwavesys.com/press-releases/d-wave%C2%A0announces%C2%A0d-wave-2000q-quantum-computer-and-first-system-order.

67. IBM Q, Building the first universal quantum computers for business and science, http://research.ibm.com/ibm-q/.

68. Google's Quantum Computer Is 100 Million Times Faster Than Your Laptop David Nield Dec 10 2015 Science Alert. http://www.sciencealert.com/google-s-quantum-computer-is-100-million-times-faster-than-your-laptop.

69. S. Wiesner, "Conjugate Coding," SIGACT News, Vol. 15, No. 1, 1983, pp. 78–88. doi: 10.1145/1008908.1008920, http://www.scirp.org/(S(351jmbntvnsjt1aadkposzje))/reference/ReferencesPapers.aspx?ReferenceID=629285.

70. Turing, A.M. (1938), "On Computable Numbers, with an Application to the Entscheidungsproblem: A correction", Proceedings of the London Mathematical Society, 2 (published 1937), 43 (6), pp. 544–6, http://onlinelibrary.wiley.com/doi/10.1112/plms/s2-43.6.544/abstract.

71. High Performance Computing (HPC) Market worth 36.62 Billion USD by 2020, 2015, marketsandmarkets.com, http://www.marketsandmarkets.com/PressReleases/Quantum-High-Performance-Computing.asp.

72. Quantum Computing Market Forecast 2017–2022, marketreserearchmedia.com March 2017, https://www.marketresearchmedia.com/?p=850.

73. Deep shift—Technology tipping points and societal impact: Survey Report, September 2015, World Economic Forum. http://www3.weforum.org/docs/WEF_GAC15_Technological_Tipping_Points_report_2015.pdf.

74. "How Things Really Work, a lecture by Gordon Bell and Carver Mead", https://youtu.be/zBpWkTETwD8?t=9m16s.

75. "Introducing a Brain-inspired Computer TrueNorth's neurons to revolutionize system architecture", http://www.research.ibm.com/articles/brain-chip.shtml.

76. "How neuromorphic 'brain chips' will begin the next era in computing" (2016), https://www.extremetech.com/extreme/236362-how-ibms-neuromorphic-brain-chips-will-begin-the-next-era-in-computing.

77. "Chip giants pelt embedded AI platforms with wads of cash" (2016), https://www.theregister.co.uk/2016/08/17/chip_giants_invest_heavily_to_boost_changes_in_embedded_ai_platforms/.

78. Furber, S. and Temple, S. "Neural Systems Engineering" J. R. Soc. Interface (2007) 4, pp. 193–206.

79. Think Fast – Is Neuromorphic Computing Set to Leap Forward? https://www.hpcwire.com/2016/08/15/think-fast-neuromorphic-computing-racing-ahead/.

80. Bekolay, Trevor et al. "Nengo: A Python Tool for Building Large-Scale Functional Brain Models." Frontiers in Neuroinformatics 7 (2013): 48. PMC. Web. 13 Apr. 2017.

81. Global Neuromorphic Chip Market to Surpass US$ 10 Billion in Revenues by 2026; Smart Machine Integration & AI Systems Driving Market Growth, http://www.futuremarketinsights.com/press-release/neuromorphic-chip-market.

82. Neuromorphic Computing Market Analysis By Application (Signal Processing, Image Processing, Data Processing, Object Detection, and Others) By End-use (Consumer Electronics, Automotive, Healthcare, Military & Defense, and Others), Expected To Reach USD 6,480.1 Million By 2024, http://www.grandviewresearch.com/industry-analysis/neuromorphic-computing-market.

83. von Neumann, John (1945), First Draft of a Report on the EDVAC, https://web.archive.org/web/20130314123032/, http://qss.stanford.edu/~godfrey/von-Neumann/vnedvac.pdf.

84. Danchin A. Bacteria as computers making computers. FEMS Microbiol Rev. 2009 Jan; 33(1):3–26. doi: 10.1111/j.1574-6976.2008.00137.x. http://onlinelibrary.wiley.com/doi/10.1111/j.1574-6976.2008.00137.x/full.

85. Next-generation digital information storage in DNA. George M. Church, Yuan Gao, Sriram Kosuri, Science Express, 16 August 2012 / Page 1/ 10.1126/science.1226355, http://arep.med.harvard.edu/pdf/Church_Science_12.pdf.

86. Igor L. Markov Limits on fundamental limits to computation, Nature 512, 147–154 (14 August 2014) doi: 10.1038/nature13570, http://www.nature.com/nature/journal/v512/n7513/full/nature13570.html.

87. H. Moravec, When will computer hardware match the human brain?, Journal of Evolution and Technology. 1998. Vol. 1, http://www.jetpress.org/volume1/moravec.htm.

88. Gitt W, Information—the 3rd fundamental quantity, Siemens Review 56 (6): 36–41 1989.

89. L.G. Valiant, A quantitative theory of neural computation, Biol, Cybern. 2006 95, http://amygdala.psychdept.arizona.edu/Jclub/Valiant_2006.pdf.

90. Reliability in the more than moor Landscape, Keynote, John Schmitz, IEEE International Integrated Reliability Workshop, October 18, 2009, http://www.iirw.org/past_workshops/09/IIRW_keynote_final_posting.pdf.
91. Nakamoto, Satoshi "Bitcoin: A Peer-to-Peer Electronic Cash System" October 31, 2008, http://nakamotoinstitute.org/bitcoin/.
92. Bitcoin Developer Guide, https://bitcoin.org/en/developer-guide#block-chain.
93. The blockchain technology, smart contracts and legal procedures. Tamer Sameeh, deep.dot.web. March 2017, https://www.deepdotweb.com/2017/03/14/blockchain-technology-smart-contracts-legal-procedures/.
94. Blockchain and bitcoin - Interview Iris Grewe, Partner Financial Services, BearingPoint, UBS Innovation Forum, December 2016 BearingPoint channel YouTube. https://www.youtube.com/watch?v=8OkDDb5igxc&t=77s.
95. Types of Blockchains, https://blockchainhub.net/blockchains-in-general/.
96. Marco Iansiti, Karim R. Lakhani, The Truth About Blockchain, Jan–Feb 2017 HBR, https://hbr.org/2017/01/the-truth-about-blockchain.
97. CryptoCurrency Market Capitalizations, http://coinmarketcap.com/.
98. James Basden, Michael Cottrell, How Utilities Are Using Blockchain to Modernize the Grid, March 2017 HBR, https://hbr.org/2017/03/how-utilities-are-using-blockchain-to-modernize-the-grid.
99. John D. Halamka, MD, Andrew Lippman, Ariel Ekblaw, The Potential for Blockchain to Transform Electronic Health Records, March 2017, HBR, https://hbr.org/2017/03/the-potential-for-blockchain-to-transform-electronic-health-records.
100. How can the blockchain technology take the security of IoT to a whole new level?, Deep.Dot.Web Tamer Sameeh, Dec 27, 2016, https://www.deepdotweb.com/2016/12/27/can-blockchain-technology-take-security-iot-internet-things-whole-new-level/.
101. Chronicled launches blockchain-registered supply chain and pharmaceutical packaging, Ian Allison, Dec 7, 2016, http://www.ibtimes.co.uk/chronicled-launches-blockchain-registered-supply-chain-pharmaceutical-packaging-1592220.
102. How does a block chain prevent double-spending of Bitcoins? Sean Ross, Investopedia June 19, 2015, http://www.investopedia.com/ask/answers/061915/how-does-block-chain-prevent-doublespending-bitcoins.asp.
103. Leslie Lamport, Robert Shostak, and Marshall Pease, The Byzantine Generals Problem, ACM Transactions on Programming Languages and Systems, Vol. 4, No. 3, July 1982, Pages 382–401. http://www-inst.eecs.berkeley.edu/~cs162/fa12/hand-outs/Original_Byzantine.pdf.
104. Minimum Viable Block Chain, Iiya Grigorik May 5, 2014, https://www.igvita.com/2014/05/05/minimum-viable-block-chain/.
105. Transaction processing for distributed systems, Jan 20, 2014, Chen Hao. Coolshell. http://coolshell.cn/articles/10910.html.

106. Contemporary Approaches to Fault Tolerance, Alex Wright Communications of the ACM, Vol. 52 No. 7, Pages 13–15 2009. doi: 10.1145/1538788.1538794, https://cacm.acm.org/magazines/2009/7/32080-contemporary-approaches-to-fault-tolerance/fulltext.
107. Deep Shift: Technology Tipping Points and Societal Impact, Survey Report, September 2015, Global Agenda Council on the Future of Software & Society World Economic Forum, http://www3.weforum.org/docs/WEF_GAC15_Technological_Tipping_Points_report_2015.pdf.
108. Eliasmith, C. Anderson, C.H. (2003). Neural Engineering: Computation, representation, and dynamics in neurobiological systems. Cambridge, MA: MIT Press.

3

Introduction to Artificial Intelligence and Cognition

Introduction

Artificial Intelligence has a long history that can be traced back to Gottfried Leibniz, who envisaged a machine that could help resolve complex legal cases using an automated reasoning machine. Leibniz made huge strides in this direction, establishing mathematical logic and the binary system as well as building the world's first four-function calculator. Nevertheless, he also inspired Gödel, whose work provided the platform from which Alan Turing launched arguably one of the most adventurous intellectual journeys undertaken by humanity—namely that of artificial intelligence.

In this chapter, we shall introduce the reader to some of the foundational concepts in artificial intelligence, while leaving the interested reader to pursue the details in books specializing in artificial intelligence, such as Russell and Norvig [1].

We begin with a brief history of how three individuals were instrumental in establishing the entire field of artificial intelligence:

- Alan Turing—who we now know was already working on these ideas back in 1942, possibly before
- Warren McCulloch, who along with Walter Pitts established an abstract model for the neuron, which not only inspired von Neumann and Marvin Minsky, but also Frank Rosenblatt, who built the first perceptron
- John McCarthy, whose efforts beginning with the infamous 1956 Dartmouth Conference have made a huge impact on this field

© The Author(s) 2018
M. Skilton and F. Hovsepian, *The 4th Industrial Revolution*,
https://doi.org/10.1007/978-3-319-62479-2_3

The section that follows, introduces the reader to cognitive concepts, which will be useful to understand how researchers we are attempting to imbue computers with these cognitive abilities, which until recently were reserved for living things—namely the ability to learn, adapt to environmental changes and to reason.

It is prudent to mention that the age of cognitively enhanced machines has been part of our community for the last twenty years. For example, we have used neural network based systems to read postal codes (zip codes) since 1998, and many banks have used neural networks to read the numerical amount on checks since that time also.

Turing, McCulloch and John McCarthy

Alan M. Turing

The notions that he had learnt while attending a course on logic by the topologist, Max Newman, fascinated Alan Turing during most of 1935. In particular, he had become very interested in Gödel's Theorem and the so-called "Entscheidungsproblem".

Gödel's Ph.D. thesis (1929) had already proved the completeness theorem for first-order logic, namely that a statement is universally valid if and only if it can be deduced from the axioms—this proved that within first-order logic the notions of "truth" and that of "provable" were essentially equal. What remained was to prove the Entscheidungsproblem (or decision) problem, namely, whether an effective method exists to decide if any well-formed formula of the pure first-order predicate logic was valid, in all possible interpretations.

In other words, to show whether there existed a method, procedure, or algorithm that would take as input a statement of first-order logic and answer 'Yes' or 'No' to the question of its validity—in a finite number of steps. The study and solution of this problem would turn out to be a pivotal point in Turing's life.

Turing realized that if he were to answer this question, he would need to give an exact mathematical description (definition) of what it means to be computable by a strictly mechanical process, which he did via the idea called a (Turing) machine,

> namely an idealized computational device following a finite table of instructions (in essence, a program) in discrete effective steps without limitation

on time or space that might be needed for a computation. Furthermore, he showed that even with such unlimited capacities, the answer to the general Entscheidungsproblem must be negative. [2]

Just one year later, Turing presented his solution to Newman, in a paper entitled "On computable numbers, with an application to the Entscheidungsproblem". Initially Newman was quite skeptical of the paper that had been presented to him, but would quickly become convinced and encouraged Turing to publish his ideas. Neither Turing nor Newman were aware that there were two other proposals that attempted to analyze the general notion of 'effective computability'—one by Gödel "General Recursiveness" and the other by Church using what he called "the λ-calculus".

Gödel explained his notion of general recursiveness in lectures on the incompleteness results during his visit to the Princeton in 1934. Nevertheless, Gödel only regarded general recursiveness as a "heuristic principle" and was not willing to commit himself to that proposal. Although,

Gödel was deeply suspicious of abstraction in computation to the point that he did not accept the λ Calculus as a model of computation until it had been proved that it computed the same functions as Turing Machines. [3]

The equivalence of the λ Calculus and Turing Machines is now known as the "Church-Turing Thesis".

Gödel, called Church's proposal "thoroughly unsatisfactory", in fact he remained skeptical of church's proposal virtually all his life, and in 1963 Gödel would identify the approach adopted by Turing as the definition of "algorithm" or "mechanical procedure" for a "formal system", in preference to even his own Herbrand–Gödel recursion and that of the λ-calculus.

Turing arrived in Princeton in 1936 to study logic under Church, nevertheless, that was not a very particularly happy relationship and would see Turing spending more time with John von Neumann—who also believed that Turing's approach was the correct one:

von Neumann ... firmly emphasized to me, and to others I am sure, that the fundamental conception is owing to Turing—insofar as not anticipated by Babbage, Lovelace and others. [4]

Turing established two life-long relationships in 1936, one with a man that would become his mentor (Man Newman), and the other with a man that he would collaborate with for years to come both in mathematics and in the burgeoning field of computer science, namely John von Neumann.

Turing continues his stay at Princeton, this time on a Procter Fellowship and decides to work towards a Ph.D. under the supervision of Church. He completed the first draft of his thesis within 14 months of arriving at Princeton—including the previous year when he was undertaking work for John von Neumann.

Turing obtains his Ph.D. in 1938 at the age of 25, and von Neumann offers him a research assistantship with him at the Institute of Advanced Studies at Princeton. Nevertheless, Turing decides not to stay in the USA and returns to Cambridge. On September 3rd, Britain declares war on Germany and Turing sets off for Bletchley Park. Turing's efforts at Bletchley Park are well known, nevertheless what is less well-known are his efforts in what he called the "child machine" and his obsession with the very notion of what would become known as "Artificial Intelligence" (AI).

Andrew Hodges describes how Turing was thinking about AI even when he wrote the famous 1936 paper in the documentary on Alan Turing made by the BBC [5]. The earliest evidence we have of this comes from recollections by those who worked with Turing at Bletchley Park. In particular Donald Michie, Jack Good and Shaun Wylie:

> Arriving at Bletchley Park in 1942 I formed a friendship with Alan Turing, and in April 1943 with Jack Good. The three of us formed a sort of discussion club focused around Turing's astonishing "child machine" concept. His proposal was to use our knowledge of how the brain acquires its intelligence as a model for designing a teachable intelligent machine. [6]

In the video "From Code breaking to Computing: Remembrances of Bletchley Park 50 Years ..." [7] Donald Michie talks about Turing's obsession regarding "Thinking Machines" that would one day "outstrip the capabilities of human thought, reason, knowledge & learning".

The friendship Turing forms with Michie, Good and Shaun Wylie continues even when the war ends. In 1947, Wylie and Michie design chess playing program called Machiavelli, to rival Turing's Turochamp program. Turing would begin to program both while at University of Manchester but would never complete [8].

In 1948, Turing takes a sabbatical from his position at the National Physical Laboratory, and returns to Cambridge to work on his ideas on AI, the result of which is a report entitled "Intelligent Machinery", which is ridiculed, then ignored by the head of Laboratory [9]. In this amazing paper, Turing defines the notion of 'discrete' and 'continuous' machinery using the notion of a path on a manifold, as well as notions that would later be recognized as Genetic Algorithms and Neural Networks.

In 1950, Turing publishes his seminal paper entitled "Computing Machinery and Intelligence" [10]. In this paper, Turing clearly states:

> The original question, "Can machines think?" I believe to be too meaningless to deserve discussion.

and suggests:

> Instead of attempting such a definition I shall replace the question by another, which is closely related to it and is expressed in relatively unambiguous words. The new form of the problem can be described in terms of a game which we call the 'imitation game'

that would permit one to establish whether a given system could be identified as 'intelligent'.

Turing describes some of the features of what he calls the 'child machine', and expresses his view that while opinions may vary as to the complexity which is suitable for such a machine, that one

> might try to make it as simple as possible consistently with the general principles. Alternatively one might have a complete system of logical inference 'built in'

and further explains that

> the process of inference used by the machine need not be such as would satisfy the most exacting logicians. There might for instance be no hierarchy of types. But this need not mean that type fallacies will occur, any more than we are bound to fall over unfenced cliffs. Suitable imperatives (expressed within the systems, not forming part of the rules of the system) such as 'Do not use a class unless it is a subclass of one which has been mentioned by teacher' can have a similar effect to 'Do not go too near the edge'

moreover,

> Most of the programs which we can put into the machine will result in its doing something that we cannot make sense (if at all), or which we regard as completely random behavior. *Intelligent behavior presumably consists in a departure from the completely disciplined behavior involved in computation*

and goes on to state,

> We may hope that machines will eventually compete with men in all purely intellectual fields. But which are the best ones to start with? Even this is a difficult decision. Many people think that a very abstract activity, like the playing of chess, would be best. *It can also be maintained that it is best to provide the machine with the best sense organs that money can buy, and then teach it to understand* and speak English. This process could follow the normal teaching of a child. Things would be pointed out and named, etc.

The final paragraph is of some significance to modern-day AI, because it is very clear that Turing's vision was to build an entire system, which included physical hardware, including sensors.

Warren S. McCulloch & Walter Pitts

In 1943, McCulloch (who was trained as a physician at Columbia University) began thinking about the notion that it should in theory be possible to translate logic into the operations of neurons in the cortex, and together with Walter Pitts, they wrote the seminal paper on neural network, "A Logical Calculus Immanent in Nervous Activity" [11].

By all accounts, this paper had a profound influence on John Von Neumann, who together with Norbert Wiener, McCulloch and Pitts had launched a series of conferences that fostered the development of what later became known as *Cybernetics* [12].

In 1961, McCulloch would write another seminal paper entitled, "What is a number that a man may know it, and a man, that he may know a number?" [13]. According to Louise Kauffman, this essay indicates a birth date for second order cybernetics, moreover

> It is through the non-numerical mathematics of the observer – the mathematics of form, reference, self-reference and logic, that arithmetic emerges into

the world, and that world learns to count and do science, even to do first order cybernetics. [14]

Louise's paper discusses the foundations of arithmetic in the non-numerical world of perception, action and distinction. There is a wonderful TED presentation on the topic of number by the logician Kit Fine, which is perhaps easier to follow then this paper [15].

The importance of numbers is best described by McCulloch himself, who states,

> I shall summarise briefly its logical importance. Turing had produced a deductive machine that could compute any computable number, although it had only a finite number of parts which could be in only a finite number of states and although it could move only a finite number of steps forward or backward, look at one spot on its tape at a time and make, or erase, 1 or else 0. What Pitts and I had shown was that neurons that could be excited or inhibited, given a proper net, could extract any configuration of signals in its input. Because of the form of the entire argument was strictly logical, and because Gödel had arithmetized logic, we had proved, in substance, the equivalence of all general Turing machines – man-made or begotten.

McCulloch goes on to state that he and Pitts had in actual fact discovered more than this, which they publish in a later paper called "How We Know Universals" [16]. The main idea in that paper was that any object, or universal, is an invariant under some group of transformations and consequently can be represented in a neural network.

According to Husbands & Holland [17]

> During the discussion session following a lecture given by von Neumann in 1948, McCulloch stressed the importance of Turing to his and Pitts' work: "I started at entirely the wrong angle ... and it was not until I saw Turing's [1936] paper that I began to get going the right way around."

Turing was a member of the infamous "Ratio Club" in Cambridge where McCulloch was a frequent visitor. It is therefore, highly likely that Turing would have been aware of the work undertaken by McCulloch and Pitts by the time he started research on his own brand of neural networks in 1947, however, there is no mention of their work in Turing's 1948 report [9].

The purpose of this section was to re-establish the relationship that has long existed between the fields of cybernetics, neural networks and artificial intelligence. With the advent of the 4th Industrial Revolution we have witnessed reunification of the two fields of research, namely, neural networks with AI, there is every reason to believe that in the near term we shall also witness the rebirth of cybernetics and the unification of all three fields.

John McCarthy: The Dartmouth Conference

In many other resources the Dartmouth Conference of 1956 [18] is marked as the birth of "Artificial Intelligence", which is apocryphal, because much effort had been expended over several hundred years with that goal in mind. Nevertheless, it is true that it was at this conference that John McCarthy coined the phrase "Artificial Intelligence".

The four people who were named as the proposers of the summer conference were:

- John McCarthy, Dartmouth College
- Marvin L. Minsky, Harvard University
- Nathan Rochester, I.B.M. Corporation
- Claude E. Shannon, Bell Telephone Laboratories

and the summary for the proposal was:

The study is to proceed on the basis of the conjecture that every aspect of learning or any other feature of intelligence can in principle be so precisely described that a machine can be made to simulate it. An attempt will be made to find how to make machines use language, form abstractions and concepts, solve kinds of problems now reserved for humans, and improve themselves.

The following were some areas of artificial intelligence selected for study:

1. Automatic Computers
2. How Can a Computer be Programmed to Use a Language
3. Neuron Nets
4. Theory of the Size of a Calculation
5. Self-Improvement
6. Abstractions
7. Randomness and Creativity

John McCarthy: The Lighthill Report

In 1973, the UK government decided to evaluate the state of AI research, and appointed Sir James Lighthill to lead this investigation, which led to the infamous "Lighthill Report" that criticized the failure of AI to achieve the objectives that were promised—the Lighthill Report led to the near-complete dismantling of AI research in the UK.

As a consequence of this report, the BBC decided to broadcast a debate from the Royal Institution of London called, "The general purpose robot is a mirage", in which had Sir James Lighthill defended his report, whereas the team of Donald Michie, John McCarthy and Richard Gregory opposed it. It was during this debate that John McCarthy provides one of the most succinct definitions for the term "Artificial Intelligence"

Definition for the Term "Artificial Intelligence"

In 1973, during the Lighthill debate [19] that John McCarthy would provide the following definition for the term 'Artificial Intelligence' that he had invented in 1955:

> Artificial Intelligence [*AI*] is a science; it is the study of problem solving and goal achieving processes in complex situations.

McCarthy further states,

> It [AI] is a basic science, like mathematics or physics, and has problems distinct from applications and distinct from the study of how human and animal brains work. It requires experiment to carry it out, it involves a very large number of parts to it, which I shall mention precisely four.

and he would go on to state that there were many areas involved in AI, but he chose four to describe during the debate. They four points are transcribed literally from this video:

1. **Processes of search**, which deals with combinatorial explosion. It seems what you said that you had just discovered that as a problem, but in fact the very first work in Artificial Intelligence, namely, Turing's, already treated the problem of combinatorial explosion.

2. **Representation of information internally in the machine**, both in Information about particular situations that the machine has to deal with, and the representation of procedures and the representation of the general laws of motion, which determine the future as a function of the past.

3. **Advice giving**, how we're going to instruct the computer, or communicate with it. At present programming that is influencing a computer program is as though we did education by brain surgery.

4. **Automatic programming**, in an extended sense beyond the way it is used normally by the computer industry—that is going from information that determines how something should be done, to a rapid machine procedure for efficiently carrying this out. This is one of the major topics.

In 2007, McCarthy would produce a document entitled, "What is Artificial Intelligence?" [20] in which he provides the layperson with answers to some common questions, and taxonomy for the various branches of AI—which he states is incomplete. Four of the question/answer pairs are produced here in their original form, in the interest of accuracy of the information being conveyed:

Question: What is artificial intelligence?

Answer: It is the science and engineering of making intelligent machines, especially intelligent computer programs. It is related to the similar task of using computers to understand human intelligence, but AI does not have to confine itself to methods that are biologically observable.

Question: Yes, but what is intelligence?

Answer: Intelligence is the computational part of the ability to achieve goals in the world. Varying kinds and degrees of intelligence occur in people, many animals and some machines.

Question: Isn't there a solid definition of intelligence that doesn't depend on relating it to human intelligence?

Answer: Not yet. The problem is that we cannot yet characterize in general what kinds of computational procedures we want to call intelligent. We understand some of the mechanisms of intelligence and not others.

Question: When did AI research start?

Answer: After WWII, a number of people independently started to work on intelligent machines. The English mathematician Alan Turing may have been the first. He gave a lecture on it in 1947. He also may have been the first to decide that AI was best researched by programming computers rather than by building machines. By the late 1950s, there were many researchers on AI, and most of them were basing their work on programming computers.

John McCarthy: Branches of AI

- **Logical AI** The encapsulation of general knowledge about the world, together with the facts of a specific situation in which the program must act, together with its goals. All of this is represented in some logical or mathematical language. By using inference techniques, the program is able to determine which actions are appropriate to undertake in order to achieve its goals.
- **Search** AI programs often face a large number of alternate possibilities (e.g. moves in a chess game) they continually assess the situation and discover how to do this more efficiently.
- **Pattern recognition** Often AI programs will make an observation of some kind, and then they are required to compare what it has observed with a given pattern.
- **Representation** This is related to the first category, namely, it is the representation of facts about the world using mathematical logic.
- **Inference** From some facts, others can be inferred. "Mathematical logical deduction is adequate for some purposes, but new methods of inference have been the focus of some recent research. The simplest kind of non-monotonic reasoning is default reasoning in which a conclusion is to be inferred by default, but the conclusion can be withdrawn if there is evidence to the contrary." (McCarthy)
- **Common sense knowledge and reasoning** This is the area in which AI is farthest from human-level, despite the fact that it has been the an active area of research since the 1950s.
- **Learning from experience** This is an area that pertains to AI programs within the specialized realm of neural networks. In addition, an AI program may be required to learn laws expressed in logic.
- **Planning** Planning programs start with general facts about the world, facts about the particular situation and a statement of a goal. From these, they generate a strategy for achieving the goal. In the most common cases, the strategy is just a sequence of actions.
- **Epistemology** This is a study of the kinds of knowledge required for solving problems in the real world.

- **Ontology** Ontology is the study of various kinds of objects, and we study what these kinds are and what kinds of basic properties they possess.
- **Heuristics** A heuristic is a way of trying to discover something or an idea imbedded in a program.
- **Genetic programming** This is a technique for getting programs to solve a task by mating random programs and selecting fittest in millions of generations.

A More Modern Definition

The current managing director of Microsoft Research's main Redmond Lab is Eric Horvitz, who defines AI as "the scientific study of the computational principles behind thought and intelligent behavior" [21]. Moreover, he states what many consider as the four main pillars of AI:

- Perception
- Learning
- Natural Language Processing
- Reasoning

Introduction to Cognition

Human beings categorize everyday objects or experiences in many ways, the two that appear commonly are the Aristotelian Categories that are based on some kind of abstract definition (or rule) and those that are based on a notion described by the philosopher Wittgenstein as *family resemblance*.

In the early 1970s the psychologist Eleanor H. Rosch conducted various experiments which showed one prominent aspect of how human beings categorize everyday objects. Rosch concluded that people appear to rely less on the classical types of categories as described by Aristotle, but appear to categorize objects based more on comparison with object which they deem to be the best representative of categories already known to them. These representatives are what Rosch names as the "prototypes" of the categories that represent everyday concepts.

In addition, Rosch demonstrated that human beings are able to categorize objects by *qualia* even in the absence of words in their language to describe the categories for the objects. Rosch argued that basic objects have an important psychological role to play in our cognition, and therefore they have a psychological import that determines how such objects are mentally represented.

Concepts: Individuals and Categories

A fundamental characteristic of human intelligence is the ability to entertain thoughts that correspond to entities or to collection of entities.

We begin by defining the word 'concept' to mean a unit of thought. There are two kinds of concepts, those that refer to 'individuals' (say the concept of a man or dog) and those that refer to 'categories', examples of which include bird or perhaps chair.

There are two basic kinds of categories:

Aristotelian Categories

Aristotelian Categories describe a collection that is relatively simple to define using basic rules. For example, a Grandmother is a person who is the mother of a parent, another example is the concept of a Prime Number, which is defined as a number whose only factors are the number 1, and the number itself. Aristotelian categories are sometimes also called *Classical Categories*.

Family Resemblance Categories

Family Resemblance Categories describe the concept for a given collection by presenting a list of common properties that are satisfied by all the members of a given category, and only the members of that category. These kinds of categories possess features quite distinct from those of Aristotelian categories.

Prototypes

Family resemblance categories typically have a 'prototype' associated with them, which is a hypothetical member of the category that possesses the largest number of traits shared by the members of that family. It is important to note that such prototypes may not actually exist in the real world.

Unclear Boundaries or Cases

Eleanor Rosch [22] demonstrated that many of our intuitive everyday concepts are more like family resemblance categories than Aristotelian ones. Moreover, Rosch discovered that given an object and a category, subjects of her experiments appear to agree among themselves on how good a member the object was for the given category—they intuitively assigned a "fitness" to the object. It is plausible that when we learn family resemblance categories what we actually remember are the prototypes, real or not, and we judge other members of the category by how similar they are to these hypothetical prototypes.

Conceptual Spaces

More recently, Peter Gärdenfors [23] has elaborated the approach to prototype theory by introducing the notion of conceptual spaces, where a category is defined in terms of a conceptual distance.

Gärdenfors defines a Conceptual Space as a geometric structure, a multidimensional space where each dimension represents one of the qualities: weight, color, taste, temperature, pitch along with the normal three dimensions of space. Within this space of qualia, the points denote objects, and the regions denote concepts. This notion of a conceptual space was part of Gärdenfors theory of conceptual learning that he introduced in the late 1990s.

Inference of Unseen Properties from Seen Properties

As we have seen there are at least two distinct ways that we, as humans, segment the world around us into manageable parts, namely by the process of forming classical categories (a cognitive process often called *abstraction*) and discovering prototypes. Abstraction is the process of filtering the informational content of an observable phenomenon, where we select only those aspects that are relevant for a particular purpose, this process results in conceptual categories, or concepts.

Nevertheless, this does not explain why humans perform such a mental task, in other words why do we categorize. The answer is reasoning. If we are able to perceive a few traits of an object, then we will place the object into a particular mental category. Then by comparing this object with the prototype for the given category, we infer that the object must also have other properties common to that category.

Reason and Reasoning

Reason is the capacity possessed by some entities that allows them to make sense of things, apply logic, establish facts, and also to modify (or justify) existing beliefs. It is a quintessential characteristic of any intelligent agent and humans in particular.

Reasoning is the ability to reason, cognitive scientists associate this ability with that of thinking or cognition. An *inference* may be defined as the process of reaching a conclusion based on evidence and reasoning.

Logic is concerned with inferences, to be more precise, logic is concerned with *valid inferences*, which are inferences where the truth of the conclusion follows from that of its premises. The word 'valid' therefore does not refer to the truth of the premises or the conclusion, but rather the form of the inference itself. An incorrect inference is known as a *fallacy*.

Charles S. Perice [24] divided inference into three kinds:

- *Deductive inference* is where conclusions are derived from premises are assumed to be true, and by using valid inferences we are guaranteed that the conclusions will also be true. In other words, in a deductive inference what is inferred is *necessarily* true if the premises from which it is inferred are true.
- *Inductive inference* is where we infer a universal conclusion from a specific premise or premises.It is common to characterize these kinds of inferences by stating that the inferences are based purely on statistical data.
- *Abductive inference* is an inference from the premises to the best explanation.
- *Statistical inference* uses mathematics to draw conclusions in the presence of uncertainty, many believe this is a generalization of deterministic reasoning.

Deductive inference tends to go from general to the specific. For example:
Socrates is a man, all men are mortal therefore Socrates is mortal.

This kind of argument is known as a Syllogism, a form of reasoning discovered by Aristotle.

Inductive Inference would typically go the other way, and there different kind of inductive reasoning. Here are two common usage:

1. Socrates, Plato and Aristotle are all men; Socrates is mortal, Plato is mortal, Aristotle is mortal therefore all men are mortal (*Inductive Generalization*).
2. 94% of all humans who live in Uberland are tall, Yano lives in Uberland, hence Yano is tall (*Strong Argument*).

In the second case above, in this case the premises ("94% of all humans who live in Uberland are tall" and "Yano lives in Uberland") make it very likely that the conclusion ("Yano is tall") is true, they don't guarantee that the conclusion is true, but they do provide good reasons to believe that Yano is tall is true. Nevertheless, if the 94% were replaced by 44% then the inference would no longer be *strong*, but considered as *weak*.

For induction, we can no longer rely on the concept of valid inference and we introduce the concept of strong/weak arguments. Notice that in the case of deduction, inferences are either valid or invalid, whereas in the case of inductive arguments strength is a matter of degree.

Inferences are logical relationships between conclusion and the associated premises, and the most intuitive way to determine whether a particular piece of reasoning is good, is to ask the following question:

> If all the premises were true, would they provide adequate support for us to believe the conclusion with a high degree of certainty?

It is important to understand that logical analysis of reasoning (namely the determination of whether an argument is strong or an inference valid) is distinct from the notion of truth for the premises.

In an *Abductive Inference* the conclusion does not logically follow from the premises, nevertheless, the conclusion is the best explanation for the situation on hand. For example,

> One day you witness John and Mary having a terrible argument and they vow never to be friends. Two weeks later you see them together outside village shop. The best explanation for this is that they made up and you conclude that they are friends once again.

Both induction and abduction are considered to be ampliative, meaning that the conclusion goes beyond what is logically contained in the premises.

Furthermore, in abduction one often appeals (implicitly or explicitly) to the best explanation for the situation, whereas in induction one only appeals to observed frequencies or statistics.

There are many ways to formulate abduction, here is just one:

Given evidence E and candidate explanations H_1,..., H_n of E, if Hi explains E better than any of the other hypotheses, infer that H_i is closer to the truth than any of the other hypotheses.

The issue here is the often the inferred explanation may not be reliable, and in this particular case it further requires an account of "closeness to the truth". Moreover, despite the fact that there is much agreement that people frequently rely on abductive reasoning, there is no such agreement with regard to which one of the various rules is the appropriate one to use—nevertheless, we may still ask if this practice is rational. Experimentalists have discovered that when people are able to provide an explanation for some possible event, they tend to overestimate the likelihood that the event will actually occur.

Normative vs. Descriptive

- Normative model is how people ought to think if they were rational
- Descriptive model is how people really do think

One example of normative model for deductive reasoning is first order logic, whereas the normative for inductive reasoning might be the mathematical laws that govern probabilities and their implications.

Theories and Models

Given a language, then informally, we can define a collection of true sentences to be a 'Theory', more often a theory consists of a set of statements (the axioms) that are assumed to be true together with all the deductions that can be made using the rules of inference.

A 'model' is somewhat more complex, and is required to provide the meaning for terms and sentences used within the theory; in particular, it is used to provide a meaning for the word 'true'. Informally, a model consists of a domain of interest together with a mapping, which takes each expression (or formula) in the theory and maps it into the domain of interest.

For example, in the language of First Order Logic, we are able to express properties of objects, and their relationships to one another in a given domain. Suppose our domain of interest consists of people in a given region together with the set of lottery tickets for that region, and one relation denoted by 'owner', such that the statement 'owner(Tom, ticket1)' is true if Tom is the owner of the winning ticket1. Notice, at this stage all we can do is state who owns which ticket we have no way of expressing the winning ticket, in order to do that we shall have to introduce a new symbol 'winningTicket', so now we can say 'winningTicket(ticket2)'.

Suppose the domain of interest is a village called "Miniscule" that consists of {Tom, Mary, Sandy, ticket1, ticket2, ticket3, ticket4}, and suppose that Tom owns ticket1 and ticket2, while Sandy owns ticket3 and Mary owns ticket4. Furthermore, on a particular day the winning lottery ticket was ticket2.

Assuming that the interpretation maps 'Tom' (the name) to Tom the person and maps the word 'ticket2' to the actual ticket that won the lottery, the set of two statements {winningTicket(ticket2), owner(Tom, ticket2)} will both be true in this setting. We call the set of two statements a "Theory", while the village is called a "Model" for this theory (let us call this model M1).

Suppose the following week, the winning ticket was ticket3, while Tom, Mary and Sandy still map to the respective people in Miniscule, the model has now changed (let's call this M2). The statement 'winningTicket(ticket2)' is not true in the new model, and therefore we say that M2 does not satisfy this theory: {winningTicket(ticket2), owner(Tom, ticket2)}.

A more sophisticated example would be given by the axioms for Euclidean Geometry, these are abstract sentences in the language of mathematics, and a plane is a good model for Euclidean Geometry.

By using deduction as our reasoning mechanism, we are able to prove true statements about the model without making any further observations—the key point here is that we are able to discover truths about our model by reasoning.

Are Models Useful?

In a recent interview [25] Vint Cerf (one of the pioneers of the Internet) was asked the question:

What kind of fundamental structures do you think might become important in the future?

To which he responded:

the most fundamental one has to do with the semantic modelling of what's going on. The thing which makes AI powerful is its ability to build models that are analytic. Right now we don't do that very well. We have neural networks whose function we don't understand.

and goes on to state

If there were a powerful addition to the computing environment that we could point out, it would be the ability to extract model of the real world, for example, or a model of an artificial world like a company and then try to understand how to reason about it.

Bayesian Statistics and Probability Theory

There are different interpretations for the notion of probability, and we are going to consider just two "Classical Probability" and "Subjective Probability".

Classical Probability

The classical interpretation of probability comes from the work of mathematicians who were attempting to figure out the mathematics of chance, typically stated as:

$P(A) =$ number of favorable cases /total number of equally possible cases

This states that the probability of some desired outcome (A) is the ratio of favorable cases divided by the total number of possible cases.

For example, consider the random trial of tossing a coin, the set of possible outcomes in this case is: $\{heads, tails\}$

$$P(\text{heads}) = \{heads\}/\{heads, tails\} = 1/2 = 0.5$$

In the case of a die, the set of possible outcomes is: $\{1, 2, 3, 4, 5, 6\}$

$$P(\text{odd number}) = \{1, 3, 5\}/\{1, 2, 3, 4, 5, 6\} = 3/6 = 0.5$$

Laplace introduced the *Principle of Indifference* to help clarify the notion of equally possible is, "We should treat a set of outcomes as equally possible if we have no reason to consider one outcome more probable than the other".

This interpretation is commonly used in cases where (a) there are a *finite* number of elementary outcomes, and (b) Laplace's principle of indifference applies.

This interpretation is sometimes called "Relative Frequency" interpretation of probability, when we say the probability of getting a head when we toss a fair coin, what we really mean is that if we toss the coin repeatedly in the long-run half the tosses would land heads. Therefore, the probability is identified with the relative frequency behavior of the coin.

Subjective Probability

The Subjective interpretation of probability is the measure of degree of belief in whether a particular event occurs, it is the reporting on the strength of the subjective degree of confidence of the outcome—this can also be thought of as the degree of belief one has in the truth for a give proposition.

$$P(X) = \text{degree of belief that } X \text{ is true}$$

Bayes' Rule it is basically the way of calculating a conditional probabilities given certain information, and it is typically used to evaluate how strongly the evidence (E) supports a hypothesis (H). The rule is often stated as:

$$P(H/E) = [P(E) \times P(H)]/P(E)$$

H is the hypothesis that a patient has an ailment given the evidence of a clinical test E.

$P(H/E)$ stands for "the probability that the hypothesis is true given that the evidence is true", this is sometimes called the *posterior probability* of H. The subjective reading for this term is, the degree of belief we should have for the truth of the hypothesis once we have learnt the truth for the evidence (posterior probability of H).

$P(H)$ represents the degree of belief we had in H before we learnt about the new evidence E (the prior probability of H).

$P(E/H)$ stands for the likelihood of the evidence of E assuming the hypothesis to be true. This is the probability that someone will test positive for E given that they have the ailment.

$P(E)$ is the total probability of the evidence E. In our example, it is the probability of all patients testing positive even if they do not have the ailment.

Let's consider an example:

Approximately 2% of patients have cancer. A patient with cancer has a 87% chance of being tested positive, while a patient without has a 10% chance of testing positive. What is the probability the patient has cancer given a positive result?

H: patient has cancer

E: a positive test

P(patient has cancer/given a positive outcome on the test)

$$= \frac{P(\text{patient having cancer}) \times P(\text{likelihood of a positive test given patient has cancer})}{P(\text{of all positive results from those taking the test})}$$

P(of all positive test results)

$= \big[$probability of no $-$ cancer and positive$(= 0.98 \times 0.10)$

$+$probability of cancer and positive$(= 0.02 \times 0.87)\big]$

$= [0.0174 + 0.098] = 0.1154$

$P() = [$probability of no-cancer and positive $(= 0.98 \times 0.10) +$ probability of cancer and positive $(= 0.02 \times 0.87)] = [0.0174 + 0.098] = 0.1154$

t has cancer/given a positive outcome on the test) $= 0.0174/0.1154$

$= 0.15$ or 15%

This example shows how the additional evidence of positive test together with the rates for a positive test can be incorporated to produce a new likelihood for cancer using Bayes' rule.

This rule provides us with a framework for how we should update the degree of belief in a hypothesis when given a new piece of evidence. With this interpretation the subjectivists Bayes' Rule functions as rational belief formation and rational inference.

A set of personal beliefs is *coherent* if and only if the set satisfies the rules of probability theory. It is in this sense that the subjective framework for probability brings with it a normative theory of probability. Therefore by following Bayes' Rule of probability theory as a principle for how we are to learn from new evidence, the only point that remains is to decide how to assign a number to a person's degree of belief, and there are various methods of achieving this goal.

The followers of this interpretation also believe that it embeds deductive logic as a subset, and this is a major issue with this particular interpretation and approach to learning. There are many non-classical logics, those who follow the Bayesian interpretation also assume that laws of classical logic are correct and make them immune to revision based on new empirical evidence.

Scientific Reasoning—Mathematical Models and Predictions

Inductive inference is also common in science, for example suppose that each day we measure the height of a plant, then plot the finite set of data points. We can then draw the best fitting line that represents the functional relationship between the two variables, Day and Height in our case.

The best fitting line that we obtained by using inductive inference (inductive generalization) is called a *mathematical model* of the finite data set. We may use the model to *predict* a value for the height on day 4 using the equation for the line that was the generalization inferred from the finite data set.

Note that the logical usage of induction is broader (allows more kinds of inductive inferences) compared to the ones acceptable to scientific reasoning, which typically focused on inferring general statements from particular ones. The important point to remember here is that when we conduct scientific reasoning we are moving from known facts, about observable phenomenon say, to a hypothesis or conclusion about the world beyond observable facts (Fig. 3.1).

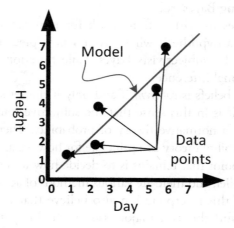

Fig. 3.1 Model and Data Points

Reasoning Systems

Historically, one of the most popular paradigms for knowledge representation was the familiar "If-then" rules, which could easily be translated into first order logic, and therefore each rule could be viewed as unit of information or knowledge. Inference rules could then be applied to create new knowledge.

Rule-based systems were the archetypes for reasoning systems, where one could apply the rules in a *forward chaining* manner to produce new pieces of information or in a *backward chaining* manner to deduce the truth of given statements.

The traditional nomenclature for this kind of system was "expert system" or "knowledge-based system" which is no longer popular; nevertheless, rule-based processing system architectures exist to this day in one guise or another. A typical rule-based system consists of three major elements:

- a knowledge base—in this scenario that would be the set of "if-then" rules and facts
- a working memory—the database of *derived facts* and data
- an inference engine—which contains the reasoning logic used to process the rules and data.

and some intelligent agent architecture still deploy this kind of architecture within each agent to perform reasoning.

It is also possible to replace the common Boolean logic and first-order logic with a *Fuzzy Logic* to deal with *possibilities* (rather than *probabilities*), enabling it to handle knowledge and facts that imprecise or vague, leaving uncertainty to a different kind of reasoning system based on probability.

Problem Solving Strategies: The Search Space and Algorithms

One of the major pillars for the field of artificial intelligence is the topic of search, in particular using search as a paradigm for problem solving, the notion of search and search algorithms were concepts that occupied Alan Turing during the early days of AI.

The *state space* approach to problem representation requires a mapping from the real-world problem to a data structure. An *initial state* together with a set of *operators* for changing the state is called the *state space* for the problem. The sequence of states produced by the valid application of the operators starting with the initial state is called a *path* in the state space.

Now that we have the definition of a path through this space, beginning with the initial state, we now need to define a *goal state* so that we are able to determine that the search is complete and we have reached a final state for the search. This is the reason for requiring an initial definition for a *goal test* that will help us determine when we have reached the goal state. Please note that in most cases defining the goal test may itself be a substantial problem.

In many search problems, not only do we wish to reach a goal state starting from a given initial state, but we would like to achieve this task with the lowest possible *cost*. Thus, we can compute the cost as we apply operators and transition from state to state—this path cost is called a *cost function*.

Effective search algorithms must cause systematic motion through the state space. *Brute-force* (or *blind*) search algorithms blindly search the state space, while *heuristic search* algorithms use feedback or information about the problem to *direct* the search by using the information to select which nodes to expand.

A search algorithm is called *optimal* if it will find the best solution from several possible solutions. A search strategy is said to be *complete* if it is guaranteed to find a solution if one exists. We must also take into consideration the efficiency of algorithms, in terms of time and space. The *time complexity* describes how long an algorithm will take to find a solution and the *space complexity* describes how much memory it will require to reach the goal state.

The best-known search strategies are:

- *Breath-first* search is a complete algorithm with exponential time and space complexity. It examines each one step from the initial state, then each state two steps away, and so on.
- *Depth-first* search has lower memory requirements than breadth-first search, but it is neither complete (it can get stuck in loops) nor optimal. In depth-first search, a single path is chosen and followed until a solution is found, or a dead end (a leaf mode) is reached. The algorithm then backs up and continues down another path.
- Another approach to problem solving using search is called *constraint satisfaction*, where the acceptable solutions are defined by expressing (or defining) a set of constraints. Therefore constraint satisfaction search uses information about valid states to help limit or constrain the range of the search.

- *Means-ends analysis* is one of the oldest problem-solving processes in artificial intelligence, it was first used by Newell & Simon [26] in their General Problem Solver.

Like any other search strategy, the means-ends algorithm has a set of states together with a set of operators that describe the transition from one state to another. Nevertheless, unlike other strategies, the operators (rules for describing the transformations) do not completely specify the before and after states.

The left hand side of the rule (commonly called the antecedent of the rule) only contains a subset of conditions, the preconditions, which must be true in order for the operator to be applied. Similarly, the right hand side of the rule identifies only those parts of the state that the operator changes. The means-ends analysis uses both forward and backward reasoning and a recursive algorithm to systematically minimize the differences between the initial and goal states.

- Large state spaces (namely those commonly found in AI problems) are particularly difficult to deal with using conventional algorithmic techniques. One relatively recent discovery is the class of algorithms called *genetic algorithms*, and the search strategy is called *Genetic Search*. Genetic algorithms have the ability to explore thousands of alternative solutions in parallel. Genetic algorithms utilize a biological metaphor to traverse the state space.

There are a few steps that are necessary for this technique to work:

- We must be able to represent the problem state (and the final solution) by strings, which are typically called chromosomes—the strings constitute the individuals in this population.
- There must exist an evaluation (objective) function that takes encoded string as an input and produces a "fitness" score. This score is then used to rank the set of strings based on their fitness.
- The strings with the highest fitness score are randomly selected to "survive" and procreate the next generation of strings. The operators are also genetically inspired and will attempt to modify the selected strings to an attempt to improve their fitness score, and help them get closer to the goal string (the goal state).
- There are two main operators, the *mutation* operator and the *crossover* operator. In the case of binary strings, the mutation operator mimics the

notion of random mutation in biology, therefore it randomly flips a few of the bits in the given string (input). The crossover operator takes two fit individual strings and combines their genetic material and forming two new offspring individuals (strings). By its very action the crossover operator injects 'noise' into the process of search to ensure the entire search space is covered.

- The various genetic operators can force widespread exploration of the search space, (crossover) or relatively localized hill-climbing behavior (mutation).

- Alan Turing knew about genetic algorithms as far back as 1948, however, their main development is due to Prof. John H. Holland and the ideas are covered in some detail in his book [27].

Summary

In this chapter, we introduced the original thoughts for a machine that could learn, think, adapt and problem solve as described by the three main pillars of the subject. In addition, we discussed the basic notions for concept representation, learning and reasoning from the field of Cognitive Psychology.

The chapter concludes by providing a simple explanation for the notions of a reasoning system and that of a "search space", which is a fundamental concept in AI.

Notes and References

1. Russell, S. and Norvig, P. (2009) Artificial Intelligence: A Modern Approach, 3rd Edition, Prentice Hall.
2. Feferman, S. Turing's Thesis http://math.stanford.edu/~feferman/papers/turing.pdf.
3. Zenil, H. (2012)A Computable Universe: Understanding and Exploring Nature as Computation, World Scientific.
4. Letter from Frankel to Brian Randell, 1972 (first published in Randell (1972) 'On Alan Turing and the origins of digital computers' in B. Meltzer and D. Michie (eds) Machine Intelligence 7. Edinburgh Press).
5. Alan Turing - BBC Horizon Documentary https://youtu.be/mdz88-fSAjM?t =7m43s and for about 15 mins.

6. Recollections of early AI in Britain: 1942–1965 (video for the BCS Computer Conservation Society's October 2002 Conference on the history of AI in Britain http://www.aiai.ed.ac.uk/events/ccs2002/CCS-early-british-ai-dmichie.pdf.

7. From Codebreaking to Computing: Remembrances of Bletchley Park 50 Years Later https://youtu.be/6p3mhkNgRXs?t=1h27m12s.

8. Shaun Wylie https://chessprogramming.wikispaces.com/Shaun+Wylie.

9. Intelligent Machinery http://www.alanturing.net/turing_archive/archive/l/l32/L32-004.html.

10. Turing A. M. (1950) Computing Machinery and Intelligence, Mind, New Series, Vol. 59, No. 236, pp. 433–460. http://phil415.pbworks.com/f/TuringComputing.pdf.

11. McCulloch, W.S. and Pitts, W. (1943) A Logical Calculus of Ideas Immanent in Nervous Activity, Bulletin of Mathematical Biophysics. 5 (4): 115–133.

12. With Jack Cowan http://thesciencenetwork.org/media/videos/52/Transcript.pdf.

13. W. S. McCulloch. What is a number that a man may know it, and a man, that he may know a number? (the Ninth Alfred Korzybski Memorial Lecture), General Semantics Bulletin, Nos. 26 and 27, p 7–18.

14. Louis H. Kauffman, What is a Number? http://homepages.math.uic.edu/~kauffman/NUM.html.

15. What are numbers? | Kit Fine | TEDx NewYork https://youtu.be/6UWhPnbZv-o.

16. Pitts, W. and McCulloch, W.S. (1947) "How we know universals: the perception of auditory and visual forms," Bulletin of Mathematical Biophysics 9:127–147.

17. Warren McCulloch and the British Cyberneticians, Phil Husbands and Owen Holland, Interdisciplinary Science Reviews, Vol. 37 No. 3, 2012, pp. 237–253, http://www.mathcomp.leeds.ac.uk/turing2012/Images/mcculloch.pdf.

18. A Proposal for The Dartmouth Summer Research Project on Artificial Intelligence http://www-formal.stanford.edu/jmc/history/dartmouth/dartmouth.html.

19. The Lighthill Debate (1973) - part 3 of 6 https://youtu.be/RnZghm0rRlI?t=10m8s.

20. What is Artificial Intelligence? http://www-formal.stanford.edu/jmc/whatisai.pdf.

21. Great Debate - Artificial Intelligence: Who is in control? https://youtu.be/rZe-A2aDOgA.

22. Rosch, E.H. (1975) Cognitive Representation of Semantic Categories, J. Exp. Psych. General Vol 104, p. 1092–1233.

23. Gärdenfors P. (2000) Conceptual Spaces: The Geometry of Thought, MIT Press.

24. Charles Sanders Peirce: Logic, The Internet Encyclopedia of Philosophy http://www.iep.utm.edu/peir-log/.

25. Fireside Chat with Vint Cerf & Marc Andreessen (Google Cloud Next '17) https://youtu.be/y9bJ8LslSZ4?t=31m10s.

26. Newell, A.; Shaw, J.C.; Simon, H.A. (1959). Report on a general problem-solving program. Proceedings of the International Conference on Information Processing. pp. 256–264.
27. Holland, J.H. (1975) Adaptation in Natural and Artificial Systems: An Introductory Analysis with Applications to Biology, Control, and Artificial Intelligence, Ann Arbor: University of Michigan Press, 1975.

Part II

Intelligent Agents, Machine Learning and Advanced Neural Networks

4

Intelligent Agents

Introduction

From sophisticated single agents to multiagent systems (MAS), intelligent agent software has come a long way since its inception. Many new branches of research in this field have emerged over the years resulting in today's agents who perform tasks such as learning, reasoning, negotiating, self-organizing, etc. that were previously only attributes that one would commonly assign to human beings.

The very notion of agency has introduced a new kind of paradigm within the software community that has evolved over the years; from software that was considered to be reactive (*reactivity*), namely software that responded to events (*stimuli*), to more sophisticated software that are autonomous (*autonomy*) and able to make their own decisions (*reasoning*). Then we saw the emergence of software that could also take initiative from plans and strategize to fulfill its goals (*proactiveness*), and it could interact with other agents (*social ability*).

The first notions of agency was originally introduced by Wooldridge and Jennings [1] for a single agent, which has evolved into a new paradigm of multiagent agent systems (MAS). These new kinds of complex agents are mobile (*mobility*) able to cooperate with one another, have belief systems, and can self-organize into a community in order to solve difficult problems. In what follows, we shall describe some of the concepts and approaches used to build such systems.

© The Author(s) 2018
M. Skilton and F. Hovsepian, *The 4th Industrial Revolution*,
https://doi.org/10.1007/978-3-319-62479-2_4

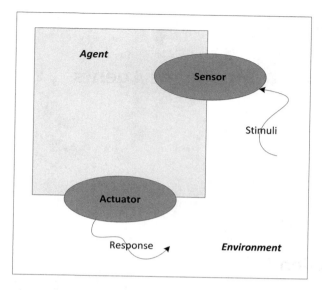

Fig. 4.1 Components of an Agent

Agent

An *agent* is an autonomous entity, which has the ability to sense its environment through the use of its sensors, and acts on the environment through the use of its actuators (Fig. 4.1).

Agents are said to be *reactive* because they typically react to events detected by their sensors via actions through their actuators. Notice this description is quite general, it does not restrict the agent to being a software entity, which allows it to be closely aligned to similar concepts (the controller) within the realm of cybernetics.

Notice this description is quite general, it does not restrict the agent to being a software entity, which allows it to be closely aligned to similar concepts (the controller) within the realm of cybernetics.

We define the *sensory history*, as the complete sequence of all sensory inputs for a given agent.

An agent can have different types of behavior, for example, the choice of action for any given instant can depend on the particular sensory input, or it can depend on the entire sensory history to date. However, it cannot depend on anything that the agent did not have prior knowledge, or anything that was not previous provided as input by its sensors.

Agent Behavior

The agent's behavior is abstractly defined as the *agent function*, which is a (functional) relationship between an action and any given sensory history.

This is an external characterization for the agent, whereas internally an agent program implements the agent function for a given agent. The two concepts are quite distinct; one is an abstract mathematical description, while the other is a real piece of software running within some physical system.

The agent's actions (often in response to some stimuli it received through its sensors) will also generate a sequence of changes in its environment, which will produce a sequence of environmental states. We can use the sequence of environmental states to measure the performance of the agent within the given environment. The performance measures should be designed with respect to the changes one actually desires in a given environment, rather than according to how an agent should behave within that environment.

Software Agent

Wooldridge [2] provides a similar definition for a software agent, namely,

> an agent is a computer system that is situated in some environment, and that is capable of autonomous actions in this environment in order to meet its delegated objectives

Rationality

We have already mentioned the general notion of rational behavior in the section on Reasoning, therefore in addition to the ability to reason and knowledge (especially prior knowledge of the environment), the other resources required by a rational agent include:

1. The performance measure that defines the criterion for success
2. The set of actions—which the agent can perform
3. The agent's sensory sequence to date

We should note that for each possible sensory sequence, a *rational agent* should select an action that maximizes its performance measure, given the resource available to it.

Task Environments

If rational agents are the solution, what is the problem? More to the point, how do we specify/describe the problem? That is where the notion of a task environment comes in—the particular type of task environment will determine the kind of design we should adopt for creating the rational agent (the solution).

Task environment is a useful concept described by Russell and Norvig [3]. It helps the designer determine the kind of architecture that would be required by the agent, and the kind of features that need to be observed by its sensors; furthermore, it also identifies the kinds of changes that need to be instigated by the agent's actuators.

The elements that constitute a task environment are:

- Performance measure
- Environment
- Actuators
- Sensors

The following table (Table 4.1) provides two examples of task environments. The second example in the table clearly demonstrates that not all rational agents will be physical entities, and that some may very well exist in a virtual environment—we refer to such agents as *software agents*.

Table 4.1 Examples of Task Environments

Agent type	Performance measure	Environment	Actuators	Sensors
Autonomous driver	Speed, compliance (legal), energy utilization	Roads, traffic, pedestrians, customers	Steering, accelerator, brake, signal	Cameras, GPS, speedometer, odometer, engine sensors
Medical diagnosis system	Healthy patient, reduced costs	Patient, hospital, various kinds of staff	Display of questions, tests, diagnoses, treatments, referrals	Keyboard entry of symptoms, findings, patient's answers

Table 4.1 is clearly vast, and therefore we need a way of classifying them Russell and Norvig [3] achieve this by using a set of seven common characteristics, four of which we describe here.

- **Observable**

For a given task environment:

- is said to be *fully observable* if the agents sensors are able to detect all aspects of the environment that is relevant for the action selected by the rational agent—what is relevant in this scenario is determined by the performance measure. Moreover, in this particular case the agent has sensors that allow it to access the state of the environment at all times.
- is said to be *unobservable* when the agent does not have any such access, which could occur for various reasons, including the lack of appropriate sensors.
- or *partially observable* in the case where it has noisy or inaccurate sensors.

- **Deterministic**

If the next state of the environment is completely determined by the current state together with the action taken by the agent, then we shall consider this task environment to be deterministic, and consider it as stochastic otherwise. Stochastic refers to the fact that the next state (the outcome of the action taken by the agent) is quantified in terms of probabilities. An environment is said to be *uncertain* if it is not fully observable or it is not deterministic.

Important note: an environment that is *not deterministic* is not the same as an environment that is *nondeterministic*, this is a subtle yet important distinction. A *nondeterministic* environment is determined by the *possible* outcomes and not by *probable* outcomes.

- **Dynamic**

Dynamic environments are those which themselves change while the agent is deliberating, an environment is said to be *static* in cases where it is not dynamic.

Dynamic task environments are significantly more complex compared to those where the passage of time has little impact on the state of the environment itself.

- **Multiagent**

The distinction between single and multiple agents is far from obvious, because we have to determine which entities within a given scenario are agents and which are objects.

Intelligent agents are essentially reactive systems, however when such agents appear in a multiagent scenario we have an additional complexity to deal with, namely the issue of communication (in other words the manner in which they will communicate with each other). Communication between the agents is an issue that must be addressed during the design stage.

Perhaps the agents are intended to compete with one another, this occurs when we are designing (or dealing with) self-interested agents, which is where we may have to introduce such notions as "auctions & voting systems" and negotiation tactics.

If the agents are benevolent, then we may need to decide how they are going to cooperate (or collaborate) with one another, in order to succeed in this kind of problem solving scenario. This is a very notion of cooperation raises some complex issues of its own, so this kind of distributed architecture is notoriously difficult even with dumb entities, let alone with intelligent ones.

Sense vs. Perceive

Consider a simple agent that does little more than 'sense' some aspect of its environment, then respond to that stimuli in a reflexive manner (these are typically called *sense-and-respond* agents or *reflex* agents). There is no cognition involved in this scenario, and in such instances the use of the term 'percept' is misleading, which is why we prefer to use the word 'sense' rather than 'percept' (the terminology used in [3]).

The separation of 'sensation' from 'perception' is also helpful when we consider the case when the agent under consideration is a human being, because we are then able to distinguish the notion of sensing a temperature from that of perceiving an object as being 'hot'. On a technical level, the sensation is a quantitative instrument producing some kind of logical or numerical value, whereas perception is a 'qualitative' cognitive concept. As we have already discussed cognitive concepts can easily overlap, in other words there may not be a clear distinction between the concept 'hot' and that of 'cold', because these categories are not well delineated nor mutually exclusive. For example, to which category does a warm object belong?

Moreover, the cognitive processing of sensory data also may deal with values that appear to be erroneous. For example, given a data reading from one of the heat sensors in our skin, which does not correspond to those of its neighbors may be ignored by the perceptual system as a mal-functioning sensor. Therefore, the perceptual system may then form a perception of the object in question using the sensors in a neighborhood but excluding the value from the malfunctioning sensor. We need to distinguish the operation of the sensory mechanism (the hardware of the intelligent agent) from that of the perceptual mechanism (a cognitive process); otherwise, we could easily lose the ability to model this important feature of an intelligent system.

Therefore, in place of 'percept' and 'percept sequence' we shall use the words 'sensory input' and 'sequence of sensory inputs', which refers to the complete history of all sensory inputs for the given agent.

Structure of Agents

Thus far we have discussed the actions of the agent (its behavior) performed given a sequence of sensations, now we shall consider the internal *structure of agents*. In the scenario where agents are used to implement a solution to a given task, the role played by AI is in the design of the agent program that implements the agent function, namely the mapping of sensation of the external stimuli into the actions to be taken by the agent.

Clearly, the agent program needs to execute in some kind of computational device, however, the agent itself needs to have an appropriate embodiment (with sensors and actuators) in order to succeed according to its performance measurements. This embodiment is what is commonly called its architecture, therefore we can state:

agent = agent architecture + agent program

The agent program needs to be designed with the agent architecture in mind, and this is where much care is needed. Many of the issues faced in designing and creating software that will have to operate some kind of machine parallels the kinds of problems addressed by *control or system engineers*.

For example, if the agent software is required to apply the brakes for a vehicle, then one must design such software with the laws of physics in mind. In the case of an autonomous vehicle, the designers must be aware that by applying the brakes the vehicle will not come to an instant resting state (because of inertia), and if the brakes are not applied gradually then such an action may cause harm to the occupants as well as the vehicle itself.

Agent Programs

Agent program combine various components in specific ways to generate actions, there are a multitude of such programs we shall consider just two.

Simple Reflex Agent

This is the simplest kind of agent, it selects actions on the basis of the current sensory input, ignoring the rest of its sensory history. The central aspect of this kind of agent program is a collection of "condition-action rules" or "if-then rules", written as:

if (condition) then (action)

As an example consider a heating agent, which has one sensor namely a thermostat, that is able to sense the temperature (T say) in some location, together with a desired temperature setting (D say) that is adjusted by some external entity. We can probably express its behavior using two if-then rules:

If the temperature T is greater than (D + 0.25) **then** turn off the heating

If the temperature T is less than (D - 0.25) **then** turn on the heating

There are two if-then rules to prevent the agent getting into an infinite loop where it turns the heating on and off without a break.

While these kinds of agents are elegantly simple they are of limited intelligence. Further, they rely on the environment being fully observable, because even the slightest amount of unobservability can cause problems.

Model-Based Reflex Agent

Partial observability is a problem for agents and one solution is for the agent to maintain an internal state that depends on its sensory history, which can at least provide some remedy for the unobserved aspects of the current state.

Periodically updating this internal state information requires two different kinds of knowledge to be part of the agent program; therefore, we need some information about

- the world and how it evolves independently of the agent (called a *model* of the world)
- how the agent's actions affect the world

An agent that utilizes such an internal model is called a *model-based agent*.

It is often not possible for the agent to determine the current state of a partially observable environment exactly, therefore it must resort to making the best guess it can. Moreover, because the model-based agent itself maintains the internal state means that it no longer has to describe, "what the world is like now" before it is able to decide on an action.

There are many other agent programs, two that are also of interest are *Goal Based Agents and Utility Based Agents.* Goal based agents act in a manner that helps them achieve their primary goal. Utility based agents act in a manner that attempts to maximize their utility function—which is the internalization of their performance measure.

Learning Agents

A learning agent can be segmented into four conceptual components as shown in the figure below (Fig. 4.2).

The *performance element* is the component responsible for selecting what actions the agent should take that will make a change in the state of its environment.

The *learning element* is the component that is responsible for helping the agent learn about its environment, the consequences of its actions, improve and update its internal model, etc.

The *critic*, which observes the environment (the world) evaluates how well the agent is performing. The learning element then utilizes the feedback it

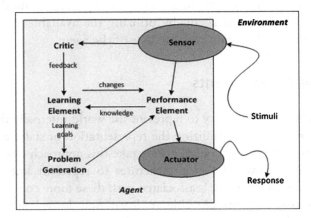

Fig. 4.2 Components of a Learning Agent

receives from the element and decides on the improvements that may be achieved if the performance element was modified in a particular manner.

The component called the *problem generator* is responsible for making suggestions that will lead to new actions, which will result in new and improved experiences. This component allows the agent to try exploratory actions that may in the future lead to better actions.

The learning element is the most powerful of all components in the agent program, because it is capable of modifying any of the knowledge components, enabling the agent to adapt to a changing environment, especially pertinent is the ability to operate in an unfamiliar environment.

The simplest example is how an agent can learn from its sensory history, because the sensory history provides a record of pairs of successive states of its environment, which provides the mechanism for the agent to improve its internal model that describes *how the world evolves*. Furthermore, its observation of the results of its actions on its environment allows the agent to improve its internal model, which determines the impact of its actions on its environment, namely they allow the agent to learn from experience of observing what *its actions do*.

Finally, we should mention that all agents aspire to achieving the universal *performance standard* of making predictions that agree with experiment. In the case where an agent possesses a utility-function the situation becomes somewhat more complex, because the external performance standard must inform the agent the impact its actions may have on its own utility. The performance standard therefore should distinguish part of the incoming sensory input as a *reward* (or *penalty*)—we often find that such performance measures as pain, hunger or elation can be best understood using this kind of structure.

In summary, learning in intelligent agents is a process of modifications of any component within the agent, by utilizing the available feedback information to improve the overall performance of the agent.

Knowledge-Based Agents

Learning agents have the ability to represent the world internally then perform some kind of reasoning, by utilizing the representation of states as the assignment of values to variables. Logical agents take this approach one step further by utilizing more powerful logical structures to represent knowledge-based notions and the reasoning that is associated with these more complex concepts.

Knowledge-based agents are able to learn new knowledge about their environment, adapting to changes by modifying their internal knowledge-base. In addition, these kinds of agents are able to accept new tasks in the form of explicitly described goals.

The central components of the knowledge-based agent is the knowledge-base (collection of statements made in the appropriate logical language) together with a reasoning engine (the collection of rules of inference for that logic). We have mentioned some of these concepts before and we shall not delve on them here, primarily because the topic quickly reaches a point where the user needs to have a deep understanding of concepts in mathematical logic, and that would detract us from the goal of this book.

Intelligent Agents

An agent exhibits intelligence if it acts rationally. Intuitively, an *intelligent agent* is a goal-directed adaptive entity that has the ability to *learn*, *utilize its knowledge* and *reason* in order to achieve its goals in an optimum manner. Intelligent agents must be able to *recognize events*, and then take appropriate *actions* within its environment based on those events.

Agents may function as individuals, or may *collaborate* with other agents and work together as a team in order to solve a given a problem, and therefore *communication* is another key attribute.

Agents may be categorized using the following three criteria:

- *Agency*—the amount of autonomy possessed by the agent
- *Intelligence*—the knowledge, reasoning and learning capabilities possessed by the agent
- *Mobility*—the ability to move in a given environment, be it physical or virtual

Agents may function as individuals, or may collaborate with other agents and work together as a team in order to solve a given a problem.

Fuzzy Agents

Fuzzy agents are intelligent agents that utilize *Fuzzy Sets* to represent the conceptual categories and *Fuzzy Logic* as its reasoning mechanism. Fuzzy sets/Fuzzy Logic approaches are not simply an alternative to probabilistic approaches, they are typically used when the conceptual categories have a degree of member for their objects rather than a simple binary membership (namely does/does not contain).

In closing we would like to mention that Russell and Norvig [3] have an important section on the nature of the various components that constitute the agent program, in particular they discuss the various internal models that help the agent represent state and the transitions between them.

Factored representation, in which each state is divided into a fixed set of variables and attributes, has the advantage that an agent has the ability to represent uncertainty, moreover, the areas of AI that utilize such representational techniques include constraint satisfaction algorithms, propositional logic, Bayesian networks and many machine learning algorithms.

It is not that factored representations are unable to represent aspects of learning and reasoning, but rather the kind of reasoning one is able to represent is restricted and may involve significantly more effort to implement and execute compared to other representational structures—in some cases it may be necessary to use more sophisticated methods.

Hence the need for more sophisticated agents need to represent the world not just as things, but also the relationship between them, this leads the designers of agent programs to consider *structured representations* in which various relationships can be explicitly expressed. Such structured representations underlie areas such as first order logic, first-order probability models, knowledge-based learning and natural language understanding.

Multiagent

The multiagent scenario is akin to a traditional distributed computing system, and as such, one must consider the manner in which agents will communicate among themselves in addition to the way they interact with their environment. This typically requires suitable protocols to be established. Nevertheless, the conventional protocols used in distributed computing, such as remote procedure calls or method invocation that may permit agents to directly change the internal state of another agent, or behavior, are simply unsuitable in this scenario.

The protocols required need to be much higher than the conventional transport protocols used such distributed systems; typically, they will be message-based systems that allow individual agents to decide how to respond, or react, to a particular message. Moreover, these protocols will typically have a richer semantics that will enable the agents to interact at an intentional level (or social level). This also provides the community of agents with the mechanism that helps them cooperate and influence one another, and thus helps them to achieve a shared goal as a collective whole.

Over the years there have been a number of approaches to modeling and creating distributed computing environment, multiagent systems provide an additional modeling paradigm that is quite distinct, mainly due to the characteristics of its components namely the collection of intelligent agents. Nevertheless, this paradigm does not preclude the system designer from utilizing other distributed notions, for example, there is no reason why an agent cannot access a service offered by a more traditional service-oriented architecture.

It is important not to confuse agents with services, for the following reasons:

- agents are autonomous and mobile, in the sense that they can move between different computing environments, allowing them to join different agencies to achieve different goals
- services are typically designed to reuse function, whereas agents should be designed to reuse entire subsystems
- agents embody knowledge, reasoning and often even beliefs via internal models and therefore hold state, services are typically stateless
- a service is often designed so that it is able to complete a given task (function) without the need to directly interact with other services, although it could be argued that both are designed with a loosely-coupled architecture in mind

Agent Development Methodologies

Designing a system of intelligent multiagents is quite an undertaking, especially as the number and complexity of the multiagents increase, much of the complexity arises initially from the very same problems we face when designing distributed computing environments, namely issues related to communication between the various components. In the case of intelligent multiagents, the problem is somewhat different, primarily because the agents are able to reason, learn and react to various events in their environment, which may result in an unpredictable behavior as a collective.

Nonetheless, this does not mean we should not establish any kind of guideline or modeling methodology. A software modeling methodology is typically intended to provide a systematic approach to the analysis, design and development for a given domain; in addition, a good modeling methodology will provide the necessary (and relevant) guidelines, principles and models.

Over the years there have been some who have endeavored to provide such a framework, although no consensus exists on to which one should use. Here is a selection of agent-oriented methodologies that extend existing approaches:

- methodologies commonly inspired by the Object Oriented software community:

  - **GAIA** [4]
  - **BDI** [5]
  - **MaSE** [6]
  - **ADELFE** [7]
  - **ASEME** [8]
  - **Tropos** [9]
  - **Prometeus** [10]

- approaches typically inspired by the Knowledge Engineering community:

  - **CoMoMAS** [11]
  - **MAS-CommonKADS** [12]
  - **Cassiopeia** [13]

We have provided links for each methodology, however, we shall only make comments on a few of the more popular ones.

Gaia

Gaia is a methodology initially proposed by Wooldridge, Jennings, and Kinny [4]; a more recent updated version was proposed by Wooldridge, Jennings and Zambonelli [14], which extends the kinds of applications to which GAIA may be applied.

Gaia is an iterative, agent-oriented analysis and design methodology, which at the analysis stage a prototypical role and interaction model. This model provides detailed information about the key roles, in addition to the interaction protocols that will be used by the agents when they need to communicate and collaborate with one another.

The design stage of the methodology requires that the designers group together the roles previously identified into agent types, then define the relationship between these types. Once the comprehensive role model has been established, then the Gaia method requires that a service model be developed that identifies the services associated with each agent type.

The purpose of the service model is to support the agent's role and activities within this system. The final stage of the analysis and design is to develop an acquaintance model from the interaction and agent model. It should be clear that this is not a classical service-oriented architecture, because the service model is there to support the roles that the agents are required to play in a given environment. Moreover, they are there to prevent one agent from directly altering the other agent's internal states, nor to permit one agent to directly invoke the other agent's operations.

Therefore, the Gaia service model is there to define the relationship between agent and service, where these services are designed to realize the agent role within an environment. The service (in this model) is part of an agent and the agent has full control over them, therefore it can be considered as one of the activities that an agent is able to perform. The Gaia method therefore takes a very different view of services compared to the conventional W3C web service architectures. Nevertheless, there is nothing to prevent the designers from adopting a SOA standard for the services, in some respects this may well help deal with non-functional engineering requirements for the system as a whole.

BDI

Belief-Desire-Intention (BDI) is an approach to modeling the internal architectural states of the agent using the following elements:

- **Beliefs**: these collectively represent the *informational state* of the agent, these typically include beliefs about the world, beliefs about itself, as well as beliefs about other agents. Included in this set is also a collection of inference rules, that permit the agent to perform reasoning and from new beliefs.
  Note how the terminology used is that of *belief* and not *knowledge*, which is often classified by the philosophers as justified true belief, primarily because there is often no way to tell if the information held by the agent at any given time may be justifiably true.
- **Desires**: represent the *motivational state* of the agent. these the possible goals the agent wishes to achieve.

- **Intentions**: represent the *deliberative state* of the agent, namely what the agent has chosen to do, these typically represent the agent's commitment to particular goal (or goals). The agent's commitment in real terms means that it has already decided on a plan/strategy and has begun to execute it, which may include intermediate goals (and plans) necessary in order for the agent to be able to accomplish its chosen desire.

  The word 'plan' as used in this context refers to a sequences of actions that an agent can perform to achieve a given goal.

- **Events**: these represent the triggers necessary for implementing reactive activity by the agent, which may include a variety of actions including, but not restricted to, updating its beliefs, inference rules, trigger a particular plan (or strategy), alter intermediate goals, etc.

While BDI is a popular model, but it does have its critics, nevertheless, the BDI method provides a systematic approach that spans the lifecycle, from modeling to realizing the BDI agents.

ASEME

The Agent Systems Engineering Methodology (ASEME) is an agent-oriented software engineering methodology (AOSE) for developing MAS.

ASEME uses the AMOLA agent modeling language [15] that provides the syntax and semantics for creating models of multi-agent systems, which cover the analysis and design phases of a software development process.

This methodology is somewhat different to the others mentioned because it utilizes a model-driven engineering approach to multiagent systems development, which is compatible with the Model Driven Architecture (MDA) paradigm.

MaSE and ADELFE

Just as Gaia was inspired by the Fusion methodology, Adelfe originated from UML and RUP [16]

For an excellent review of these two methodologies see [17]. In which the authors present material that is part of a broader project that aims at analyzing important aspects of modeling different multiagent systems using different methodologies, the first one of which was a study in a medical domain using Adelfe methodology.

Foundation for Intelligent Physical Agents (FIPA)

On their website [18] FIPA state:

> FIPA is an IEEE Computer Society standards organization that promotes agent-based technology and the interoperability of its standards with other technologies

FIPA is essentially an international organization that is dedicated to openly developing specifications that support interoperability among agents and agent-based applications. Compliance with FIPA specifications provides some specific advantages, for instance being compliant to FIPA guarantees the system's architecture conforms to well-tested protocols that enable agent cooperation and interoperability. Nevertheless, it is up to the individual researcher or organization to decide whether their solution needs to be FIPA compliant.

Support Tools

Artificial intelligence solutions are quite complex and solutions that work well within one context may perform poorly in another, requiring not just a reimplementation but often a new set of algorithms, representation schemas, etc. to be custom developed for that specific problem.

The AI community is collecting many of these algorithms, representation, learning and reasoning techniques and approaches into various frameworks or libraries. Nevertheless, these kinds of libraries are often only useful to those who are already experienced in constructing such systems, and are intended to reduce the time required to develop a solution rather than open the way to anyone who wishes to create this kind of software.

It is a major undertaking to compare tools, first one must establish a criterion that will be used for the study, then decide on a subset of tools that are available at that time. Then follow the process to for each product so that a fair comparison can be reported. Given that such an extensive study [19] was undertaken recently, we shall only mention some of the pertinent points from this study leaving the interested reader to follow up with the study should they require a more details.

FIPA Compliance (Table 4.2).

Security management overview (Table 4.3).

By combining the first two tables, we get products that are FIPA compliant and secure (Table 4.4).

Platform properties (Table 4.5).

Despite the choice of twenty-four agent development platforms that were tested, the JADE (Jave Agent Development Environment) remains the most popular platform that is FIPA compliant and secure, while supporting different operating systems on the web. Moreover, it is open source and has a lively community.

Table 4.2 FIPA compliance

Full compliance	JADE, Jadex, JACK, EMERALD
Partial compliance	JAS, Jason, AGLOBE, agent factory, SeSAm, GAMA
No compliance	Cougaar, swarm, MASON, INGENIAS development kit, cormas, repast, MaDKit, cybelePro, JIAC, agentscape, anylogic, netlogo, JAMES II

Table 4.3 Security management overview

Name	End-to-end security	Fair	Platform security	Publication	Available
Agentscape	Authentication, private logging	Yes	Good	Oey et al. 2010	AgentScape 2014
AnyLogic	Authentication	Yes	Strong (closed system)	Borshchev 2013	AnyLogic 2014
EMERALD	Signature and encryption, HTTPS support	Yes	Strong	Kravari et al. 2010	EMERALD 2014
JACK	Authentication domain protection mechanisms in JDK	Yes	Strong	Winikoff 2005	JACK 2014
JADE	Signature and encryption, HTTPS support	Yes	Strong (jaas API, user authentication)	Bellifemine et al. 2003	JADE 2014
JADEX	Powerful and flexible security mechanism based on shared secrets	No	Strong	Braubach and Pokahr 2013	JADEX 2014
MaDKit	Authentication	No	Good	Gutknecht and Ferber 2000	MaDKit 2014

Table 4.4   Security management overview and FIPA Compliant

Name	End-to-end security	Fair	Platform security	Publication	Available
EMERALD	Signature and encryption, HTTPS support	Yes	Strong	Kravari et al. 2010	EMERALD 2014
JACK	Authentication domain protection mechanisms in JDK	Yes	Strong	Winikoff 2005	JACK 2014
JADE	Signature and encryption, HTTPS support	Yes	Strong (jaas API, user authentication)	Bellifemine et al. 2003	JADE 2014
JADEX	Powerful and flexible security mechanism based on shared secrets	No	Strong	Braubach and Pokahr 2013	JADEX 2014

Table 4.5   Platform properties

Name	Developer/ Org	Primary domain	Latest release	License	Open source
EMERALD	LPIS group, Aristotle University of Thessaloniki	Distributed applications composed of autonomous entities	EMERALD v1.0 (23/01/2012)	LGPL	Yes
JACK	AOS	Dynamic and complex environments	JACK 5.5 (02/09/2010)	Commercial, academic license	No
JADE	Telecom Italia (TILAB)	Distributed applications composed of autonomous entities	Jade 4.3.1 (06/12/2013)	LGPLv2	Yes
JADEX	Hamburg University	Distributed applications composed of autonomous BDI entities	Jadex 2.4.0 (20/12/2013)	LGPLv2	Yes

JADE is written using the JAVA programming language and therefore provides a comprehensive API (Application Programming Interface) in JAVA, which facilitates the implementation of various functional aspects of the agent program. Moreover, it includes an implementation of the Agent Communication Language (ACL) as defined by FIPA for multiagent coordination required when implementing a MAS.

Nevertheless, if the reader is serious about developing an intelligent agent solution the comparison study that we have mentioned is worth reading.

Summary

In this chapter, we introduced some of the fundamental concepts that underpin the notion of an intelligent agent and machine learning, providing real world examples along the way.

Much of the current focus on AI remains firmly focused on machine learning and deep learning in particular, nevertheless, we believe that it is only a matter of time before the community begins to demand the Internet of "smart things" rather than the "Internet of Things" and that's when intelligent agents will play a prominent role.

Notes and References

1. Wooldridge, M. and Jennings, N.R. (1995) Intelligent agents: Theory and practice, The Knowledge Engineering Review, vol. 10, no. 2, p. 37.
2. Wooldridge, M. (2009) *Introduction to Multiagent Systems*, Wiley.
3. Russell, S. and Norvig, P. (2009) Artificial Intelligence: A Modern Approach, 3rd Edition, Prentice Hall.
4. Wooldridge, M. Jennings, N.R., Kinny, D. (2000) "The Gaia Methodology for Agent-Oriented Analysis and Design" Journal of Autonomous Agents and Multi-Agent Systems 3(3) 285–231.
5. Rao, M. and Georgeff, P. (1995) BDI-agents: From Theory to Practice. In Proceedings of the First International Conference on Multiagent Systems (ICMAS 95).
6. DeLoach, S. A. (1999) Multiagent Systems Engineering: A Methodology and Language for Designing Agent Systems, Agent-Oriented Information Systems '99 (AOIS'99), Seattle WA, 1 May 1999.
7. Henderson-Sellers, Brian & Giorgini, Paolo (ed). (2005). Agent-oriented Methodologies. 1ed: Idea Group Inc, London, UK, ISBN 1-59140-581-5, p. 412.
8. Spanoudakis N., Moraitis P. (2010) Model-Driven Agents Development with ASEME. In: 11th International Workshop on Agent Oriented Software Engineering (AOSE 2010), Toronto, Canada, May 10–11, 2010.
9. Castro, J., Kolp, M. and Mylopoulos, J. (2001) A Requirements-Driven Development Methodology, In Proc of the 13th International Conference on Advanced Information Systems Engineering CAiSE 01, Interlaken, Switzerland, June 4–8, 2001.
10. Padgham, L. and Winikoff, M. (2000) "Prometheus: A Methodology for Developing Intelligent Agents". Proceedings of the Third International Workshop on Agent-Oriented Software Engineering, at AAMAS'0.

11. Glaser, N. (1996) Contribution to Knowledge Modelling in a Multi-Agent Framework, Ph.D. Thesis, L'Université henri Poincaré, Nancy I, France.
12. Analysis and design of multiagent systems using MAS-CommonKADS, In AAAI'97 Workshop on Agent Theories, Architectures and Languages, Providence, RI, July 1997. ATAL. (An extended version of this paper has been published in INTELLIGENT AGENTS IV: Agent Theories Architectures, and Languages, Springer Verlag, 1998).
13. Agent Oriented Design of a Soccer Robot Team, In Proc. of the Second Intl. Conf. on Multi-Agent Systems, Kyoto, Japan, Dec 1996.
14. Zambonelli, F. and Jennings, N.R. and Wooldridge, M. (2003) Developing Multiagent Systems: The Gaia Methodology, ACM Transactions on Software Engineering and Methodology, Vol. 12, No. 3.
15. Spanoudakis, N. and Moraitis, P. (2008) The Agent Modeling Language (AMOLA). In: Proceedings of the 13th International Conference on Artificial Intelligence: Methodology, Systems, Applications (AIMSA 2008), Springer, Lecture notes in Computer Science (LNCS), Volume 5253/2008, Varna, Bulgaria, September 4–6, 2008.
16. Rumbaugh, J., Jacobson, I. and Booch, G. (2004). The Unified Modelling Language Reference Manual, Second edition, Addison-Wesley.
17. Vera Maria B. Werneck, Rosa Maria E. Moreira Costa and Luiz Marcio Cysneiros (2011) Modelling Multi-Agent Systems using Different Methodologies https://cdn.intechopen.com/pdfs-wm/14487.pdf.
18. http://fipa.org.
19. Kravari, Kalliopi and Bassiliades, Nick (2015) 'A Survey of Agent Platforms' Journal of Artificial Societies and Social Simulation 18 (1) 11 http://jasss.soc.surrey.ac.uk/18/1/11.html.

5

Machine Learning

Introduction

It is common to encounter terminology such as, neural networks, deep learning and reinforcement learning, all of which are a form of machine learning. There are two major kinds of machine learning tasks: classification and regression.

As the name suggests the classifiers are intended to categorize data, typically into either concepts or collection that utilize the notion of family resemblance. Regression typically extrapolates the trends present in the data to help the system make some kind of prediction based on those trends.

Machine Learning: A Cognitive Perspective

A central aspect that one associates with intelligent behavior is that of being able to adapt or learn from experience, because at the point of its creation one cannot foretell all of the situations that a given system will encounter during its lifecycle. Therefore, it is of considerable importance that we design intelligent systems with the ability to adapt to changes in its environment and be able to learn from experience.

An agent that has the ability to adapt and learn will clearly have an advantage over those that cannot; moreover, this aspect of the agents behavior elevates the agent to a higher level of ability—from a cognitive perspective.

© The Author(s) 2018
M. Skilton and F. Hovsepian, *The 4th Industrial Revolution*,
https://doi.org/10.1007/978-3-319-62479-2_5

Weight Adjustment

Consider the situation where we know what factors are important in a decision, however, what we don't know is the contribution each factor makes towards the final solution. A common approach is to provide a weight for each of the factors and allow a learning system to adjust the weights over time, so as to improve the likelihood of achieving a correct result. This is the approach adopted by neural network learning systems.

Induction

Induction may be thought of as learning by example in which we try and extract the important characteristics of the problem on hand, thereby allowing us to generalize to novel situations. Decision trees and neural networks both perform induction and can be used for classification or regression (prediction) type problems.

Clustering

We have mentioned this in a previous section when we discussed concepts and how we, as human beings, use this kind of learning algorithm to grouping together complex entities that possess many attributes. Moreover, we utilize prototypes for such clusters in order to determine the similarity of a given member with the prototype for that cluster. The similarity measure can be used to assign meaning to that cluster.

It is prudent to mention that machine learning techniques, especially induction for classification and prediction and clustering, is used by the Data Mining community to discover (and extract) patterns of information that were previously unknown. This distinguishes the learning process from the process of reasoning, which may involve some prior knowledge of the data set, or the knowledge used within its reasoning system.

Before we continue deeper into this topic, let us consider a definition for what is formally meant by the term *"learn from experience"*.

A computer program is said *to learn from experience* E with respect to some class of tasks T and performance measure P, if its performance at tasks in T, as measured by P, improves with experience E. [1]

This should make sense given our previous discussion of intelligent agents.

Neural Computation

Typical (Biological) Neuron

A typical cortical neuron has the following (simplified) structure: the neuron has a body and a region called the *Axon hillock* that generates the outgoing spikes—whenever there is sufficient charge collected from the energy that has flowed in at the synapses with its *Dendritic tree* to depolarize the cell membrane.

Notice how there is a tree of dendrites to collect the charge whereas there is only one axon that leaves the body, then branches (Fig. 5.1).

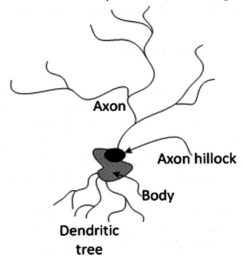

Fig. 5.1 Components of a natural neuron

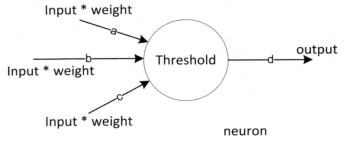

Fig. 5.2 Components of an artificial neuron

The Computational Simplification of a Biological Neuron

While Turing was fully aware of that he would need to better understand the concept of how the network of neurons were able to undertake computation and learning, it was McCulloch and Pitts [2] who first formalized the notion in 1943.

During the early 1950s, Marvin Minsky built a reinforcement-based learning network, which formed the basis of his PhD thesis at Princeton [3]. A few years Later, Frank Rosenblatt began to experiment with the notion of using such a framework for pattern recognition, which represented the first practical model of an Artificial Neural Network (ANN) and he called his invention a *perceptron* [4] (Fig 5.2). This was followed by the famous text on perceptrons by Minsky and Papert that explained some of the limitations of this particular approach and indicating directions for overcoming them [5].

A Simple Example: Perceptrons

The notion of a perceptron was quite advanced for its time, the idea was to network abstract neurons together, not simply by connecting their inputs and outputs together, but also multiplying the various inputs by a weight to provide the notion of less/more influence on the output value. The neuron had a threshold that would determine if the neuron fired, providing a binary output value based on the sum of the input values.

This is very much like a voting system; suppose the voting system required a majority vote, and the incoming values votes were: yes, yes, no (assuming a similar weight of importance for all) then in this case the neuron would output a yes value.

Now imagine that for this simple neuron, its inputs were actually certain features for a given collection of objects, then it is not difficult to see that the neuron could function as a classifier, by splitting the given collection into two, those that pass the threshold and those that did not. Such algorithms are called *Binary Classifiers*.

During the training stage an external entity needs to provide the inputs, then provide the correct output so that the perceptron could adjust its weights in order to obtain the desired output, this is called supervised learning.

Technically, the perceptron is an algorithm for supervised learning of binary classification, which may be expressed as:

$$Let\ z = w_1x_1 + \cdots + w_nx_n + b = \sum_{i=1}^{n}(w_i x_i) + b$$

$$y = \begin{cases} 1, & if\ z < 0 \\ 0, & otherwise \end{cases}$$

for the case where the artificial neuron has n inputs and one binary output.

Intuitively one can think if the expression in the first line of this function as the equation for a line, and the constant b simply move the line away from the origin, it is called the *bias*.

The perceptron is a good starting point, as it simple enough to help one understand what is meant by classification, with more sophisticated techniques the kinds we simply extend the ability of what can be classified, the basic concepts remain the same.

This all appears to be quite civilized, so where do the problems appear? Real data sets are nowhere near as pleasant as the one shown above, where we could linearly separate the data points using a straight line. Often the data sets are both multidimensional and non-linear, meaning linear methods will fail to classify the points correctly.

Moreover, even parametric methods often used in statistics perform poorly, due mainly to the nonlinear nature of the underlying phenomenon that produced the data set in the first instance. In order to obtain the correct classification boundary we shall have to use machine learning algorithms that are nonparametric.

Example Applications of Machine Learning

Assuming that we have more sophisticated techniques and lager collection of data, what sorts of things can supervised learning help us achieve (Table 5.1)?

Table 5.1 Example uses of machine learning

Market Segment	Problem	Example application
Call centers	Speech recognition	Automated call centers often request the ability for an intelligent system to be able to understand a user's request and make every effort to fulfill that request
Financial	Stock trading	In this scenario an intelligent agent predicts the performance of a given stock based on the current and past stock movement
	Detecting anomalies	Based on the usage pattern for a given client, the particular financial institution is able to identify transactions that are potentially fraudulent. As well as other kinds of security anomalies
	Biometrics	Voice recognition, fingerprint recognition, palm and retina recognition, are all now enhanced by various techniques from the realm of machine learning
	Credit risk assessment	This is more of a classification type problem well suited to machine learning techniques
Retail banking	Cash machine usage	Banks want to keep their cash machines adequately stocked with cash, without hitting the two extremes (overfilled or empty). Siemans have developed a very successful neural network for this task
Social Media	Face detection	This is becoming a prominent aspect within the realm of social media websites, as well as some financial institutions. This feature enables an intelligent agent to tag a person across many digital photographs
	Potential suicide prediction	A major social media provider explained that it may be possible to identify a potential suicide victim from their social media activities
Retail	Product recommendation	Many people shop online each day, and retailers are able to preserve the history of purchases for each shopper, and use machine learning techniques on this data to make recommendations of products that may also be of interest to them. Amazon has been very successful in using this kind of feature on its website
Manufacturing	Defect identification	It is possible to determine manufacturing flaws using machine vision and machine learning techniques

(continued)

Table 5.1 (continued)

Market Segment	Problem	Example application
Legal	Legal augmentation	AI-based systems are now employed by legal firms, both in Europe and the US, that assist attorneys within the legal areas of *due diligence* and *bankruptcy*
Patents Search	Patent Analytics	Machine learning methods are used for organizing and prioritizing documents
Utilities	Demand forecasting	Machine learning can help utility organizations to predict energy demand patterns
Education	Personalized learning	Intelligent agent tutors can answer 80% + of a typical students questions within an eLearning environment. They can provide explanations ad nauseum without becoming impatient with the student. They can also evaluate a student's performance and make recommendations
Bioinformatics	Protein structure	Prediction of protein structure and function
Medicine	Expert diagnosis	IBM's Watson and Google's Deep Mind have both been helping radiologists diagnose potential cancer cases from their x-rays, in some cases surpassing the performance of human radiologists
	Drug repositioning	Predict whether an approved drug may be useful for an off-label indication, which typically involves genomics data

When to Apply Machine Learning

(See Table 5.2)

Types of Learning Problems (for machine learning)

Machine learning has various kinds of problem that it has the potential to solve, as depicted the in the picture.

Categories of Learning Problems

- Classification
- Clustering
- Regression
- Optimization (Table 5.3)

Table 5.2 When to apply machine learning

Case	Description
Human expertise is unavailable	Consider the mars rover, it is millions of miles away and it must make decisions of its own, because help is hours away
Humans have no explanation for their expertise	Speech recognition, perceptual tasks in human vision, natural language
The solution is likely to change during its operation (or even its lifetime)	Temperature control of an intelligent building, is somewhat more complex than simply operating a thermostat, the sun heats up one side while the other is cold, requiring not just different zones but also control of the heating/cooling for the zones in order to keep the building at a comfortable temperature while minimizing energy usage
The solution needs to adapt	Various cases involving personalization, including education & shopping
The search space for the solution is too big for humans to cope	A good example here is determining webpage ranking
Anything humans can do that takes less than one second of thought	This is a statement that Andrew Ng (formerly, Chief Scientist of Baidu) often uses when asked the associated question
There is sufficient amount of data available	Current model of machine learning require both ample amounts of data in order to train the neural network, and the availability of powerful computers

Table 5.3 Categories of learning problems

	Supervised	Unsupervised
Discrete	Classification or Categorization	Clustering
Continuous	Regression	Dimensionality reduction

Classification problems: in this category we are expecting the machine to learn to classify the individuals contained with a data set into discrete classes. The similar to asking the machine to categorize them into Aristotelian categories.

Clustering problems: in contrast to classification problems, we may be looking for some kind of pattern in the data. Typically we are going to be asking the machine to categorize the individuals using a family resemblance relationship.

Regression (or prediction) problems: we provide the machine with historical data and ask the machine to help us predict real-valued output for each individual, whether it was contained within the data set or not.

Optimization problems: these are of a different nature to the other three kinds of problems, because they're not normally involved with deriving the model in the first instance, but improving the model obtained via evaluation and iteration.

Machine Learning Paradigms

There are various paradigms have been utilized over the years within the field of machine learning.

Types of Machine Learning

- Supervised Learning
- Unsupervised Learning
- Model-based Learning
- Memory-based Learning
- Deep Learning
- Reinforcement Learning.

Supervised Learning

The agent is trained by using examples from the problem space together with the desired output or action. Then the agent is provided with an input without the additional desired output and is required to make a prediction of the associated output, if the output differs from the desired output then the agent is required to adapt (typically by being adjusted in some manner) so that it is able to produce the appropriate output for the given input.

The process continues until the agent is able to produce an accurate output (or prediction) when given an input. In other words, the agent is given inputs along with corresponding outputs, and asked to find the *correct* output for a test input.

Classification, is where the agent is required to assign each input to a finite number of discrete categories. The agent determines the boundaries that separates the categories by utilizing the training date to determine a model (this step is essentially an inductive inference), followed by a decision stage where the agent uses the model to make an optimal category assignment.

Regression, where the agent learns the continuous input-output mapping from a limited number of examples. Sometimes, regression is called *curve-fitting*.

If we consider the training for these kinds of supervised learning, in the case of classification, the target output is a class label, whereas in the case of regression the target output is a real number (or a vector of real numbers).

Suppose we have a input vector x, and a target output t, then we can begin the learning process by selecting a *model-class* (*f* say):

$$y = f(x \, ; \, W)$$

then for each input vector **x**, the model-class *f* will use the numerical parameters (**W**) to map **x** into a predicted output y. Then learning (within this framework) means adjusting the parameter values to reduce the discrepancy between the target output (t) and the actual output (y) produced by the model. Clearly, this is an iterative process, since we adjust the weights, run the model again with a member of the dataset and obtain a new discrepancy, then repeat until the discrepancy is within an acceptable tolerance.

Unsupervised Learning

These kinds of algorithms are used to train agents that are required to recognize similarities between inputs or identify features in the data provided. The agent is required to classify the provided data into clusters, or segments the data into groups of similar entities. The training process continues until the agent is able to consistently segment the provided data—in other words the same data set as input will result in the same classification as output.

In other words, the agent is given only inputs and required to find some kind of structure in the space of inputs. The common algorithms used to implement this kind of structure discovery learning are:

Clustering, where the agent discovers clusters of similar individuals within the data.

Density estimation, where the agent determines the probability density distributions for the data within the input space.

Dimensionality reduction, this is sometimes called projection, namely it takes the input space and projects it down to a space of lower dimension.

Compression coding, the agent is required to discover a function, such that for each input the function computes a compact code from which the input may be reconstructed.

Reinforcement Learning

These are algorithms that are used when the kind of training data used in the case of supervised learning, namely, clearly demarcated *desired outputs for given inputs* are unavailable. Because this kind of learning fails to provide the same kind of error information that is commonly available with supervised learning, reinforcement learning often takes much longer and is less efficient when compared to supervised learning algorithms.

In reinforcement learning, the agent is required to react to inputs from its environment by taking the appropriate action on the environment that will maximize its performance measurement. This is animals learn, the performance measurement is the natural reward or punishment mechanism that's integrated into their nervous system.

While introducing the concepts of machine learning we should also mention two related concepts, namely memory based learning and model based learning.

Memory-Based Learning

The key to learning is not simple recall of data stored in some manner, but it embraces the notion of *generalization*(we have mentioned this before when we discussed the notion of inductive reasoning and natural categories formed using family resemblance), namely given an input the agent should have ability to determine the correct output or behavior, especially for those inputs that were not part of the training data.

Recall that family resemblance categories typically have associated with them a prototype for each category, which we can now use to determine to which category the new input best *fits*. We need to compute the similarity measure (distance) between the input and each stored prototype, and we can achieve this as follows:

- nearest neighbor: choose the category for the prototype that has the least distance from the input
- k-nearest neighbor: choose the category that has the majority among the k nearest prototypes

These techniques are not without their challenges, for example, as the number of prototypes increases, so does the amount of computation required to determine the appropriate category.

Model-Based Learning

This is one of the more interesting and useful techniques, where the agent builds a model that is a useful approximation to the training (input) data, or by constructing an explicit description of the target function. Issues that need to be considered in this case are,

- linear vs. nonlinear
- parametric vs. nonparametric

The main advantage this has over the memory-based learning is its computational efficiency, and the efficient manner in which memory is used, primarily because the agent is able to discard the training data once it has processed them.

The challenge for this kind of approach is called a learning or inductive bias, which is the collection of assumptions that the learner uses to predict an output for each given input that it has not previously encountered.

One way to encapsulate this notion is to express it as a formula in logic, then use it with the training data to logically infer the hypothesis generated by the learner. Although elegant, this approach often fails in real world cases, where the inductive bias can only be given as a rough description.

As an example, consider the k-nearest neighbor algorithm we previously mentioned, in this case the inductive bias is the assumption that individuals near each other belong to the same natural category.

Example of a classifier model is the perceptron, and we can use the traditional method for curve fitting to obtain a model for regression. The perceptron is a good example of linear model (classifier) and as a model of a regression.

Deep Learning

During the last decade there have been some major breakthroughs by the machine learning research community, particularly when dealing with problems to do with images and voice. The specific kind of neural networks that were developed for these kinds of applications were called *Deep Neural Networks*, where each layer had the ability to recognize a set of features that would be used by the next layer in the network, moreover, the weights assigned to the connections between the nodes emphasized the importance of the particular feature. The sub-field has become known better known as *Deep Learning*, and includes more advanced neural networks such as *Convolutional Networks* and *Deep Belief Networks*.

Bias and Variance

In supervised machine learning the goal of the algorithm is to best estimate the mapping function (also called the *Target Function*), f(x), which produces an output for some given input data. It is best understood in the case were the model is going to be used to make predictions.

Different sources of error helps us improve the data fitting process and thereby produce a more accurate estimate for the target function, and a better quality model.

Within a machine learning scenario, the algorithm is going to repeat the model building step a number of times, using new data, producing a new analysis for the model each time. The various models will produce a range of predictions, primarily due to the random nature of the data set being used.

Bias measures the difference between the correct value and the predictions from these models. The *variance* measures the variability of the predications made for a particular data point as given by the different models.

The prediction error at a point x given by given by the following function:

$$Err(x) = Bias^2 + Variance + Irreducible\ Error$$

(for details, see: [6] or [7])

The final terms in this equation is the 'noise' term, which cannot be reduced or removed by any model. It is generally the case that non-parametric algorithms have a high variance, and correspondingly low

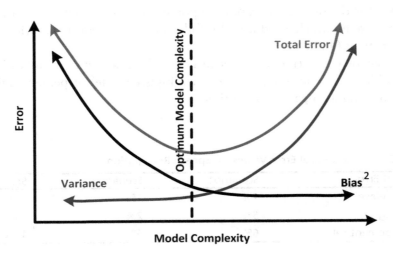

Fig. 5.3 Bias variance tradeoff

bias, whereas parametric algorithms are the reverse. This is known as the *Bias-Variance Tradeoff* (Fig. 5.3), because increasing the bias will decrease the variance and vice versa.

If we consider the model as a curve, then a machine learning algorithm may be thought of as "curve fitting", and therefore the notion of bias and variance then become properties of curve fitting, namely issues that deal with over-fitting and under-fitting.

As more parameters are added to the model, the complexity of the model increases, as does its variance while its bias decreases.

Understanding bias and variance is critical for understanding the behavior of prediction models, and the optimal complexity of a model is the point at which the increase in bias is equivalent to the reduction in variance.

In a recent presentation, Andrew Ng expressed the importance of have a sound understanding of bias and variance; he believes it is critical for understanding the behavior of deep learning models, and thereby being able to fix difficulties that arise while building such models. Ng describes the classical partition of a data set into

- *Training* (70%)
- *Development*, or *validation* (15%)
- *Test* (15%)

and states that the best way to determine how to improve the performance of a model is to look at the nature of errors that arise (and the relationship with other errors).

Consider the development of a (hypothetical) human-level speech recognition system, which produces the following hypothetical scenarios upon measurement (Table 5.4):

In scenario1, the Training-set error is significant and it is an indication of a high bias, a solution might be to use a **bigger model** or perhaps training this model for a longer period of time.

Table 5.4 Hypothetical Error Values for Speech Recognition

Type of Error	Scenario1	Scenario2	Scenario3
Human-level	1%	1%	1%
Training-set	5%	2%	5%
Development-set	6%	6%	10%

In scenario2, the Development-set is significant, and this is indicative of a high variance type problem, another words it is an over-fitting problem. In this case, one might try **more data**, or try adding regularization.

We face a challenge in scenario3, because a high bias is accompanied by a high variance and therefore a more complex solution is required.

This is a significant change from the early days of classical machine learning, when we lacked both adequate amounts of reliable data and significantly powerful (and affordable) computing resources, which often meant we could not build the bigger models that we do today.

The kind of development where we create a model, analyse the kind of errors we find, make some changes to the model, then repeat the whole process is reminiscent of iterative techniques used in other areas of (modern) software engineering. Later in this chapter, we shall describe a preliminary outline for the kind of lifecycle that may best suit these kinds of machine learning software.

Artificial Neural Networks

An Artificial Neural Network (*ANN*) is a generalization of the perceptron idea that we have already mentioned.

Formally, a perceptron consists of the components shown in Fig. 5.4, we split the processing at each node (neuron) into two; the first part (called the *integration function*) sums the various inputs:

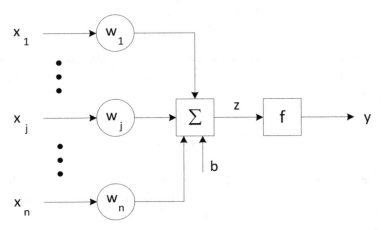

Fig. 5.4 Components of a perceptron

$$Let\ z = w_1x_1 + \cdots + w_nx_n + b = \sum_{i=1}^{n} (w_i x_i) + b$$

then the second part, called the *activation* function, is defined by:

$$y = \begin{cases} 1, & if\ z < 0 \\ 0, & otherwise \end{cases}$$

In order to generalize this, let
$$y = f(w_1x_1 + \cdots + w_nx_n + b)$$

or

$$y = f(\mathbf{W}.\mathbf{x} + b)$$

where $\mathbf{x} = (x_1, \ldots, x_n)^T$ *is the input column vector, and*

$\mathbf{W} = (w_1, \ldots, w_n)$ *is the weight row vector*

$$z = w_1x_1 + \cdots + w_nx_n + b = \sum_{i=1}^{n} (w_i x_i) + b = \mathbf{W}.\mathbf{x} + b$$

In the case of a simple perceptron the activation function is described as a *step function*:

$$f(z) = \begin{cases} 1, & if\ z < 0 \\ 0, & otherwise \end{cases}$$

We are free to choose the particular activation function that would work in our particular case, for example, we could choose the activation function to be a sigmoid:

$$Sig_c(z) = \frac{1}{\left(1 + e^{-cz}\right)}$$

where the constant c can be selected arbitrarily, its reciprocal $1/c$ is called the temperature parameter in stochastic neural networks. The shape of the sigmoid changes according to the value of c, the higher values of c make the sigmoid look more like the step function. In all our examples we shall assume that $c = 1$.

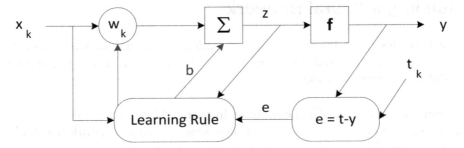

Fig. 5.5 Learning rules for a perceptron

Learning Rules

Learning rules (also known as *training algorithms*) adjust the weight and biases in order for the artificial neural network to perform a desired task (see Fig. 5.5). We shall now describe the three main types of training algorithms.

Supervised

For a given set of input pairs $\{(x_k, t_k)\}$, where x_k is the input and t_k is the corresponding target value for the output y, the learning rule will update the weights and bias values.

Reinforcement Learning

This is similar to supervised learning, however, instead of being provided with the set of pairs $\{(x_k, t_k)\}$, the algorithm is only provided with a score that measures the neuron's performance.

Unsupervised Learning

The input of data into the neural network causes the weights and biases to be adjusted–according to the learning algorithm in use. Many such algorithms are available that can cluster the input into a finite number of classes, and thereby discover 'patterns' in the input data.

Building a Neural Network

We have described the basic unit for building a neural network, namely the binary threshold unit (a perceptron), so let us now consider a recipe for building a neural network:

1. understand and specify the problem in terms of inputs/outputs
2. at the first attempt, select the simplest kind of neural network that looks like a possible candidate for solving your problem
3. split your training dataset into a training set and a testing set (the generalized version of this idea is called *Cross-Validation*)
4. from your training dataset, select a small subset and discover the connection weights and activation function that will be produce the right result for your small training data
5. increase the size of the training dataset in 4 and repeat that process until the network is able to respond with an appropriate output for a given input from your training dataset
6. test the performance of your network with a member from the remainder of your training dataset
7. if the network did not perform well, return to step 4, and repeat
8. if you reach this step then there are two possible reasons; first, the problem was ill-defined, so you could return to step 1 and ensure that you had a good understanding of the problem and there were no conceptual inaccuracies in your specification. The second, is that the problem you have chosen may not lend itself to this kind of solution, and therefore you should look elsewhere.

Step 4 is often called the *training phase* for the neural network, which should be a systematic procedure for determining appropriate connection weights, this systematic procedure is called *learning*.

In the case of the perceptron (described earlier in this section), which we assumed a set of input/output pairs $\{(x_k, t_k)\}$, where e was defined as x−t, and this was used to classify inputs into two linearly separable classes. We can now express these notions using the following general form:

$$\boldsymbol{W}^{new} = \boldsymbol{W}^{old} + e\boldsymbol{x}^{T}$$

$$b^{new} = b^{old} + e$$

Machine Learning Lifecycle

There is no consensus on the kinds of tasks we should undertake in order to develop and deploy machine learning models into our intelligent agents (or other applications). Nevertheless, it is prudent declare some steps that should be taken during this process (Fig. 5.6).

1. Goal:

   a. define the goals and assumptions,
   b. determine the problem type—for example, is it for a classification or regression kind of problem?

2. Data:

   a. collection of data
   b. data preparation: preparing historical data for training of the machine learning algorithms

3. Model:

   a. Building: including the use of training data to build the model
   b. Evaluation: use the data to improve the model
   c. Optimization: improve the accuracy and scalability of your model

4. Prediction:

   a. see if your model is able to make valid predictions
   b. how the model performs on new data

It is important to note this is not a waterfall kind of process, but rather an iterative one, because each step in this process will need to be visited more than once in order to achieve a satisfactory solution.

The first step of this lifecycle is shared with so many others within the development community, it is important to decide what kind of data you have, and the kind of problem that you intend to tackle using the resources available to you. For example, if you only have images of dogs it is unreasonable to expect your machine learning algorithm to learn to recognize cat images. Moreover, at this stage of the machine learning lifecycle, one must also determine (and define) what 'human-like' errors means in this context.

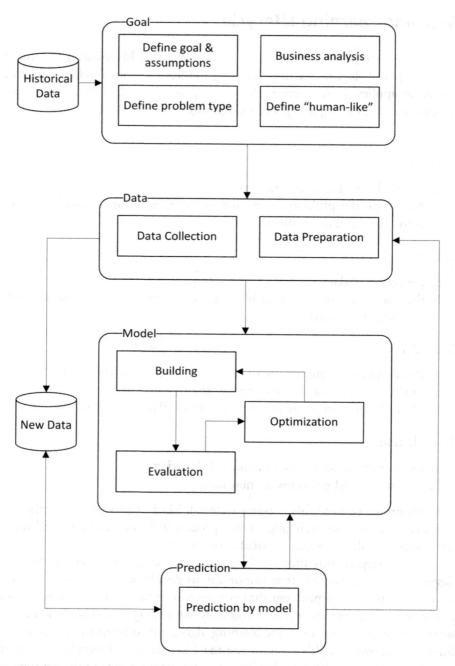

Fig. 5.6 Machine learning lifecycle

The second step involves the preparation of data, it is easy to underestimate the importance of this step, especially where data is going to be used for training purposes. If you are going to use a supervised learning algorithm, then you must ensure an adequate collection of clean, appropriately labeled data that will be used for training. Similar (relevant) data must be saved, which can later be used to test the model that has been built by the algorithm.

In manner in which data is collected is particularly important for technical, practical and training reasons. Specific knowledge of the domain can provide deep insight and help to extract additional value from the collected dataset, which can highlight certain kinds of features before the main model building begins. This kind of data preparation is sometimes called *feature engineering*, and it is so important in real world ML that in some high profile examples the feature engineers may hand-engineer synthetic data.

Step three is really a composite step, it involves using the algorithm to create a model, then using the various resources to evaluate the performance and adjust the model accordingly. This is a peculiar step, because the human creates the environment in which a learning algorithm can operate, while the rest is (partially) undertaken by the machine learning algorithm; we say partially because a human being often determines what may need to be done to improve the performance of such an algorithm.

Step four is related in spirit to the presentation by Andrew Ng, in that we must have a way to access the algorithm, and the model, which it has constructed before we release it into the wild.

The one step that we have omitted is that of feature extraction, or feature engineering, in which valuable information may be extracted from seemingly uninformative data set.

Types of Machine Learning Algorithms

- Clustering
- Decision Trees
- Dimensionality Reduction
- Kernel Approaches
- Bayesian
- Regression Analysis
- Deep Learning.

Machine Learning Algorithms

Thus far we have discussed some of the ideas centered on the notion of a neural network, let us now consider some of the other kinds of machine learning algorithms.

Decision Trees

Design trees are a well established technique in classification and prediction, where the root is the input for all information and outputs are the leaf nodes. For example, in the case of classification, the information enters the decision tree at the root and the leaf nodes represent the classified results.

More formally, a function that consists of comparisons statements, each branch may lead to another comparison branch or to a leaf, is represented by a decision tree.

To make a decision, the path starts at the root and navigates recursively down the various branches of the tree until it reaches the desire leaf node.

For example, suppose we wish to classify the diagram of blue-dots and red-triangles (Fig. 5.7). We could use a decision tree inducing algorithm called CART (Classification and Regression Trees) which creates a binary tree, meaning at each there are always two branches

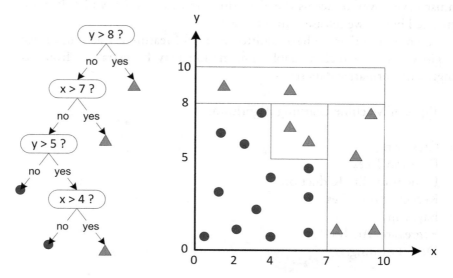

Fig. 5.7 Decision tree

that emanate from it. There are various ways to manage the complexity of this tree as it grows, for example, one can adopt a cost-complexity pruning mechanism such as the Gini index.

Note:

- there can be several decision trees representing the same problem
- there needs to be a termination criteria that will determine when to stop building the tree
- the depth of the tree is proportional to the number of features selected (in our example, we selected two features, x and y). In general, a decision tree of depth n can handle 2^n classes
- the output of the tree is always in the form of simple rules.

Entropy and Information

Entropy is a concept that belongs to *Information Theory*, and intuitively, it measures the concentration of a variable into one or more values—in other words it measures the *randomness* of the outcome for that variable.

Suppose our random variable x can assume the following five values (events) {a, b, c, d, e}, with the following corresponding probabilities for their outcome {0.25, 0.1, 0.35, 0.1, 0.2}.

The entropy H(x) of a random variable x is given by:

$$H = -\sum_i p_i \log_2 p_i = \sum_i p_i \log_2 (1/p_i)$$

we shall use a form that emphasizes the variable x with values x_i

$$H(x) = \sum_i p(x_i) \log_2 (1/p(x_i))$$

In our case the entropy for the random variable x will be:

$$H(x) = 0.25 \log_2 5 + 0.1 \log_2 5 + 0.35 \log_2 5 + 0.1 \log_2 5 + 0.2 \log_2 5$$

$$H(x) = \log_2 5 = 2.32$$

Note, the reason for using log to base 2 is because it makes the units of entropy, 2, which is why the units are called 'bits'.

Information gain provides us with a way to utilize the notion of entropy to help us segment our data. Information gain essentially measures the change in randomness, which tells us how much a piece of information will alter an outcome.

In the case of 8 red-triangles and 12 blue dots, our random variable x will take two values, {blue-dots, red-triangles} with probability {3/5, 2/5}. The entropy for x can be calculated as follows:

$$H(x) = 0.8 \log_2 (1.67) + 0.4 \log_2 (2.5) = 0.8(0.74) + 0.4(1.32)$$

$$H(x) = 0.59 + 5.28 = 5.87$$

Now consider the segmentation of this set using the line labeled 'A' (Fig. 5.8), the distribution to the left now contains 12 blue-dots and 4 red-triangles, and the one on the right contains 4 red-triangles. Let us calculate the entropies for these two sets:

Left of line A (with probability 16/20, or 0.8—which represents the proportion of blue-dots and red-triangles that belong to this region out of the total number of blue-dots and red-triangles)

$$H(x) = 0.75 \log_2 (1.33) + 0.25 \log_2 (4)$$
$$= 0.75(0.41) + 0.25(2) = 0.81$$

Right of the line A (with probability 4/20, or 0.2)

$$H(x) = 0$$

The entropy of the right hand side is 0, because the it is deterministic, they are all red-triangles.

The *information gain* is the weighted difference of entropies (namely, before and after the segmentation)

$$= 0.8(5.87 - 0.81) + 0.2(5.87 - 0) = 0.8(5.06) + 0.2(5.87) = 5.22$$

In the case for the segmentation using line labeled 'B', for the left-hand side we would get:

$$H(x) = 0.67 \log_2 1.5 + 0.33 \log_2 3 = 0.67(0.58) + 0.33(1.58) = 0.91$$

and 0 for the right-hand side, however, the information gain would have been

$$= 0.9(5.87 - 0.91) + 0.1(5.87 - 0) = 5.05$$

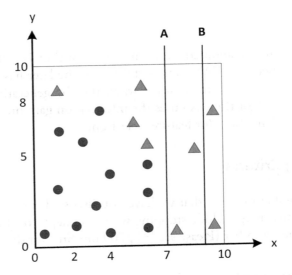

Fig. 5.8   Information gain

Therefore the segmentation using line 'A' is better than the one using line 'B'.

Decision Tree Algorithms

There are various algorithms that one can use, including CART that we have already mentioned. The main goal of a decision tree algorithm is to segment a given dataset (V say) into subsets {V_i} that will eventually become the set of classification classes.

The difficult part is determining the appropriate set of tests, which given a data point will produce the corresponding output value.

Cart

We have just been describing an algorithm for the CART decision algorithm, which is essentially a binary tree, where the leaf nodes contain the outputs.

C4.5

One other commonly adopted decision tree algorithm is called C4.5; the main difference between CART and C4.5 is that the later has the capability to split the decision node in multiple ways, thereby generating more than binary trees. This algorithm also uses the information gain measure to determine the optimal attribute (or feature) selection.

Terminating Criteria

There are a number of issues that we have not discussed, such as terminating conditions, which may include stopping when the depth of the tree exceeds a pre-determined number (Please see [3] p709 onwards for details).

Decision Trees for Regression

Decision trees may be used for regression in similar manner, where each region corresponds to a leaf node in a binary decision tree. In this case, the leaf nodes contain a real-valued number for the target that corresponds to that region.

Random Forests

High dimensional data is a common problem for machine learning algorithms, and one way to manage the complexity is to use a special kind of decision tree called *Random Forests.*

The main impediment to decision trees is the addition of new data, if they fail to follow precisely the same distribution as the training set, then the algorithm's performance may be put at risk. One can mitigate this risk by using a collection of decision trees, and when it is time to produce an answer one approach is to use the majority of the votes or means.

Random forests are nonlinear, accurate, algorithms that are widely used in many real world classification applications, and they are a good solution for handling noisy datasets.

Pros and Cons of Decision Trees

Decision trees do have significant advantages that include:

- they are relatively easy to build
- they can handle high dimensional data and operate on large datasets
- can be combined with other decision techniques
- they are robust and relatively easy to understand.

although there are disadvantages also:

- they can become quite unwieldy is many outcomes are linked, and in cases where values are uncertain the calculations will become rather complex, and a different architecture may become necessary.

Nearest Neighbor

The nearest neighbor is a memory-based learning algorithm, this algorithm is based on the idea that points behave in a similar manner to their nearby or neighboring points—using some notion of similarity or distance.

In the case of regression, when the algorithm is given a new data point it will search in its database for the nearby points, and return the target value for the one that is nearest. In the case of classification, let us assume that our measure of distance is the Euclidean Distance given by:

$$d(x, y) = \sqrt{\sum_i (x_i - y_i)^2}$$

We need to take a moment to describe one of the most important structures in computational geometry, namely the *Voronoi Diagram*, whose formal definition follows:

Let $P = \{p_1, p_2, \ldots, p_n\}$ be a set of points in the plane (or in any dimensional space), which we shall call sites. Then $V(p_i)$, the Voronoi cell for p_i, is the set of points q in the plane that are closer to p_i than to any other site, that is:

$$V(p_i) = \{q | d(p_i, q) < d(p_j, q), \text{ for all } j \neq i\}$$

The veronoi diagram of a set of points in the plane partitions the plane into non-overlapping regions that are the voronoi cells of those points.

Given a data point set P, and a test point q, then one way to determine the nearest neighbor for q is to compute the Voronoi Diagram for P and locate the cell of the diagram that contains q.

The nearest neighbor algorithm does have problems with outliers, and one way to remediate this issue is to consider more than one neighbor, which helps to stabilize the model. The modified version is called *k-nearest neighbor algorithm* (*kNN*).

For classification: suppose we have a set of data $\{(x_i, y_i)\}$, where x_i are the features and y_i represent the corresponding class labels, and we are then given a test point x to label. The k-nearest neighbors algorithm (assuming we have selected the Euclidean distance) is as follows:

- compute the distance $d(x, x_i)$ for each x_i and rank them according to shortest distance
- select the k vectors that have smallest distance from x
- use a voting system to determine which class label appears most frequently among the k ranked vectors, and return the class y that that corresponds to the class to which x belongs.

Training for kNN models is trivial, we simply store all the training data and when a test point arrives we simply follow the procedure above.

The kNN algorithm is successfully used in recognizing handwritten digits—especially in the case of postal codes on envelopes. In this case with a 7NN algorithm its accuracy rating is approximately 95% and that compares with human beings at 97%.

The value k in kNN is a critical factor because it can influence the final result, and the best way to choose the value k is to use cross-validation techniques. Clearly, it is not just the value k that has an influence, but the specific distance function used to compute the shortest distance can also be significant. Consider the Minkowski Distance function

$$d(x, y) = \sqrt[p]{\sum_i |x_i - y_i|^p}$$

this is a very interesting metric, it is a generalization of the Euclidean distance, where the value p is now parameter that we can change. For example,

- $p = 0$ gives the Hamming Distance, which behaves like a logical AND, it simply sums the number of features that are different
- $p = 1$ gives the Manhattan Distance, or the city block distance
- $p = 2$ gives the familiar Euclidean Distance
- as $p \to \infty$ the distance function begins to behave like logical OR.

Clustering Algorithms

Clustering is one of the most common forms of unsupervised learning, in these kinds of learning algorithms we are attempting to learn something about the pattern (or structure) of the dataset, rather than prediction about a particular value.

These kinds of techniques are used to better understand the underlying patterns inherent in the dataset, and therefore enable the researchers to undertake data mining to explain the patterns, provide suggestions for missing data values, or provide feature generation or selection for the members of the dataset.

One of the tasks for a clustering algorithm is to look for subsets of the dataset and determine some information about them, such as:

- how many subsets are there and what can we determine about the size of these subsets?
- do members of the subsets share any common properties or features?
- do the subsets themselves contain some kind of structure?

The idea here is to find these subsets of members of the dataset that are similar to one another, and group dissimilar members into different subsets. These subsets are called *clusters*. Some good examples of clusters include:

- Marketing, often uses notion from clustering, from categorizing customers according to various similarity relations, such as campaigns or product preference
- Financial Services, uses clustering for their customers according to various criteria related to credit scores, assets, spending habits
- Document Management Systems, use clustering to organize documents.

Clusters come in two flavors, *hard clusters*, where the clusters do not overlap and *soft clusters* where they do. These are analogous to the notions of Aristotelian Categories and Family Resemblance categories that we mentioned in the section on cognition, and as in that section soft clusters may also involve the notion of degree associated with a given member.

We should also mention that clustering methods can produce clusters that are *partitions* of the dataset, where the subsets of the dataset are not further decomposed into subsets, and those that produce a *hierarchical* decomposition of the dataset.

There are various algorithms for clustering, here are few common ones:

Hard Clustering: the commonly used algorithm is the *K-Means Clustering* algorithm, although it has some limitations with regard to initialization methods that are overcome by the use of *K-Means ++* algorithm that selects initial sites that are far away but in a random manner.

Soft Clustering: it worth considering *Gaussian Mixture Models* are useful and flexible model of probability distributions used here for clustering. The parameters for the Gaussian mixture models can be learnt using *Expectation Maximization* algorithms.

Bayesian Learning

Statistical models generally have an underlying assumption, namely, a probability model that assigns a probability to an instance of a particular class. The goal of this supervised learning technique is to develop a probability distribution for the class labels, moreover, the Naïve Bayes is broadly based on Bayes' theorem, which is central to Bayesian Learning methods.

Before we continue there are a couple of items that we should mention:

- Prior and posterior probability: the probability that a given event will occur, without any further knowledge, is called the *prior probability*. Nevertheless, conditions change so suppose that we update our probability values for the aforementioned event, then these new probabilities are called *posterior probability*.
- Given a hypothesis (H, say) and a dataset of observations (D, say) then Bayes Theorem can be stated as:

$$p(H|D) = \frac{p(H)p(D|H)}{p(D)}$$

where:

- $p(H)$ is the probability of the hypothesis H before any observations from D becomes available (the prior probability)
- $p(D)$ is the probability of the dataset D (the evidence)
- $p(H|D)$ is the probability of the hypothesis once we have observed the dataset D (the posterior probability)
- $p(D|H)$ is the probability of the dataset D given the hypothesis H (the likelihood).

Example: Suppose half of your business trip flights results in you catching the flu, whereas normally you have a 1/20 chance of getting the flu, and on any given day there is a 1/30 chance of you taking a business trip flight (basically once per month). Furthermore, suppose I observe that you have flu, can I predict (and with what probability) that you were on a business trip?

Let

$$BT = event\ that\ you\ were\ on\ a\ business\ trip$$

$$Flu = event\ that\ you\ have\ flu$$

$$p(BT) = 1/30$$

$$p(Flu) = 1/20$$

$$p(Flu|BT) = 1/2$$

Using Bayes Theorem we have:

$$p(BT|Flu) = \frac{p(BT)p(Flu|BT)}{p(Flu)} = \frac{(1/30)(1/2)}{(1/20)} = 1/3$$

In this scenario, given a model of how long flights may cause one to catch the flu (given by the probability $(Flu|BT)$) together with some background probabilities and the observation that you have flu, we can compute the probability of some underlying cause for the flu.

Let us express Bayes theorem in a form that will be more useful for the Bayes Classifier.

$$p(y|x) = \frac{p(x|y)p(y)}{p(x)}$$

where

$p(y|x)$ is the probability of the class given the observation and $p(y)$ is the probability overall of each class outcome. The law of complete probability allows us to express $p(x)$ as

$$p(x) = \sum_c p(x|y = c)p(y = c)$$

giving us

$$p(y|x) = \frac{p(x|y)p(y)}{\sum_c p(x|y = c)p(y = c)}$$

How do we use this for classifying some data? Suppose that we are given a table of observed data (training data) Table 5.5 remember that the classifier is attempting to map observed values of x into predicated Table 5.6 values of y. Table 5.7 shows the prior probability for each class, $p(y)$, it also shows the distribution of features given the class, $p(x|y = c)$, so for each of the classes the algorithm learns a model for the set of observations represented by x.

So the steps that we have taken are:

• estimate $p(y)$ for each class $p(y = c)$

Table 5.5   Observed data (training data)

Features	Class1 (y = 0) Sweet Potato	Class2 (y = 1) Broccoli
x = 0 (Vitamin A)	120	6
x = 1 (Vitamin C)	30	220
x = 2 (Calories)	100	45
Totals	250	271

Table 5.6   Predicated values of y

Features	Class1 (y = 0)	Class2 (y = 1)
x = 0	120/250	6/126 = 0.05
x = 1	30/250	220/271
x = 2	100/250	45/271
Totals	250	271
p(y)	250/521 = 0.48	271/521 = 0.52

Table 5.7   Distribution of features given the class, p(x|y = c)

Features	$p(y=0|x)$	$p(y=1|x)$
$x = 0$	0.95	0.05
$x = 1$	0.12	0.88
$x = 2$	0.69	0.31

- for each class c, estimate the probabilities for the feature within that class $p(x|y) = c$
- calculate $p(y = c|x)$ using Bayes rule
- choose most likely class c.

Naïve Bayes

The process described above may work well for small number of discrete features, however, the table will grow exponentially with the number of features and that is simply unmanageable for machine learning systems.

One solution is to make some simplifying assumptions regarding the set of features, namely, that they are independent of one another. This allows us to simplify the Bayes equation:

$$p(y|x) = \frac{p(x|y)p(y)}{p(x)}$$

by allowing

$$p(x|y) = \prod_i p(x_i|y)$$

which significantly reduces the computational complexity of the contingency table.

Learning Based on Regression Methods

Regression methods are typically used in statistics to model the relationship between two or more variables. Using a statistical methodology called *Regression Analysis* we are able to measure the strength of the relationship between variables, and may be used to address both classification and prediction problems. Regression techniques are commonly used within the realm of supervised learning.

In contrast to Bayesian methods use probability to model a given situation, regression methods use methods that are more statistical, notions such as the Covariance:

$$\rho_{xy} = \frac{\sum_{i=1}^{n} (x_i - \bar{x})(y_i - \bar{y})}{n}$$

for a dataset comprising of two variables (x and y) The covariance is best used when it is normalized to a number between -1 and 1, which is achieved by normalizing the covariance with the standard deviation of both variables, and the result is called the *Correlation Coefficient*:

$$\rho(x, y) = \rho_{xy} = \rho_{xy}/\sigma_x \sigma_y$$

The correlation ($\rho(x, y)$) measures the strength of linear dependence between the variables x and y.

In order to give this an intuitive understanding suppose we are given a dataset of two variables (x and y), and we produce the regression equation that represents the mathematical model for the relationship between the variables. The question we would like to answer is how good is the model? In other words how good is the fit of the regression equation to the dataset that we were initially provided?

This is where the correlation coefficient (technically, it is the Pearson's correlation coefficient for linear regression) helps us to quantify how well the pairs of points matches the regression equation. The goodness of fit of the data to the mathematical relationship can be thought of as a measure of how well one variable can predict the other, given the context of the data.

For example, a *Linear Regression* between an independent variable (x) and a dependent variable (y) is captured by the equation, $\hat{y} = w_0 + w_1 x$, which enables us to predict values of y for a given value of x. *Multiple regression* is a simple extension of linear regression where there are more than one independent variables (x_i) used in predicting the value for dependent variable (y). So why is the dependent variable (y) expressed as ($\hat{y}$)? That's because when we use the equation to predict a value for (y) it is the *estimated* or *predicted* value (namely, $\hat{y}$) and not the *actual* value (namely, y) this is an important difference.

The relationship between the independent and dependent variable may not be best represented by a line, but a curve of some kind, cases like these are called *Polynomial* or *Non-linear Regression.*

We use a method called *least squares* is used to fit a polynomial regression model to the data primarily because it minimizes the variance in the estimation of the coefficients. Now consider the equation:

$$\hat{y} = w_0 + w_1 x$$

where the coefficients w_0 and w_1 are discovered by minimizing the sum of the errors squared (if you do not square the errors before you sum them, they will typically cancel one another out and you will end up with a sum of 0).

$$S = \sum_i e^2 = \sum_i (y_i - \hat{y}_i)^2 = \sum_i (y_i - (w_0 + w_1 x_i))^2$$

the error e is often called a residual, namely the difference between the actual value and the value predicted by the model (the sum and the mean of the individual residuals, one for each point, is equal to zero).

This is an example where we have one dependent variable and one independent variable, together with two parameters, which we shall now generalize as:

$$e_i = y_i - (w_0 + w_1 x_i)$$
$$= y_i - f(w, x_i)$$

where w is the vector that holds all of the values of all values w_i and the minimum of the sum of squares of the errors is obtained by setting the gradient to zero:

$$\frac{\partial S}{\partial w_i} = 2 \sum_i e_i \frac{\partial e_i}{\partial w_i} = 0, \quad for\ i = 1, \ldots, n$$

What is important here is not the precise statement for the equations, but rather the concept, namely that we begin by guessing the degree of the polynomial that we believe best describes the data, then allow a given method to determine the set of parameters, w_i, that will minimize the residuals (errors) and thereby provide us with the best possible fit for the data.

Logistic Regression

Logistic regression is an extension of linear regression where the dependent variable is a categorical variable, in other words the it is used to classify the observations represented by the independent variable (typically a binary variable taking two values 0 and 1).

We have seen the same form as this function before when we discussed perceptrons:

$$y = f(w_1 x_1 + \cdots + w_n x_n + b)$$

or

$$y = f(\boldsymbol{W}.\boldsymbol{x} + b)$$

which we can reduce simply by letting the constant $b = w_0$ to $y = f(\boldsymbol{W}.\boldsymbol{x})$

Therefore we can say that in linear regression we were attempting to predict the value of y using a linear function $y = f(\boldsymbol{W}.\boldsymbol{x})$, in logistic regression what we are attempting to do is predict the probability that a given example belongs to class 1 rather than class 0. More precisely, we are attempting to learn a function of the form:

$$p(y = 1|x) = f(W.x) = 1/1 + e^{-W.x}$$

Much as in the case for linear regression, we wish to minimize some "error" or "cost" function, therefore we define the cost function to be:

$$S(W) = \frac{1}{2} \sum_i (y_i - \hat{y}_i)^2 = \frac{1}{2} \sum_i (y_i - (w_0 + w_1 x_i))^2$$

However, the concepts are analogous.

Summary

In this chapter, we introduced the reader to the notion of an artificial neuron, and explained its relationship with a basic biological neuron commonly found in nature. This enabled us to present the notion of a perceptron, one of the first structures used in neural machine learning, and a network of these abstract neurons form an Artificial Neural Network. Basic learning types of learning algorithms were introduced that included, supervised, unsupervised, and reinforcement learning.

Furthermore, we introduced various common kinds of machine learning algorithms; including decision trees, regression analysis, and k-nearest neighbour. In keeping with the spirit of the book, we provided examples of applications that use machine learning, when to apply machine learning and categories of learning problems that could be addressed by these methods.

Finally, we have included an outline of the steps that would be prudent to include in a machine learning lifecycle.

Notes and References

1. Mitchell, Tom M. (1997). Machine Learning, McGraw-Hill.
2. McCulloch, W. S. and Pitts, W. (1943). A Logical Calculus of Ideas Immanent in Nervous Activity, Bulletin of Mathematical Biophysics. 5(4): 115–133.
3. Minsky, M. L. (1954). Theory of Neural-Analog Reinforcement Systems and Its Application to the Brain-Model Problem. Ph.D. thesis, Princeton University.
4. Rosenblatt, F. (1958). The Perceptron, a Probabilistic Model for Information Storage and Organization in the Brain, Pscyh. Review, 62: 386.
5. Minsky, M. and Papert, S. (1969). Perceptrons, MIT Press.
6. Fortmann-Roe, S. (2012). Understanding the Bias-Variance Tradeoff, http://scott.fortmann-roe.com/docs/BiasVariance.html.
7. Hastie, T. et al. (2009). The Elements of Statistical Learning: Data Mining, Inference, and Prediction. 2nd Ed, Springer.

6

Advanced Neural Networks

Introduction

In the previous chapter, we considered various approaches to machine learning, including a basic single layer perceptron that can be quite successful in handling linearly separable classification type problems. Nevertheless, the current success for machine learning emanate from a class of methods collectively called multi layer networks, which include deep learning networks.

In this chapter, we shall introduce various kinds of neural network architectures, including the infamous convolutional network that revealed how these kinds of networks (when combined with the backpropagation algorithm for minimizing the errors) could perform perception-type tasks. For example, a network of this kind is used by the US postal service to recognize handwritten zip codes (postcodes).

Multi Layer Perceptrons

Single layer networks are only suitable for linearly separable classification problems, many real-world problems are not of this kind, and therefore it is important to find ways to circumvent these limitations. Fortunately, there are various ways in which we can achieve this, for example, we can define a multiple feed-forward layered network, which functions by mapping input (or stimulus) values to output (or response) values (Fig. 6.1).

© The Author(s) 2018
M. Skilton and F. Hovsepian, *The 4th Industrial Revolution*,
https://doi.org/10.1007/978-3-319-62479-2_6

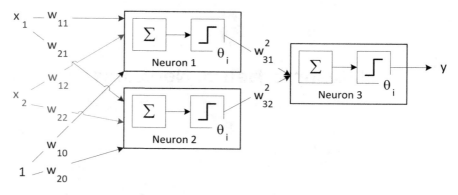

Fig. 6.1 Multi layer perceptron

We have also taken the opportunity to standardize the notion and symbolism often used by researchers working in this field:

- The activation function f is often given the symbol that indicates whether it is a step function, a linear function, etc. and it often accompanied by the set of parameters denoted by θ_i
- The weights are also enumerated using the last subscript for the input, and the first subscript for the destination neuron
- Superscripts are sometimes used to indicate the layer to which the weights belong, so for example in case of w_{31}^2 the weight belongs to the second layer (first neuron-to-neuron connection) and is between neuron 1 and neuron 3
- The threshold in a single unit is equivalent to having a negative bias, therefore it is prudent to include the bias as an input that always has the same activity, namely the number 1, then we can assign weights to the connection to change its value. Moreover, with this modification, learning the bias is the same as learning the weights for activities

The perceptron as a binary output classifier can be provided with the following training procedure:

- ensure we have modified the unit to remove the bias (as mentioned above)
- pick training cases using any policy that ensures that every training case will be repeatedly selected

  - if the output unit is correct, retain its weight
  - if the output unit incorrectly yielded a value 0, then add the input vector to the weight vector
  - if the output unit incorrectly yielded a value 1, subtract the input vector from the weight vector

This procedure will find a set of weights that will produce the correct response for all training cases, *if such a set exists*. We mentioned "if such a set exits", because there are many cases when they do not—these are the tasks that a binary threshold neuron is unable to achieve. For example, a binary threshold output unit is incapable to determining if two single bit features are equal:

Positive case	$(1, 1) \rightarrow 1$
	$(0, 0) \rightarrow 1$
Negative case	$(1, 0) \rightarrow 0$
	$(0, 1) \rightarrow 0$

This is was the beginning of a whole set of problems associated with these kinds of neurons, the general statement of which appears as the Minsky and Papert's *Group Invariance Theorem* [1]. These kinds of transformations are problematic for binary threshold perceptrons, because they need to use multiple feature units in order to recognize transformations of informative sub-patterns. Therefore the difficult part is handled by the hand-coded feature detectors and not the learning procedure.

One answer is to use multiple layers of adaptive, nonlinear hidden units, although this presents a whole new sleuth of problems of its own. For example, we would need to find a way of adapting all the weights, not just the last layer—and that is very difficult in practice, placing a demand on both computational resources (processing, memory, etc.) as well as huge well tuned datasets. Moreover, the learning that takes place for the weights in the hidden units are equivalent to learning features.

Of course this begs the question, what was Alan Turing's intuition telling him about groups of symmetry transformations that would induce him to spend the last years of his life studying, what would become one of the most important fields in mathematical physics, namely, *symmetry-breaking* [2].

Neural Network Architectures

Often diagrams show a lot of detail, which is unnecessary for conveying the high-level architecture, therefore we shall only show the units, inputs and outputs.

The *architecture* of an artificial neural network is determined by:

- Number of inputs and outputs of the network
- Number of layers

- How the layers are connected to each other
- The activation function of each layer
- Number of neurons in each layer

Activation Function

There are a variety of activation functions, here are a few commonly used ones (Table 6.1):

In a deep neural network the activation function may change from one hidden layer to the next.

Feed-Forward Networks

The diagram (Fig. 6.2) shows an example of a multi-layer *Feed-Forward* network, where the layer containing the three neurons is called the *Hidden Layer*. By convention, any multi-layer network with more than a single hidden layer is called a *"Deep Network"*. In this example, the output consists of two neurons, and therefore both the inputs and outputs are each considered to be a vector of values.

Information flows in a single direction in a feed-forward network, typically from layer n to layer n + 1, and cannot skip over layers.

Table 6.1 Activation functions

Activation function name	Equation	Comment
Linear	$f(z) = z$	The simplest of all functions, simply returns the input value, typically used as the output in a linear regression layer
Step	$f(x) = \begin{cases} 0, & x < 0 \\ 1, & x > 0 \end{cases}$	Typical "threshold" function
ReLU	$f(x) = max(0, x)$	Also known as the "rectifier"
Logistic	$f(x) = 1/1 + e^{-x}$	This is also known as the "Sigmoid"
Gaussian	$f(x) = e^{(-x^2/2)}$	Typical bell curve function
Hyperbolic Tangent	$f(x) = (1 - e^{-2x})/(1 + e^{-2x})$	This is the typical 'S' curve - somewhere between a step and sigmoid with values are between −1 and +1

In this particular neural network, the input values are considered as layer 0 and the output vector of values as layer 2, layer 0 stores the current input pattern and is therefore not a true layer, because no processing takes place at that layer.

Special Kind of 2-Layer Networks

These kinds of networks often have one or more hidden layers, all of which have a sigmoid activation function, together with an output layer of linear neurons, all of which have a linear transform function.

Two layer neural networks of this kind are known to be capable of approximating many functions arbitrarily well, when given sufficient neurons in the hidden layer.

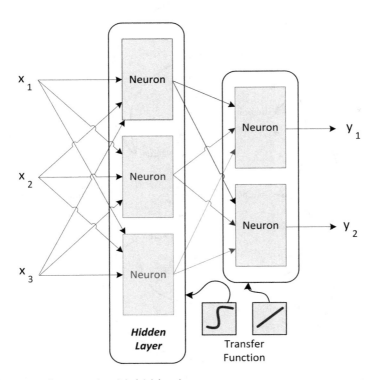

Fig. 6.2   Neural network with hidden layer

Recurrent Neural Network

Recurrent Neural Networks (RNN) differ from a free forward network by having at least one feedback connection, so the activations can flow in a loop (Fig. 6.3).

This enables a RNN to do temporal processing and learn sequences, in other words it can perform sequence recognition or temporal association (prediction).

Recurrent neural networks may take many forms, the one we have depicted here is a very common sort, consisting of a multi-layer perceptron (MLP) plus some added loops, which provides the network with the ability to exploit some of the nonlinear aspects of MLP and provide the network with a *memory*.

A fully recurrent network is an MLP where the previous set of hidden unit activations feed back into the network along with the inputs.

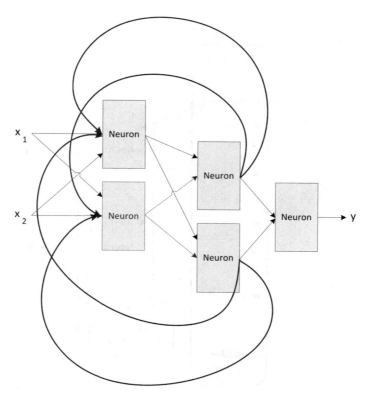

Fig. 6.3   Recurrent neural networks

These kinds of networks are very good for motor control, because they have the ability to exhibit oscillatory behavior. Another feature comes from their dynamics, namely, they can settle to point attractors, which is useful for retrieving things from memory. However, they can exhibit chaotic behavior, which makes them unsuitable for general information processing tasks.

The distributed hidden states within a recurrent neural networks gives it the ability to (efficiently) store information about the past, and their non-linear dynamics allows them to update their hidden *states* in very complicated ways. Which leads us to this remarkable that describes the computational capabilities of recurrent neural networks of this kind:

> All Turing machines may be simulated by fully connected recurrent networks built out of neurons with sigmoidal activation functions. [3]

But this computational power comes at a price, they are very difficult to train.

Associative Memory

One of the differences between human and computer information processing is the manner in which humans utilize memory, namely they use what is typically called associative memory, which they access through the content rather than location. The idea here is to use a recurrent neural network and allow the memory content to be a pattern of activations on the nodes of the network.

Hopfield Network

One way to implement an associative memory is to use the Hopfield Network, which is a fully recurrent neural network of N neurons, whose activations are normally ±1, rather than the conventional 0 and 1. The neuron activation equation is:

$$x_i = sgn\left(\sum_{i=1}^{n}(w_i x_i) - \theta_i\right) \quad where, \ sgn(z) = \left\{ \begin{array}{l} 1, if \ z \geq 0 \\ -1, otherwise \end{array} \right.$$

the activations here are time dependent, and will continue to change until they have all settled down to some stable pattern. Those activations can be updated either synchronously or asynchronously.

A *Hopfield Networks* is a *symmetrically connected network* that does not have any hidden units. Symmetrically connected networks are generally much easier to analyze, nevertheless they are constrained in terms of what they are able to do, because the model for such a network must obey an *energy function*. For example, such a network is unable to model cycles (of information).

Boltzmann Machines

Geoffrey Hinton and Terrence Sejnowski introduced a variant of the Hopfield Network in 1985 [4], and called it a *Boltzmann Machine*, primarily because of its stochastic nature. This was the first of this kind of recurrent neural network that was capable of learning internal representations. These kinds of networks are generally more powerful than Hopfield Networks but less powerful than recurrent neural networks.

Boltzmann machines are one type of a *generative neural network*, which we obtain by connecting binary stochastic neurons using symmetric connections. We can significantly improve the computational aspects of the learning process simply by restricting the connectivity in a special manner.

Incidentally, if we were to connect binary stochastic neurons in a directed acyclic graph we would get another type of generative neural network called a *Sigmoid Belief Network*.

Let the state of a given unit, be denoted by s_i (where $s_i = 1$ if unit i is *on* and 0 otherwise), furthermore, let the connections between nodes i and j be given by w_{ij}. Unit i updates its binary state by first calculating

$$z_i = b_i + \sum_j s_j w_{ij}$$

where b_i is its own bias and $\sum_j s_j w_{ij}$ is the sum of all the weights on units that are active and connected to it. The probability that unit i will then turn on is given by the following logistic function:

$$p(s_i = 1) = sigmoid\left(b_i + \sum_j s_j w_{ij}\right)$$

If the units are updated in a sequential order of any kind, the network will eventually reach a *Boltzmann distribution* in which the probability of a state vector, **v**, is determined solely by the "energy" of that state vector relative to the energy of all possible binary state vectors:

$$P(v) = e^{-E(v)} \bigg/ \sum_u e^{-E(u)}$$

The term:

$$\sum_{u} e^{-E(u)} = Z$$

is called the *partition function*, which ensures $P(v) = 1$.

In both Hopfield Networks and Boltzmann machines, the energy of state vector **v** is defined as

$$E(v) = -\sum_{i<j} s_i^v s_j^v w_{ij} - \sum_i s_i^v b_i$$

where s_i^v is the binary state assigned to unit i by the vector **v**.

It is common to see this expressed as

$$E(x) = -x^T W x - b^T x$$

where x is binary random vector (the units) and W is the weight matrix of model parameters and b is the vector of bias parameters—assuming all the units are *visible* (or *observable*).

Suppose we chose the connection weights w_{ij} such that the energies of the state vectors represented the cost of those vectors, then the stochastic dynamics of a Boltzmann machine can be viewed as a way of looking for a low-cost solution. This search can be improved by using simulated annealing that scales down these weights and energies by a factor, T, which is analogous to the temperature in a physical system.

In order to discuss the learning in a Boltzmann machine we need to look at the case where it contains hidden units, and those that do not separably.

Suppose we are given a training set of state vectors, which is our data, and we are dealing with a Boltzmann machine *without* hidden units. In this context, learning is considered to be the process of finding the weights and biases (the parameters for the network) that define a Boltzmann distribution in which the training set of state vectors have a high probability.

We can obtain the following by differentiating the energy equation for the state vector (**v**) for this system:

$$\partial E(v) / \partial w_{ij} = -s_i^v s_j^v$$

and

$$\langle \partial \log P(v) / \partial w_{ij} \rangle_{data} = \langle s_i s_j \rangle_{data} - \langle s_i s_j \rangle_{model}$$

Suppose the Boltzmann machine samples the state vectors from its equilibrium distribution at a temperature of 1, which will give us an expected value expressed by $\langle . \rangle_{model}$. The expected values in the data distribution is given by $\langle . \rangle_{data}$. To perform gradient decent in the log probability, the w_{ij} is incremented by a small learning rate times $\langle s_i s_j \rangle_{data} - \langle s_i s_j \rangle_{model}$ (the learning rule for the bias b_i involves a similar term, except the term s_j is omitted).

Now suppose the Boltzmann machine consists of some *visible* units, whose states can be observed, and some *hidden* units whose states are determined by the observed data. The hidden units act like *features* that allow the machine to model distributions over visible state vectors that cannot be modeled by the interaction between the visible units themselves. Nevertheless, the learning rule remains the same, which makes it possible for the machine to learn (binary) features that capture higher-order structure within the data.

With the hidden units, the expectation $\langle s_i s_j \rangle_{data}$ is the average of the expected values of $s_i s_j$ when a data vector is frozen (technically, *clamped*) in the visible units, then the hidden units are repeatedly updated until they reach equilibrium.

An alternate way of stating the joint probability distribution, when the units are partitioned into visible and hidden units, is given by the following formula:

$$p(x, h) = exp\left(-E(x, h)\right)/Z$$

where

$$Z = \sum_{x} \sum_{h} exp\left(-E(x, h)\right)$$

and the energy function is given:

$$E(x, h) = -h^T W x - a^T x - b^T h$$

$$E(x, h) = -\sum_{j} \sum_{k} W_{jk} h_j x_k - \sum_{k} a_k x_k - \sum_{j} b_j h_j$$

this comes from the analogous situation in physics, where the probability of observing a particular configuration of variables of interest is given by the exponential of the negative of the energy function. The term Z represents an normalization constant (partition function) which sadly for a Boltzmann machine is intractable. However, the conditional probabilities are tractable

$$p(h_j = 1|x) = 1/\left(1 + \exp\left(-(b_j + \mathbf{W}_j \cdot \mathbf{x})\right)\right)$$

$$p(h_j = 1|x) = sigmoid\left(b_j + \mathbf{W}_j \cdot \mathbf{x}\right)$$

where W_j is the jth row of W and a similarly:

$$p(x_k = 1|h) = sigmoid(a_k + \mathbf{W}_k \cdot \mathbf{x})$$

A Boltzmann machine with hidden units is no longer limited to modeling linear relationships between the variables, instead it becomes a universal approximator.

Unfortunately learning is quite slow in general Boltzmann machines, these difficulties can be overcome by placing constraints on the connectivity of the network and restricting the learning process to one hidden layer at a time—restricted Boltzmann machine satisfies both constraints (Fig. 6.4).

A *Restricted Boltzmann Machine (RBM)*, is a shallow 2-layer network that are the most common building blocks of deep probabilistic models, in which the first layer is called the visible layer and the second layer is the hidden layer.

In a restricted Boltzmann machine, there are no intra-layer links, the nodes are connected to each other across layers, but no two nodes may be

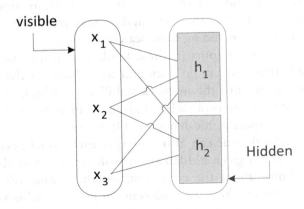

Fig. 6.4 Restricted Boltzmann Machine

connected at the same layer, moreover, the hidden units are conditionally independent given the visible states. In addition, there is no direction in restricted Boltzmann machine.

In the original paper that described the underlying ideas of a RBM, the author [5] states:

> In harmony theory, knowledge is encoded as constraints among a set of well-tuned perceptual features. These constraints are numerical and are embedded in an extremely powerful parallel constraint satisfaction machine: an informal inference engine.

The learning algorithm is very slow in networks with many layers of feature detectors, however, on can improve the performance by using a many layer network consisting of single layers of RBM, whose feature activations in one layer serves as the data for the next.

Boltzmann machines are used to solve two different kind of problems:

- Search Problem: in this scenario, the weights on the connections are fixed and represent a cost function, which enables us to sample the binary state of vectors that have low cost function values.
- Learning Problem: in this case the Boltzmann machine is shown a set of binary data vectors and required to learn to generate these vectors with high probability, which it does by finding weights on the connections so that the data vectors have low cost values.

This is not quite as straight forward as it initially sounds, because in order for a Boltzmann machine to learn it must make many updates to the weights of the data vectors, and each update may require the machine to solve various problems, including some search problems.

Notice there are no outputs in these kinds of unsupervised networks. The idea here is that you can go back and forth between the visible layer and the hidden layer until the network stabilizes, at which point the hidden units will present the probability a given input vector will produce an activation for that specific hidden unit. Of course, given the symmetric nature of the network, one can also state that each visual node represents that probability that a given hidden vector will activate that visible node.

We already know about the constraints on the connectivity, moreover, the hidden units are conditionally independent given a visible vector, therefore we can obtain unbiased samples from $\langle s_i s_j \rangle_{data}$ in one parallel step. To sample from $\langle s_i s_j \rangle_{model}$ is a different story, because we need multiple iterations that alternate between parallel updates of the hidden units and parallel updates of the visible units, this means we need to replace $\langle s_i s_j \rangle_{model}$ with $\langle s_i s_j \rangle_{reconstruction}$ which is obtained using the following process:

1. Start by instantiating the visible units with a data vector, then perform a parallel update all of the hidden units
2. Update all the visible units in parallel, this is essentially the *reconstruction* of the values for the visible units
3. Now update all of the hidden units in parallel

This efficient learning process is described in Hinton [6].

Deep Learning Networks Using Restricted Boltzmann Machines

Once one hidden layer has gone through the process of learning, the next step might be to use the activity vectors of that hidden layer as data for training another RBM - this is an effective way to compose the RBM. Of course we need not stop there, we can then take the activity vectors of the second hidden layer and use that as training data, and so on. Once the machine has been allowed to learn using the multiple layers of hidden units, it is only reasonable to view the entire network as a single multi-layer *generative* model—called a *Deep Boltzmann Machine* (DBM).

This is an efficient way to build (an unsupervised) deep learning neural networks, with many hidden layers, where the highest level of features are typically more useful for classification than the lower ones. These deep networks can be further fine-tuned to be more effective at classification, or dimensionality reduction, by using a *backpropagation* (or *gradient descent*) algorithm.

Backpropagation Algorithm

One of the best explanations of the back-propagation algorithm may be found in the original article [7], in which the authors state

There have been many attempts to design self-organizing neural networks. The aim is to find a powerful synaptic modification rule that will allow an arbitrarily connected neural network to develop an internal structure that is appropriate for a particular task domain. The task is specified by giving the desired state vector of the output units for each state vector of the input units. If the input units are directly connected to the output units it is relatively easy to find learning rules that iteratively adjust the relative strengths of the connections so as to progressively reduce the difference between the actual and desired output vectors. Learning become more interesting but more difficult when we introduce hidden units whose actual or desired states are not specified by the task.

The learning procedure we are about to describe is for multi-layered networks that have a layer of input units at the bottom, a number of intermediate layers, and a layer of outputs at the top. Inter-layer connections nor connections from higher layers to lower layers are permitted (Fig. 6.5).

An input vector is presented to the network by setting the states of the input units - in our diagram this means we assign values to a, b and c. Next, we assign states to each layer by using the following equations:

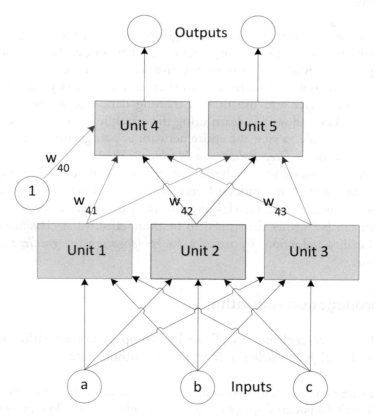

Fig. 6.5 Backpropagation

$$x_j = \sum_i y_i w_{ji}$$

$$y_j = 1 \big/ 1 + e^{-x_j}$$

where x_j represents the total input to unit j and is clearly a linear function of the outputs, y_i of the units that are connected to unit j multiplied by the appropriate weights w_{ji} for those connections. Notice the bias is represented by an input of 1, multiplied by the appropriate weight for that input, namely, w_{40}, this helps with the clarity of the equations that we need.

If we follow the diagram, this means the total input for *Unit4*

$$U4 = 1 * w_{40} + U1 * w_{41} + U2 * w_{42} + U3 * w_{43}$$

where $U4$ is the value assigned to *Unit4* (its state). The output of *Unit4* is given by

$$U4 = 1 \big/ 1 + e^{-U4}$$

note that each unit has a binary state, on or off, but has a real-valued output, y_i, which is a non-linear function of its total input. This means we have a linear equation that combines the input values into the unit, along with the appropriate weights, then a non-linear function going out.

The aim here is to discover a set of weights (w_{ji}, *or* **W** *the weight matrix*) such that for each input vector the corresponding output vector is sufficiently close to the desired output vector.

Given a fixed set of input/output cases from our dataset, we compare the desired output value with that computed by the network in every case, and thereby obtain a value for the total error, which is defined by:

$$E = \frac{1}{2} \sum_c \sum_j \left(y_{j,c} - \hat{y}_{j,c} \right)^2$$

where c is the index over the input/output cases, j is an index over the output units, y is the actual state of an output unit and $\hat{y}$ is the desired state.

To minimize E, by gradient descent, we need to compute the partial derivatives of E with respect to each weight in the network. The partial derivatives of Error with respect to each weight are computed in two passes, the forward pass which we have already described, and the backward pass that propagates derivatives from the top back to the bottom.

The following is a detailed description of the mathematics that underlies back propagation, and is included here for the benefit of those who wish to see the underlying mathematics for this process. The reader is free to skip this derivation.

The backward pass is much more complicated than the forward pass, and we begin by computing $\partial E / \partial y$ for each of the output units, which we do for a particular case, c (and therefore suppress the index c):

$$\partial E / \partial y_j = y_j - \hat{y}_j$$

now apply the chain rule from calculus to compute $\partial E / \partial x_j$

$$\partial E / \partial x_j = \partial E / \partial y_j \cdot dy_j / dx_j$$

however, since we have

$$y_j = 1 \,/\, 1 + e^{-x_j}$$

$$dy_j / dx_j = y_j (1 - y_j)$$
$$\partial E / \partial x_j = \partial E / \partial y_j \cdot y_j (1 - y_j)$$

this tells us the change in the total input x to an output unit will affect the error. For a weight w_{ji}, from i to j, the derivative is

$$\partial E / \partial w_{ji} = \partial E / \partial x_j \cdot \partial x_j / \partial w_{ji}$$

$$\partial E / \partial w_{ji} = \partial E / \partial x_j \cdot y_i$$

for the output of the ith unit, the contribution to $\partial E / \partial y_j$ resulting from the effect of i on j is given by

$$\partial E / \partial x_j \; \partial x_j / \partial y_i = \partial E / \partial x_j \cdot w_{ji}$$

so collecting together all the connections for a given network that will impact the ith unit, we have

$$\partial E / \partial y_j = \sum_j \partial E / \partial x_j \cdot w_{ji}$$

This calculation shows us how to compute $\partial E / \partial y$ for any unit in the penultimate layer given $\partial E / \partial y$ for all units in the final layer, therefore we can repeat this process to compute such a term for earlier layers, computing $\partial E / \partial w$ for the weights at each stage.

The simplest version of gradient descent is to change each weight by an amount proportional to the accumulated $\partial E / \partial w$, namely:

$$\Delta w = - \in \partial E / \partial w$$

While not as efficient as other methods, this approach has two advantages; first, it can be implemented by local computations in parallel (which is significant given that we now have such hardware readily available at a reasonable cost able to perform those kinds of computations) and secondly, it is much simpler than calculating second derivatives. There are also ways to accelerate this process, see [7].

Symmetry is an issue, for example one task that cannot be solved by simply connecting the input units to the output units is the detection of symmetry, for that we need the intermediate layers. To break the symmetry the authors recommend that the process begin with small randomly generated weights.

Convolutional Neural Networks (CNN)

Convolutional neural networks are networks that have a known grid-like network topology, such as image data that are essentially a 2-dimensional grid of pixels. Moreover, the name "Convolutional" indicates that the network employs a mathematical operation called a *convolution*, which is a specialized kind of linear operation. In a multi-layer neural network in which the matrix multiplication has been replaced by the use of these convolution operators (in at least one of their layers) is called a *Convolutional Neural Network (CNN)*.

The mathematical definition of the term convolution is as follows:

Given two functions, $f, g : \mathbb{R} \to \mathbb{R}$ the *convolution* $f * g$ is defined as:

$$s(t) = (f * g)(t) = \int\limits_{-\infty}^{+\infty} f(\tau)g(t - \tau)d\tau$$

Suppose the parameter t represents time, then we can interpret the convolution

$$s(t) = (f * g)(t)$$

as the weighted average of the function $f(t)$ at the moment, where the weighting is given by $g(-\tau)$ is shifted by t, thereby emphasizing different parts of the input function.

In the case when the functions are defined on the set of integers, $f, g : \mathbb{Z} \to \mathbb{Z}$ then the convolution is given by:

$$s[n] = (f * g)[n] = \sum_{m \in \mathbb{Z}} f[m]g[n - m]$$

however, in the interest of simplicity and uniformity we shall use the following notation, because it is consistent with the literature on neural networks:

$$s(t) = (x * w)(t) = \sum_{\tau \in \mathbb{Z}} x(\tau)w(t - \tau)$$

The convolution operator is commutative, meaning we can also write the same operation as:

$$s(t) = \sum_{\tau \in \mathbb{Z}} x(t - \tau)w(\tau)$$

The function $x(t)$ is called the *input*, and $w(t)$ is called the *kernel*, the convolution $s(t)$ is referred to as the *feature map*.

Think of the standard convolution operation, using one kernel, as extracting one kind of feature. We may apply a number of them in parallel at different locations, however, in a multilayer neural network we want each layer to extract many kinds of features, at different locations.

Many of the instances we meet are far more complex than a simple grid, even when they initially appear to be a simple case. For example consider a color image split into its red, green and blue components (essentially, three images, one all red, one all blue and one all green) stacked as playing cards one on top of another. In order to address a given value, we need one index to tell us which color and two further indices to describe the spatial location within each channel (Fig. 6.6).

It is common to find examples of multidimensional arrays of data in machine learning applications and the kernel is a multidimensional array of parameters that are adopted by the learning algorithms—the two arrays must be stored separately within the software. It is often the case that some elements of these arrays will be zero, and given the convolution operation there is little point in storing those, therefore we store only non-zero values and make the assumption that any other value in the array is zero.

We can also use convolutions over multiple axis at a time, for example, in the case of an image given by the 2-dimentional array $I(m, n)$ as our input,

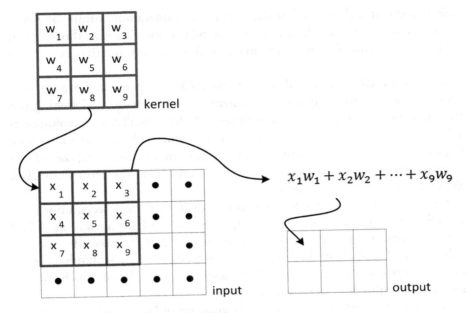

Fig. 6.6 Example of general convolution

we can use a 2-dimensional kernel $K(p, q)$. The convolution in this case becomes: $S(i, j) = (I * K)(i, j) = \sum_{m} \sum_{n} I(m, n) K(i - m, j - n)$

however, commutativity of the convolution operation gives us:

$$S(i, j) = (K * I)(i, j)$$

$$= \sum_{m} \sum_{n} I(i - m, j - n) K(m, n)$$

The commutative property of convolution arose primarily because the kernel is flipped relative to the input, that is to say the index into the input increases while the index into the kernel decreases.

Despite the fact that the second form is preferable when it comes to implementing the algorithm in software, many libraries implement a related operation called *cross-correlation*, which is the same as convolution but without flipping the kernel:

$$S(i, j) = (I * K)(i, j) = \sum_{m} \sum_{n} I(i + m, j + n) k(m, n)$$

This is the first indication that the convolution operation within the realm of neural networks is different to the standard one, because this kind of multi-channel convolution is not guaranteed to be commutative, even if the kernel is flipped.

Convolutional networks also need the ability to perform learning, and therefore be able to compute the gradient with respect to the kernel, given the gradient with respect to the outputs. Mathematically, a convolution is a linear operation and therefore we can represent such an operation using matrices. This means we can use multiplication by the transpose of the matrix defined by the convolution, to back-propagate the error derivatives through the convolutional layer.

Convolution networks were initially designed for pattern recognition, and therefore dealt mostly with color images, which we have already described are 3-dimensional objects. This enabled the designers to take advantage of this fact and constrain the architecture accordingly. These kinds of neural networks have a wide range of applications, examples of which include image recognition and recommender systems.

A *Convolution network* (or *CovNet*) is made up of layers, each one of which has a simple API that transforms an input 3D volume to an output 3D volume using some differentiable function that may, or may not, contain parameters.

Typically, there are three layers that constitute the CovNet:

- *Convolutional Layer*
- *Pooling Layer, and*
- *Fully-connected Layer*

An example of such an architecture is the LeNet5 architecture from 2001, which was a very successful 7-layer network that was discovered by Yann LeCun [8], and subsequently used by banks for hand written numerals on checks and the US postal service for automatic recognition of zip codes (Fig. 6.7):

Convolutional Layer:

The parameters at this layer are not simple numbers, but a set of learnable filters, and while each filter may not be very big (say 3x3 or 5x5) there will be three of them—one for each of the color channels (R, G, B). In this layer, the system will pass each filter across the image performing a convolution at each step, until it has covered the entire image.

This may now be considered as a map, namely, the response of the filter at every spatial location of the input image—or in other words, the value

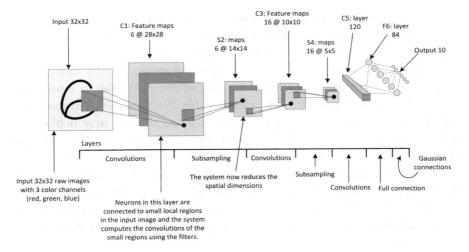

Fig. 6.7 LeNet5 Architecture

produced by the convolution operation between the filter and the image, at a given pixel. This map is called an *activation map*.

The network will eventually learn, which filters correspond to which kind of features that occur in input images—for example, some filters will be quite good at identifying a visual edge in a given image. Note that there will be a separate 2D activation map for each filter.

By stacking the activation maps together one on top of another (much like playing cards in a deck) we can produce a volume that represents the output of this layer.

The size (height/width) of a given filter, intuitively determines the neighboring neurons that will be taken into consideration when we perform a convolution operation. For example, a 3x3 filter only takes into consideration immediate neighbors, whereas as 5x5 filter also takes into consideration their neighbors.

When dealing with images (for instance 32x32 pixel images) it is simply impractical to connect one neuron to all neurons in the previous layer. One technique is to connect a given neuron in this layer to a region of the input volume—this local region is called the *receptive field* of the given neuron (which incidentally, corresponds to the chosen filter size).

Please note, that the extent of connectivity along the depth axis remains the same as the input image, in other words, a three channel image will remain retain this value even after being processed by this layer.

This explains the connectivity between the neurons in the first Conv layer to the input layer, and the input volumes that it receives and processes into output volumes, which are themselves controlled by three parameters:

Depth, of the output volume is a hyperparameter, which corresponds to the number of filters we choose to use, where each filter is sensitive to a given feature in the input. For example, this first Conv layer receives raw pixel images as input, therefore the kind of filters that we may deploy may seek the presence of a visual edge at a particular orientation. The collection of neurons that look at the same region of the input is called a *fiber*.

Stride, is the number of pixels that we slide the filter along the image, so for example, if we slide it along by one pixel then the stride is one, but we could move it along two or even three pixels at a time, which would have strides of two or three respectively. The larger the stride, the smaller the output volume (spatially).

Zero-padding, the best way to explain this is to consider an image with a 3x3 filter, the target of the filter is the cell in the center of this 3x3 grid. Clearly, the target cannot be matched with the edge pixels as things stand, therefore one solution is to pad the outer edge of the image with cells that have zero as a value. The size of this zero-padding is also a hyperparameter (Fig. 6.8).

Here is modified version of the example we discussed earlier while describing the convolution operation, where we have zero-padded the input by one, and increased the stride to two. We can now see the equation for determining the output volume given an input volume:

$$O_{H} = (I_H - R + 2Z)/(S + 1)$$

Where:

O_H: Height of Output size
I_H: height of Input size
R: Receptive field size
Z: the amount of zero padding
S: the stride used

There will be an analogous formula for the width.

One can easily see that in our case using these formulae, we get a 3x2 output. Clearly, there will be times when O turns out to be a decimal number, this is considered to be an invalid case, and in such cases we have to be careful and re-design elements of the architecture to ensure that the sizes workout correctly.

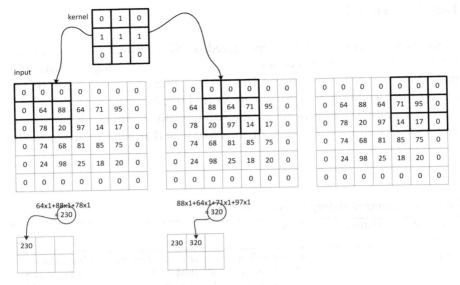

Fig. 6.8   Zero-padded input image

One more useful technique is that of *Parameter Sharing*. For example, given an input as an image of 32x32x3, we may decide to look for the same feature at different spatial locations but at the same depth (which we call a depth slice). This helps us control the number of parameters used because we can constrain the neurons to share the same weights and bias.

Pooling (Subsampling) Layer:

Pooling is a technique used to reduce the spatial size of the various representations in the ConvNet, to control the number of parameters and hence reduce the amount of computation required by the network. Pooling layers operate independently on every depth slice of the input.

Max-pooling, which is a form of nonlinear down-sampling partitions the input image into a set of non-overlapping sub-regions, then for every sub-region it outputs the maximum value—in contrast, *average-pooling* outputs the average of the sub-region.

A very common example is max pooling using a 2x2 kernel (filter) with a stride of 2.

Full Connection Layer:

Neurons in this layer are fully connected to all activations in the previous layer, which means their activations may be computed using a matrix multiplication together with a bias offset—this is akin to a classical multi-layer perceptron together with logistic regression (Table 6.2).

We are not going to provide a full taxonomy, but a simple taxonomy consisting of an example from each of the categories that are mentioned in this text (Table 6.3).

Table 6.2 Examples of deep convolutional NN

Name of convolutional network	Comments
LeNet-5	A pioneering convolutional network developed by Yann LeCun, et al., that classified handwritten digits, and was successfully used to read postal codes and by banks to recognize hand written numbers on checks [1]
AlexNet	Developed by Alex Krizhevsky, Ilya Sutskever and Geoff Hinton, that significantly outperformed traditional method of image processing during the 2012 ImageNet ILSVRC challenge. The runner-up in the competition had an error of 25%, AlexNet produced on average an error of just 16% [7]
GoogleLeNet	2014 ILVSRC winner, this network introduced a new concept called an Inception Module that reduced the number of parameters in the network to 4 million (down from 60 million in AlexNet) [6]
VGGNet	The runner-up in 2014 was a network from Karen Simonyan and Andrew Zisserman, which clearly demonstrated that the depth of the network plays a critical role in its performance [8]
AtomNet	In 2015, a deep neural network called AtomNet was the first neural network to be used for structure-based rational drug design [9]
ResNet	2015 winner of ILSVRC was a network developed by Kaiming He et al., which showed that by skipping connections and using batch normalizations one could further improve the performance of certain types of networks. Kaiming He et al. have recently published a paper [7], on the topic of *Identity Mappings in Deep Residual Networks*, which is considered to be the state of the art in Convolutional Neural Network models

Table 6.3 Taxonomy of deep learning networks

	Supervised	Unsupervised
Shallow	Perceptrons logistic regression	Restricted Boltzmann Machines
Deep	Recurrent neural networks Deep neural networks	Deep Boltzmann Machines

Reinforcement Learning

Let us review some of the kinds of neural networks that we have considered thus far:

Supervised Learning, in which the network is operating to a known expectation, and the dataset members are all *labeled*. The algorithms for these kinds of networks typically focus on discovering a relationship between the input attributes and the output attributes, that is to say to discover a function (f say) such that given input x the goal of the network is to speculate an appropriate y such that: $f(x) = y$.

Unsupervised Learning, there are times when we simply do not have labeled datasets, or we are seeking to discover any structures that may exist within the given dataset—many (if not all) of the attributes for the dataset are often unknown for this class of problems. These kinds of datasets are called *unlabeled*.

Semi-supervised, these kinds of networks before, but the dataset for these kinds of networks contain both labeled and unlabeled data.

Reinforcement Learning, is the process of learning and adapting to a changing environment. In this approach, intelligent agents learn from direct interaction with the environment they are placed in, for which they may have little information let alone a complete model. The intelligent agent learns by getting feedback about its actions in terms of rewards or punishment, therefore it is different to both supervised and unsupervised learning, because at no stage is the agent given any kind of confirmation or denial.

During the learning process, the agent will map situations to actions to be taken in an environment, and the learning algorithm's main focus is to maximize the rewards received during its interaction with the environment and to establish a mapping of states to actions as a decision-making policy.

One challenge faced by reinforcement learning methods that do not occur in other kinds of learning is the trade-off between exploration and exploitation, which is the trade-off between exploiting previously tried (and successful) actions, against exploring new kinds of actions in order to make better actions choices in the future. The dilemma here is that the agent must balance amounts of exploration and exploitation to ensure that it succeeds with its goals.

Another factor that reinforcement learning agents have to contend with is not just unknown, but also uncertain, environments, which raises the issue of having to address the problem of goal-directed interaction within such an environment.

The main difference between supervised learning and reinforcement learning is the absence of input-output pairs, instead the agent is told the immediate reward and subsequent state once it has chosen an action to take, furthermore, it is not told which action would have been in its best interest. To make matters more interesting, the agent's learning is concurrent with the evaluation process.

Every day our expectations from intelligent systems increases and traditional data-based intelligence techniques are rapidly approaching their limits. We need systems that are able to solve complex decision problems in environments that are unfamiliar to them, of which they have little information and are often highly uncertain. They need to exploit their existing knowledge and explore new paths, learn to take new actions and then have its internal critic evaluate its effects and provide feedback, which it can use to improve its overall performance.

Some of these notions were also discussed in the section on Learning Agents. While this is an active area of research it is outside the scope of this book.

Machine Learning Frameworks and Languages

Many programming languages are used in developing machine learning systems, and much of it depends on what you are attempting to achieve, whether you are at the concept/prototyping stage or planning on delivering a solution, as well as the background knowledge (preference) of the programmers themselves (see Appendix A).

Summary

The general consensus appears to be that in the near future one of the main goals for machine learning research is unsupervised learning, which include Reinforced Learning techniques using various kinds of neural networks, including Recurrent Neural Networks.

Gunnar Carlsson and his team at Ayasdi have discovered that by combining techniques from the nascent world of Topological Data Analysis, with the familiar ones from machine learning can produce superior results within the realm of unsupervised learning. These two approaches appear to complement one another rather well, see [9] for more details.

In order for a system to build a model of its environment and be able to update it in a continuous manner, it must possess some kind of short-term memory. Recurrent networks possess loops that enable it to remember certain artifacts, however, they can only remember things for a very short time, and one solution appears to be to combine LSTM (Long Short Term Memory) [10] with a recurrent network. There is an interesting approach adopted by the research team at Google's DeepMind called Differentiable Neural Computing (DNC) [11, 12], in which the authors claim:

> ... demonstrate that a DNC can successfully answer synthetic questions designed to emulate reasoning and inference problems in natural language

This approach is one attempt at emulating natural reasoning, an alternate approach is adopted by Hinton [13], using something he calls a 'thought vector' and describes some very interesting ideas in the referenced video.

Bengio [14] also talks of the importance of memory and reasoning, and in his presentation he states it as "The Next Frontier", although he mentions that the immediate or "hot" frontier is Deep Generative Learning, an interesting article discusses the use of such an approach for location-invariant word recognition [15].

LeCun [16], talks about the failure of traditional attempts to enable machine to reason using symbolic systems (logic in particular) and believes that we should be replacing the symbolic system with a continuous system, where the logical operators are replaced by continuous mathematical operations. This is an idea that originally lead Zadeh [17] to instigate an entire field called *Fuzzy Sets* and *Fuzzy Logic*.

Given a set of medical results, the question often asked is, what disease might a given patient have? Sometimes it is necessary to solve this kind of problem before we are able to perform other kinds of tasks. We often try to use a probabilistic model in such circumstances, where we need to predict the value of some variable given the value of some other variables, or predict a probability distribution over a set of variables.

These are examples of what we have been calling an *inference*—however, for most deep models these kinds of inference problems are often intractable.

One approach used in deep generative models is called Approximate Inference see [18].

Notes and References

1. Minsky, M. and Papert, S. (1969). Perceptrons. MIT Press.
2. Turing, A.M. (1952). The chemical basis of morphogenesis. Transactions. Royal Series B, Biological Sciences, 237 (641): 37–72.
3. Sieglmann and Sontag (1991). Applied Mathematics Letters, 4, 77–80.
4. Ackley, D.H., Hinton, G.E., and Sejnowski, T.J. (1985). A learning algorithm for Boltzmann machines. Cognitive Science, Elsevier, 9 (1): 147–169.
5. Smolensky, P. (1986). Information processing in dynamical systems: Foundations of harmony theory. In Rumelhart, D. and McLelland, J.L. (1986) Parallel Distributed Processing: Explorations in the Microstructure of Cognition, Vol.1, pp.194–281. MIT Press, Cambridge.
6. Hinton, G.E. (2002). Training products of experts by minimizing contrastive divergence. Neural Computation, 14 (8): 1711–1800.
7. Rumerlhart, D.E., Hinton, G.E., and Williams, R.J. (1986). Learning representations by back-propagating errors. Nature, 323 (9): 533–536.
8. Lecun, Y., Bottou, L., Bengio, Y., and Haffner, P. (2001). Gradient-based learning applied to document recognition. In Intelligent Signal Processing. IEEE Press, pp. 306–351.
9. Topological Data Analysis and Machine Learning: Better Together (2015). http://cdn.ayasdi.com/wp-content/uploads/2015/02/wp-tda-and-machine-learning.pdf.
10. Hochreiter, S., and Schmidhuber, J. (1997). Long short-term memory. Neural Computation, 9 (8): 1735–1780.
11. Graves, A. et al. (2016). Hybrid computing using a neural network with dynamic external memory. Nature, 538, 471–476 (27 October 2016).
12. Differentiable neural computers, https://deepmind.com/blog/differentiable-neural-computers/.
13. Hinton, G. (2016). Google's AI Chief Geoffrey Hinton how neural networks really work, https://youtu.be/EInQoVLg_UY.
14. Bengio, Y. (2015). Scaling up deep learning, http://www.iro.umontreal.ca/~bengioy/talks/IBM_13Oct2015.pdf.
15. Di Bono, M.G., and Zorzi, M. (2013). Deep generative learning location-invariant visual word recognition. Frontiers in Psychology, 4, 635. doi: 10.3389/fpsyg.2013.00635.

16. LeCun, Y. (2017). Facebook's Yann LeCun: Predictive learning: The next frontier in A.I. https://youtu.be/qjI8lJn8Mss.
17. Zadeh, L. (1965). Fuzzy logic. Information and Control, 8, 338–353.
18. Rezende, D.J., Mohamed, S., and Wierstra, D. (2014). Stochastic backpropagation and approximate inference in deep generative models. In ICML'2014. Preprint: arXiv:1401.4082.

Part III

The Cross-cutting Concerns of Artificial Intelligence

7

Impact of Architecture on Intelligent Systems

Introduction

In this chapter we explore major cross-cutting themes that are pervading the 4th Industrial revolution. Observations in how the early genesis of the internet has given rise to a global phenomena of connected devices and things that have reach much further than the original web of content and services. The nature and scale of computing power, storage and advances in algorithms have enables new kinds of feedback and connectivity at the macro and micro to nano scale that are creating 4th industrial revolution insights and changes. There are new policy, operating, economic, legal and personal consequences from this massive scaling that are having serious impacts on cyber security, personal privacy and surveillance laws in countries.

We explore these themes with recognized international experts in these fields to draw practitioner experience and guidance to the significance and mean of these cross-cutting concerns.

Topics covered in this chapter include the historical underpinnings of the internet and internetworking and how this is evolving into the networks of the future.

A New Kind of Network

I have seen and been involved in several recent research topics that are considering legal implications of machine learning with personal data privacy. This has been driven by cloud computing and how devices, smart gadgets and the

© The Author(s) 2018
M. Skilton and F. Hovsepian, *The 4th Industrial Revolution*,
https://doi.org/10.1007/978-3-319-62479-2_7

IoT and cloud typically now go together [1]. There has also been work looking at machine learning that is using these technologies and the implications of legal liability of machine learning [2]. Machine learning is transforming legal and technical issues around responsibility, autonomy and accountability [3].

The spring of machine learning was around the year 2000 with the transformation of the internet into mass data capture and leading to mass surveillance, replacing the traditional advertising market research analytics and targeting advertising. The root of this was the accidental discovery by Google's two founders Larry Page and Sergey Brin while they were Ph.D. students at Stanford University. They were originally just trying to construct a better search engine that was not gameable, because it had been observed from all the previous search engines people had been boosting their ranking by various tricks.

The idea of page rank is not actually an original idea, it goes back to the 1950s when information retrieval was simply to make it dependent on everyone else, not on what you gave, you can't influence everyone else except having a better page or more relevant page. So page rank became a powerful method but the really clever bit that they accidently realized was that having got the relevance ranking right then if you have adverts associated with the pages it had commercial value that you could measure by the page clicks.

This evolved into two things, one you could build your own index of all the web pages so you now know what's in them all, and is the method used in how you search the internet. You are not actually "searching the internet", but in fact it is the index that is built which you are just returning the result of what people put in. Secondly, since you now know what people actually like, you can charge advertising directly.

This became a new kind of insight to people who had effectively relied on a combination of other mediums. Previously, for example, in TV advertising you broadcast a TV program you have absolutely no idea how many people are actually watching and what you should be paying for that advertising from a commercial view point. So then you have to rely on ratings agencies with sampling studies and very clever statisticians working for who these agencies calculating ranking. They would literally put a box on top of your TV, monitor the programs you are watching, and phone you up and ask questions. With the internet they have automated that, but you have not only automated that process but you have also indirectly created a complete surveillance over that activity and associated information in terms of internet TV and viewing behavior. You have literally collected and potentially computational data on everything relating to the consumer and the medium through the internet. This was the arrival of a new kind of interaction where people started to think about analytics.

Of course, the page rank is pretty simple, there is a lot more behind the interaction data to figure out what in the pages is important. Page rank is not simply counting the images, often there needs to be considerations taken into account to stop various tricks people may try to boost page ranking by creating new links from search terms that are more likely to be used. You can de-game that by for example using machine learning natural language processing on the pages to resolve how page searches might be used. You can also stop people doing collusive attacks on the system by counting how may pages the links are actually similar and so are probably created by the same people and may therefore probably be related to a clique trying to boost their rankings. All this and many other scenarios will involve the need for increasingly more computing power to process and resolve massive dataset and association graphs forming on the internet.

The google search engine started around 2000 after the AltaVista web search engine of 1995 and the Yahoo! Search engine that launched the same year and several others. This is just a mere fifteen plus years ago, at the time nobody thought of them as having any intrinsic commercial value themselves, all that was required was a large data center to just do the search. The big shift primarily led by Google from AltaVista specialist DEC Alpha workstations, was the introduction of massive scaling by use of low cost commercial off-the-shelf computing power in the data center enabled by the fall costs from the commodification of PCs. Combined with this was the ability to distribute the computation out over many commodity machines to enable cost effective scalable concurrent computations and storage at a massive scale on what we call "embarrassingly parallel tasks".

This started around 2005, scaling out and virtualization of computing resources and the development of distributed concurrent activities that led to the emergence of data analytics and the indexing, searching or targeting adverts. The emergence of analytics tools such as Google's MapReduce as an open source version of Hadoop and companies such as, VMware, Citrix, Amazon and Cloudflare and many others offering rent time on their cloud computing platforms saw a major shift in the internet from a searchable web pages to a scalable analytics and computing resource.

This second shift in the evolution of the internet enabled really cheap computing building blocks that individuals and enterprise businesses could use on-demand as your business scales and if your income goes up with demand then you buy more boxes and the prices of boxes goes down. This is the scaling effect of the internet where by subsequent large cloud computing companies like Google, Amazon, Facebook and others could inherit a large fraction of advertising revenue, social media users or market capacity but at a incrementally decreasing cost enabling large margins. This is the effect of digital two-sided markets where you can apparently give something for free, but what you are actually giving them is something in exchange without them potentially realizing you are data mining everything they do. Search engines become a monopoly as a result and this kind of effect spreads to many other systems as a result of the internet scaling effects.

The Nature of the Internet is Changing

This is today's business model, but the future business model might involve machine learning and artificial intelligence. The internet that we know today is the same internet that was created in CERN in the early 1990s or ARPANET by the US Department of Defense in the late 1960s. So the nature of the Internet is changing.

The main thing was historically the internet had been a computing resource that was very centralized and you push all the data into this central system. The emergence of web pages enables this to move from centralization to a highly-decentralized internet architecture it gave access to data from millions. By 1992 we first web server but within a year there were a 1000, another year there were 10,000 and it just continued to multiply. But we are now in a third wave of network evolution decentralization has reversed and now we are pushing all this information back to a very small number of very big data centers that gain the cost and performance benefits of scaling properties of what we call "hyperscaling". In this third wave we are also seeing the rise of another massive scaling of the Internet of things IoT creating even more information collection into this network.

Cloud computing providers are invested in many IoT providers to develop this next generation of connected systems whether they are smart home heating, smart TVs and entertainment and the next step of this is something that has already happened in the automotive industry. Today most automotive engines have engine management computers that log performance. When you take your car to be serviced, the mechanic plugs it into a computer and reads out the logs, most cars these days such as BMW are connected and continuously feedback the logs that machine learning can exploit. What they are doing of course is monitoring classes of use against wear-and-tear so that they can figure out when to do recall, or replace parts and how to manage cost of warranty and liability. The aim is not mass surveillance but more engaged in optimizing the value delivery legally.

The Value Topology is Changing

I see the key fundamental learning point here for practitioners is the value topology of the internet is changing. We are moving from a decentralized world a centralized world and a situation of "embeddedness" into things that are then becoming generators of machine learning information and towards self-diagnosis. This pattern of using machine learning and artificial intelligent for surveillance and new value propositions is being followed by Google and search and gmail, Facebook and your login activity; twitter and on to IoT devices that you use. Webo and Alibaba in China are building the same services with their own versions, with over 600 million social media users in china it is exactly the same situation and same company style. With globalization and internet scaling these companies can reach around the globe launching direct competition with the US so you can get all your stuff from Alibaba instead of Amazon nowadays.

The same is happening in IoT services from high value items that have wear-and-tear you want to optimize maintenance through life costs to wearables for healthcare.

This era is creating an increasingly "rich data picture", where the simple transactional world is moving to a micro-location, spot cloud kind of existence, the nature is looking at attributes of this information, the richness and the type of data is fundamentally changing.

The combining of this information for personal data services in health or personal lifestyle to social activity services is one area that has not happened widely yet but it will lead to wellbeing services from fitness devices and mobile services. The combining of the personal data and the internet of connections to your home, retail and work experiences is where the real value is. This idea has sometimes been called the Internet of People IoP and is leading to new platforms such as the-hub-of-all-things or HAT that is a kind of personal data marketplace to trade and development this new business model [4]. This where extra internet style value will appear, in the combinational effects of this information.

This is happening in many areas in existing products and services including the automotive market. For example the connected car BMW or Audi vehicle will email the garage to call the owner for their next maintenance inspection with a list of what is coming to replace or check on the car before they go wrong because statistical analytics and machine learning algorithms had determined from past histories when the components are going to go wrong in the next month.

While many of these things is not artificial intelligence, it is just statistics that use well known often high school level math such as meantime between failure and variance analysis on attributes. With artificial intelligence this is a new higher level of math where you can start to do clustering algorithms and classifiers of data to find more advanced associations. For example, the type of driving behavior that might exacerbate some wear-and-tear with lots of short journeys compared to longer journeys. By being able to record more things about the vehicle from start and stop times to other variables it is possible to start to do more clever things with AI.

50 years ago you could log into an IBM mainframe and have a database query that would look up all the attributes and all the people for a given population of data for some field greater than x and then do statistics. You would write a Cobol program to find the mean and variance of this, given all the people under the age of 50 that drink more than x units per day?, what is the incidents for health when they have this type of condition compared to the mean? and what is the variation to confirm the actual risk? This can now develop much further if we want to know other things such, do you have ginger hair?, or born north of Watford?, or some combination. We do not know if these are related but it is possible to mine this data and look for associations and causalities by bring together many different disparate sources and types of information that the original data on its own could never do. This is leading to the development of deep learning that is now widely applied in many industries.

The Rise of Deep Learning

Deep Learning really refers to Neural Nets, and "deep" refers to the depth of the neural net in terms of the number of layers used to fit the training data. It is a particular type of learning technology and today there any many different types of learning technology. The most commonly used one is the thing called "decision forests" to a whole collection of techniques that rely on training sets of data and they are either supervised or unsupervised. We now have the compute power and economic costs to do these kinds of large scale processing that 40 years ago while we had the models, they were unable to afford the cost of the computer processing, or more importantly, did not have access to enough training data.

Deep learning is different, the problem with Deep Learning is that Neural nets have no explicit model in the neural net, it is literally you feed a whole collection of inputs in and you train it for the types of connections. There are many uses for this approach with a collection of weights on the connections between the nodes and the neural net which can be layered into a complicated architecture but it does not have internally a representation of what it is modelling. The earlier systems did have an approach to writing down the math as a description of the system, it would be the equations and what are the parameter values that describe the behavior of this system but this has since advanced rapidly into highly complex models with multiple layers.

There is a whole bunch of clever tricks that are now possible with deep learning. For example, a Bayesian inferencing system can actually figure out what are the relevant latent variables. Without instructing the model, it can work out what is important parameter. The result can be expressed so you can go look them up after you have trained the model up and see the latent variable or dependent variable. Then we get into one of the big issues.

One of the Big Issues of Deep Learning

One of the big issues in designing a neural net is if you have a lot of dimensions to a deep learning model it can become increasingly complex and difficult to understand its structure and how it effectively works out its forms of hill climbing, a term used to broadly describe a process of what is called gradient decent to find an optimal fit in a neural network. They are trying to find the right place to match the data effectively. This has surfaced as an issue recently on the popular media press this has surfaced in instances where some practitioners stating they don't know how the deep learning networks [5]. Another is the lack of visibility and transparency in "black box" machine learning algorithms [6]. The underlying main issue is how this might be used for good and bad things. How should this be governed and what type of regulation is needed?

This is not easily explainable to a lay person. You can explain how you trained the neural net, you can even give the training data to another neural net and get it to end up in the same place, assuming it is not doing anything stochastic and random. What data is in the computer memory of the neural network does not explain what it is doing.

This can have consequences when considered from the legal perspective, you are not allowed, for example, to prioritize through distinguishing on the basis of gender a decision to accept or decline car insurance for example. To illustrate this, consider a situation where someone is typing in online "give me the cheapest car insurance?", the online insurance quote computer program asked them a set of questions in a form which can be used to compare the market when the form is submitted. This data can be used to calculate insurance rates and can be fed into a deep learning training system. Whether you are using a decision tree forest or some other neural net, you need to be able to examine and check they are not accidently creating variables that correspond to gender, because otherwise they are breaking European law.

So for example, "what is your favorite color of car?", and you say "pink" and then "how many journeys and what time of day do you typically drive?", and you say "I drop the kids off at school typically around 9.00 am and pick them up at 3.30 pm". This is fairly obvious, not one hundred percent, most places in North America it has a stereotypical view. If you use that to set insurance, you have effectively learnt something that you are not supposed to. If you had just said what type of car or the color of the car or if you knew the person was a female you could show there was a strong correlation then you would exclude that rule. In this way it is possible to "learning things" that correlations between is it pink and 3.30 pm may not have any obvious relation to the topic, unless you are deliberately trying to identify something so you can offer a discount that is not to particular insurance plan.

It's a Bit Like Learning to Ride a Bicycle

Neural nets might do this based on strengths of all the acquired connections, you learn some things but you don't really know how. it's a bit like people learning to ride a bicycle and the first thing you have to do is you have to try not to consciously balance the bicycle. The reason is that while you can explain to someone how to be stable on a bicycle, this learning system for humans is exactly wrong for actual conscious control. It has to be internalized through some learning process as just teaching the theory is actually going to destabilize you because you cannot react fast enough to keep stable. You have to do it predictively. What you do when you learn to ride a bicycle is to distract people at the last second, you push them and let go.

We Do not Have to Understand All the Detail

In business context if we are optimizing the outcomes, we can use these kinds of concepts and technologies to try to optimize the desirable outcomes, we don't necessarily have to understand all of the engineering and detail to achieve this.

The state of the art that is happening right now that exemplify these different approaches is probably self-driving cars because they use different approaches for different parts of the controlling space.

So typically the will be a combination of very classical rule based systems which are not very clever to do validation of vehicle mechanical conditions that use algorithm for classifications. Certain types of neural net learning will be used to recognizing objects on a road, pedestrians, cycles or other vehicles having been trained on a large data set of these objects. The outputs if these systems could then go into a number of classifications for a rule base system to steer the vehicle.

When we talk about the law, most people may be pretty happy with that structure because the rule will say "don't run over pedestrians", "don't run over cyclist", "if you hit another vehicle that is not a cyclist and not endanger yourself or a pedestrian; then if you exceed this speed, it is ok". So now you are making decisions about avoiding obstacles with a priority, that is a simple rule based system. But the thing that does the determination of objects is probably some kind of deep learning system. You test the hell out of that, test many examples of test data, trained and checked. Every now and then it will go wrong, the legal opinion on this is that as long as it as least as good as a human, that is fine. Its pretty easy to make it that level, it is actually easier because one of the rules is "don't break the speed limit" which the machine control will always be better than the accuracy of a person driving. Particularly in a built up area with a speed limit below 20, then if the self-driving car does hit something then there is a very high chance it will survive. So the actual outcome for the consumer is always better from a picture of survival rates by speed limits viewpoint [7]. Another example is the impact of speed on Carbon emissions for example [8].

It is Like Being on Venus

This causality in the event time frame and the wider environment outcomes illustrates the need to consider both micro and macro context. How the car is driven can affect the local conditions and outcomes of drivers and pedestrians but can also have an impact on the wider environmental situation. The challenge is being able to identify the classifiers and attributes just enough to be able to control these outcomes with artificial intelligence.

Dimensionality is a famous curse in debugging of big data. It is not that you just have a billion people or a trillion stars your radio telescope, but it is also for each thing that can have many parameters. This is sometimes confusing, people see image processing as a learning problem and classifying things in an image. It is said the dimensionality of an image is the number of pixels. A 4K UHD screen resolution can be 3840 pixels × 2160 lines for 8.3 megapixels and an aspect resolution of 16:9. For a typical high resolution, high definition TV, you might have several million pixels or more. But it is not a million dimensions because there is only a few things in the picture. You could mathematically describe it as a million that is fine but that is a weird way to think about it. For example, we are sitting here in this room reading this book, there is a carpet and a celling and a number of other things in this space. You might still use high dimensionality but you might want to reduce the dimensions to be able to processes them quickly to discover the information. A difficulty arises if you then have a new thing that you have not seen before, then you may need to use deep learning to create a new training and learning algorithm. That is like being on the planet Venus, you point a camera out at the world and you have no idea what the world looks like and you have atmospheres pressure and different chemicals and so on, all unknown.

Theorize the number of dimensions in an image to be able to recognize specific objects on that image can be done by specific algorithm classifiers but what level of accuracy? Then what is the criteria when you need deep learning to identify something unknown? It seems the former condition of training data establishes declarative probability rules based on prior learning. Other issues of unknown objects requires transfer learning or other techniques. In practice, it is a combination of machine learning and sensor and actuator methods that is starting to enable artificial Intelligent to be applied to many situation.

Behind the Meter and in Front of the Meter

Another example of what is possible today with the discovery of new insights and control can be seen in the installation of smart energy meters in homes. It is possible by just recording the electrical energy consumption signal from the electric mains connected to the house during each day over 24 hours to determine right down to which specific type of electrical appliance is working in that home.

In Fig. 7.1 this is a smart meter readings for one day in a house. We can identify what all the consumption peaks activity where just by their electrical power consumption signature. The fan oven is really easy to spot, it is the fan going on and other activities. We crowd sourced people recording activity during the day and built up a set of training data across many homes with this system. We could determine many activities just from the electrical signal alone.

Today a combination of machine learning algorithms and deep learning can generate algorithms and patterns that can tell you what you are up to in a particular moment in the house based on electrical demand usage. This can be developed through further training to understand the characteristics of that house building structure and its appliances and occupant behavior in the

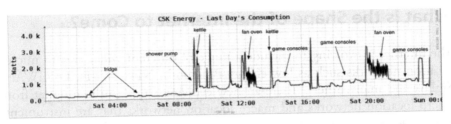

Fig. 7.1 Smart energy meter electrical signal. With permission from Prof. Jon Crowcroft Nov 2016

household. It is information that can then be used to potentially control appliances, optimize energy consumption and occupant behavior in what is called "in front of the meter" services. These could be connected to retail and maintenance services so that automation can follow and optimize the occupant lifestyles and building services. In "behind the meter" services this data can be used by power generation companies to optimize load and maintenance schedules using machine learning algorithms. But equally the consumer occupant could move to new business models such as renewable energy and solar power and sell their spare energy to their neighbors or back to the local grid. Such systems are already in place in New York City with solar energy micro-grids and the use of blockchain for smart contracts and energy trading [9].

Multi-Algorithms and Hybrid AI

This is just one example of the many machine learning algorithms that will come together to cooperate or have competing priorities. Nowadays there are many toolkits that do various kinds of machine learning and you can glue these things together with simpler plumbing so you can build these hybrid systems. Algorithms will become the competitive advantage and intellectual property of organizations today and in the future. There are also companies, such as CognitionX, that are an Algorithm marketplace broker platform started by Charlie Muirhead, a British Internet entrepreneur and co-founder with Tabitha Goldstaub and serial startup from Imperial College originally. They have establish marketplaces for algorithms and act as a shell company for listing of machine learning expert company of different areas of expertise. They have a large and growing catalogue of algorithms where you go to them with a specific problem and they advise who may have solution for that kind of problem or this combination of solutions [10].

What is the Shape of the Internet to Come?

The internet is evolving to include a range of different wider area to micro-location networks such as low energy Bluetooth, NFC, Wi-Fi, LoRaWAN, SigFox and many others. There an new evolving strata to the internet from micro-location networks and macro location networks that are instrumenting connected building or a connected city and down to the individual person or object. For me it is kind of reshaping the topology of networks.

It seems to be a continuum of different issues of coverage and performance. For example did you know London, Cardiff, Bridgton, Leeds, Edinburgh, Manchester and Liverpool have their own internet exchange points IXPs. What they are looking for is really low latency and performance. But there are also other areas in a geography that has minimal or no internet coverage then no internet services reach those locations.

One evolutionary path that has definitely already happened in the paste five plus years is that there has been a move to putting big server farms inside internet exchanges. While there are big data centers there is now this move in what has been described as "flattening put the internet" to decentralize and distribute computing power to the edge of the network for better performance and lower latency. This is the reason why Netflix and Amazon just build a data center every time there is an internet exchange point, to enable better local service delivery of content.

The next step of this is kind of running out of physical real estate to put everything in the internet exchange points. So the next step is to replicate the data centers into the pox, points of presence of the ISPs, so then a typical point of exchange POX might be serving 50,000 or 100,000 not 10 million, so you need a much smaller data center. You are replicating the data and data services there, but then it is even nearer, so they gain maybe one hop, they are going through their DSL line, home broadband, their fiber and they land on their TV media service provider and there in the data center it has all the videos that they want to see. Maybe it is backup their smart home, or serving a smart table or serving as a mirror for that.

This is all somewhat making the internet flatter.

The Rise of Augmented Reality

Today there are devices that enable the ability to scan three dimensional physical objects into render as a digital model of the physical object. We see this happening now in examples such as geospatial lidar scanning or Google project tango to enable 3D scanning of a room with a mobile phone to create a spot cloud. This is all generating "digital twins" of the physical world. This perspective is also generating a new depth of field spatial proximity information collected through sensors and scanners and enabling new kinds of virtual reality and augmented reality. With this kind of multi-dimensional information you can augment objects with additional views and capabilities. This is augmentation that instruments up the space, digitized objects and activities into a multi-dimensional rich data environment and representation or facsimile. In order to bring this potential about have to have a mandate to be able to develop the infrastructure, the internet and networks to be able to support this kind of data loads and real-time responsive performance. This in tern will drive huge demand for bigger and faster networks and the storage to deliver this volume of 3D data.

For example Google and YouTube has 3000 data centers in the world now and this from a situation where they just had two. They realized that if you are trying to serve somebody in a physical location, for example Pakistan, to stream YouTube videos for example where advertising for companies in Pakistan, doing this from the US was not ideal. So by putting a big YouTube service inside the main Pakistani ISP service resolves this performance issue.

If you go to augmented reality, IoT, health tracking, this is creating huge amounts of high volume local data that is all going to be very near to us. As you move around it will use the tracking to migrate the thing that is running your digital twin. This is likely the viable way to do it with computing moving to a decentralized at the edge network, powerful computing will need to be near you in your hand or location for fast ultra low latency immersive experience.

Machine Reasoning

Generic algorithms and evolvable programs is a possible future development in machine learning [11]. Will computers able to "program themselves"? Will this be science fact or fiction using genetic programming that allows computers using "natural selection" to generate programs is another possibility [12]. Part of this goal is the field of machine reasoning and inferencing that aims to tackle such complex problems. Examples such as Isabell/HOL developed since the late 1980s by Barry Paulson at Cambridge University was a generic proof assistant that can use mathematical formulas to test correctness of solutions. Isabell/HOL has been used with economists for reasoning about trading in markets and trying to infer what people are doing [13].

Machine reasoning in this context example today is useful in analysis of big software systems, where we can now buy a lot of bug free systems because we can effectively remove bugs semi-automatically for large systems. This is a typical challenge in business today with large software systems that are messy and complicated. Facebook actually check all their checked in code. Programmers are not allowed to check code in if the system infers there could be bugs in it with some probability. This saves time for programmers removing the need for rechecking and the possible customers complaining about bugs.

With the spread of the network and these emerging capabilities, new kinds of intelligence will emerge.

Summary

The architecture of the internet is changing as algorithms and the topology of networks evolve to include new hybrid models of network connectivity.

The 4th industrial revolution will drive new kinds of networks and devices that will represent a new level of scalability unprecedented in human history. It will also challenge the rights and issues of personal data privacy in particular and establish new challenges to preserve these rights while attaining the potential of the new 4th industrial revolution era.

Notes and References

1. Dimitra Kamarinou, Christopher Millard, Jatinder Singh, "Machine Learning with Personal Data", Queen Mary School of Law Legal Studies Research Paper No. 247/2016 https://papers.ssrn.com/sol3/papers.cfm?abstract_id=2865811.
2. Jatinder Singh, Ian Walden, Jon Crowcroft, Jean Bacon "Responsibility & Machine Learning: Part of a process", October 27, 2016 https://papers.ssrn.com/sol3/papers.cfm?abstract_id=2860048.
3. Chris Reed, Elizabeth Kennedy, Sara Nogueira Silva "Responsibility, Autonomy and Accountability: legal liability for machine learning", October 17 2016 Queen Mary School of Law Legal Studies Research Paper No. 243/2016 https://papers.ssrn.com/sol3/papers.cfm?abstract_id=2853462.
4. Hub of all things https://hubofallthings.com/.
5. Machine learning works great – mathematicians just don't know why, Wired, Ingrid Daubechies, 12 December 2015 https://www.wired.com/2015/12/machine-learning-works-greatmathematicians-just-dont-know-why/.

6. Machine learning requires careful stewardship says Royal Society, 25 April 2017 https://royalsociety.org/news/2017/04/machine-learning-requires-careful-stewardship-says-royal-society/.

7. Vision Zero: A Vision for Safer Streets for All, IGC 27 March 2017, https://www.lgc.org/safer-streets-for-all/ Source: U.S. Department of Transportation, National Highway Traffic Safety Administration (1999).

8. The impact of speed on Carbon emissions for example, RAC foundation, August 2012, http://www.racfoundation.org/assets/rac_foundation/content/downloadables/speed_limits-box_bayliss-aug2012.pdf.

9. In New York, neighbors trading solar energy electrify community, March 30, 2017 http://www.reuters.com/article/us-energy-usa-blockchain-idUSKBN171003.

10. A Community and Directory for All Things AI http://cognitionx.com/.

11. W.B.Langdon, S.M.Gustafson, Generic Algorithms and Evolvable Machines: Ten years of review. Genetic Programming and Evolvable Machines, 11, 321–338 (2010) http://www0.cs.ucl.ac.uk/staff/wlangdon/ftp/papers/gppubs10.pdf.

12. William B. Langdon, Adil Qureshi Genetic Programming, Computers using "natural selection" to generate programs - Dept of Computer Science, UCL http://www0.cs.ucl.ac.uk/staff/ucacbbl/ftp/papers/surveyRN76.pdf.

13. What is Isabelle, https://isabelle.in.tum.de/overview.html.

8

Impact of Security on Intelligent Systems

Introduction

Many years ago we developed fingerprint recognition in the late 1970s that by the early 1990s had evolved into an integrated automated fingerprint identification system which later became part of the field of biometrics combining many types of identification. At the time machine driven finger print recognition was wonderful, but nobody was interested even if you "do not need keys anymore" but they could not see it. Ten years later, 911 happened and all of a sudden everyone wanted finger print recognition. Over that period of time all of this biometric information gets stored somewhere as digital information. As soon as that happens it is not the security of it that is the main worry, it can get copied, moved or deleted. Modification is a bigger worry, if somebody gets to the data and changes a link how do you then prove who you are if the original reference data has been edited?

All Eggs in One Basket

We need guiding principles here, and one of the guiding principles that would be helpful for business be they new businesses being created or existing ones, is not to collect together a knowledge base, a collection of information that you are not able to adequately protect. This is really important.

One of the things often seen is people are very disparaging about "dragons den" the UK TV program, and it is superficial in lots of ways but when you see

© The Author(s) 2018
M. Skilton and F. Hovsepian, *The 4th Industrial Revolution*,
https://doi.org/10.1007/978-3-319-62479-2_8

people with great ideas but they do not scale, it is just a hobby, it will not become a business, it is not some something someone will invest in, you cannot protect your Intellectual property IP. The other thing that does not seem to be considered is whether it is sensible from a cyber security perspective?

You might have this wonderful idea for a business, perhaps Industrie 4.0 pulling together sensors input throughout an entire supply chain. As a business you might be able to offer to business enterprise as-a-service rather than they do this themselves. You have worked out how to do this, on your platform you state that you will pull all of your sensor data centrally to be able to coordinate your supply chain. But that is a very attractive cyber attack target for a lot of people but your business model might not producing enough revenue for you to be able to properly secure what you are doing. It would not take many months before there was some form of cyber security breach. So you need to consider the cyber aspects of the business as you are developing it. This is really important.

Ultimately the overall business outcome goal is seeking to create competitive advantage. We are trying to transform processes to lower cost or new capabilities because the benefits can be past on to consumers and then everyone in a nation or across the planet benefits from prosperity indirectly. We increase wealth people have by not having to pay as much for the things that we want. The internet and its network effects have a whole heap of benefits that we get but there are dangers as well that we can see.

Protecting the World We Want

When we look at IoT devices they are horrendously insecure, criminally insecure. One of the things everyone involved in Industrie 4.0 and the 4th industrial revolution and in respect of smart and future cities and societies need to understand is that we are trying to create well governed spaces that are both in the physical world and increasingly now in the virtual world too. For example, we like working in the UK, it is generally cheap to do business. I don't need to take somebody out for three months to get a personal trust relationship to then be able to transact because we believe in the rule of law, we have property rights, and there doesn't seem to be an awful lot of corruption or nepotism. It is a great space. That is the space we also want in our virtual cyber-physical environments too, it needs governance and it needs protecting.

What Is a Dangerous Space?

The minute somebody can create something, it is possible for somebody else to waltz in and steel it for free and then exploit it. The minute that everything you own is capable of being modified to damage you or to further somebody else's agenda with no normative barriers in place, this is a dangerous space. That is one of the things we are trying to change. This is an overarching theme of the 4th industrial revolution.

Governmental policies are evolving as people are becoming more aware of what the consequences and risks. Often people do not know what are the risks in cyber-physical spaces or where the perimeter of security is for that matter?, where it is safe to go?, what data, devices and networks should you use? I think from observing cyberattack events after they have occurred, people do not know what and where the risks areas are and how to perceive how information works across cyber-physical spaces.

There is no menu, "oh follow these five steps and you will be fine". This becomes even more difficult when the goal or the game of hackers seems to be in trying to break the protection and barriers put in place.

A key question is what is the role of intelligence and machine intelligence from the prevention side or the attackers side? We are starting to see more sophisticated uses of machine learning that may be used in cyberattacks. Likewise, in prevention and the use of artificial intelligence to scan and monitor and respond to attacks.

Focusing on the Adaptive Parts of a Space

Both the user and hacker sides can use intelligent, adaptive, smart systems for increasing their ability to respond in an agile way to changes in the environment. So, when an opportunity arises, both sides will use it. The thing you have to understand from the defensive side is that lots of people think that the answer to cyber security defense is some great big electronic super brain that will sit rather like a general on a hill overseeing the theater of battle. The General watching what's going on and making wonderful decisions and changes within the space to be able to protect an organization or a Nation or whatever. But when you look to attack a system using cyber hacker techniques, you look at what you focus on. You focus on the adaptive bits of the system, the network, the company organization and people involved. So, ninety-five percent of all attacks will start with a phishing email or something. You are going after the adaptive human. Then you will focus, if you are doing a technical attack, on the adaptive protocols. So you may, for example, go after and adjust address resolution protocols [1], and the Span entry protocols [2] that dynamically reconfigures all of the switches into a network in an enterprise.

Cyber Security Homunculi

You will look at all of these adaptive bits of a system as points for cyber-attack and protection. I am sure that if you have seen those homunculi where you have a little model of a naked human but with the parts of their body in proportioned to how many nerves they have so they have big hands, a great big tongue and is a metaphor for these kinds of adaptive parts. If you were to take a "computer system homunculi" and do the same and scale it by how much adaptation it is. Then do a completely separate one where you scale it by how likely it is attackers are targeting those bits, I think that is the same diagram. As a consequence anyone who thinks that they can create this wonderful new smart system to defend, thinking it is sitting on the sidelines like an-all-seeing general. It is not, it is right in the middle of the battlefield with a great big target painted on it. We absolutely need smart systems that recognize the distributed and decentralized nature of the real situation today. You need them to be developed by people who know how to develop distributed system protection that are robust to attack because you are increasing your attack surface in the 4th industrial revolution.

Perimeter Is the Wrong Way to Think About Cyber Security

The risk profile and the perimeter of what is a systems are changing. Do we know where the perimeter is one thing in the sense of knowing where your attack surfaces might be? Often the issue in security might be outside your domain of control so therefore it is an *ecosystem mindset* that is required. In an organization the securing of assets or people and activities might be outside the domain of control of that organization. This means it is an ecosystem mindset needs to consider inside and outside threats and protection in cyber security.

Perimeter is probably a wrong way now to think about cyber security in general for individuals, enterprises, governments and societies. If we think about how we secure our cities, the city of London physically for example, we do not have a clearly defined perimeter, there is no great wall around London. We may have a rim of steel in the middle metaphorically made up of an awful lot more monitoring that goes on, nevertheless you do not have to cross a check point and people who would be considered highly risky can be right at the heart of your city are allowed almost up to the front door of No. 10 Downing street. The approach that is taken is a combination of cultural awareness so that people will report and watch each other and some architectural changes which are designed in.

So there are technical and non-technical approaches to protecting our spaces and we need to take that approach and bring it into the cyber virtual world. The old view of this is an organizational boundary and this is a perimeter of the organizational owned IT system and will protect it. For example a building management system that is probably being controlled by estates and not by the occupant; or it could be your production control system coordinating a complete distributed supply chain. System ownership can be different in reality.

Cyber Is not Information Security

We can follow information security rules such as those found in ISO27001 but in reality its easy to steal information potentially from organizations. The security approach of information that you care about, knowing where it is, encrypting it when you are sure nobody is looking over your shoulder, decrypt it and work with it, and then re-encrypt it doesn't work when the thing you care about isn't information. If you are managing a production line or if you are travelling in a car travelling down a motorway, or using an insulin pump; you can't encrypt it and then decrypt it when you want to squirt some insulin. It is a physical process that is being digitally controlled and the way that we protect that has to be using different principles from the principles we use to protect information. But people are still talking about cyber security as some kind of physical process with strong authentication, strong encryption, collect your assets together. Well the Americans tried that in Pearl harbor in 1941, they put many battleships, planes and ammunition as well as the Commander in Chief of the Pacific

Fleet Command together in very centralized places and then it became a target that is very easy thing to hit. By arbitrary comparison, look at the country of Estonia, they have their government online, even if the country was invaded they can virtually move everything that they do in government to any other part of the world they like. They can use servers to bounce around the world. This is the opposite of sticking it in a box and making it sure nobody can get into it.

It Is a Cultural Overhang

When we first invented the electric kettle, before that we had kettles that we put on open fires to heat the water by the first underneath. The handle was on the top because if it was on the side you would burn your hand. Then we invented the electric kettle and we still have the handle on the top, when you poured the electric kettle, steam burnt your hand. Suddenly someone realized it is no longer over an open flame, and could put the handle on the side. But for while this was not the case. This is the *cultural overhang* often seen in moving from the old era of a technology to the new and the residues of old thinking conditioned by previous social norms, beliefs and artifacts. We have the same cultural overhand when viewing from a cold war, military, hierarchically organize perspective. Here the organization believes it owns its own Information Technology (IT) perspective, and that is the way we treat cyber security in many cases today. Sooner or later we will come to the realization that the internet and the IT landscape and the data, artifacts, places, people, behaviors and networks in it is more like a *global commons*. That it is a shared space that we want to contribute to as stakeholders to it being well governed and the approach to do that is necessarily technical but also equally necessarily cultural and behavioral.

Cyber-Physical Systems CPS to Cognitive Cyber-Physical Systems CCPS

If we are talking about cyber-physical, perhaps we ought to be talking about cognitive cyber-physical systems because that human habitat is in many ways the most important.

This is describing the anthropic perspective and impact of physiological and psychological issues of protecting this space. It is to particularly to do with the psychology of dealing with humans and spaces that can jump and mix between physical behavior and virtual online behavior. There is also the speed of effectiveness issue, as with the insulin pump or in the case of the self-driving car we are faced with situations that are both wicked problems that have difficult life or death consequences of being able to automate and being able to make decisions fast enough to protect the human or the pedestrian. It is having systems that are able to sense make and be appropriately fast enough to fix the problems or opportunities at the speed the situation requires. In the case of the self-driving car this could be milli-seconds to make crash avoidance decisions. With the case of cyber security policy making it often assumes that a human is required for making decisions but there can also be situations happening so fast such as in the case of machine learning that humans cannot be part of that equation, because you cannot interact fast enough. So the other issue is the machine to machine attack vectors which are not about humans specifically as they are functionally not part of it. There are machine learning algorithms now that can come in and attack spaces.

World's First All-Machine Cyber Hacking Tournament

On the August 4, 2016, DARPA (U.S. Defense Advanced Research Projects Agency) held a $2m Grand Challenge for "fully automated" cyber defense systems [3].

Seven high performance computers were set to play an all-machine Capture the Flag contest, reverse engineering unknown binary software, authoring new IDS signatures, probing the security of opponent software, and re-mixing defended services with machine-generated patches and defenses.

Starting with over 100 teams consisting of some of the top security researchers and hackers in the world, the Defense Advanced Research Projects Agency (DARPA) pit seven teams against each other in the Cyber Grand Challenge final event. During the competition, each team's Cyber Reasoning System (CRS) automatically identified software flaws, and scanned a purpose-built, air-gapped network to identify affected hosts. Cyber Reasoning system (CRS) is a term that refers to systems to automate tools that not only uncover vulnerabilities, but have the intelligence to automatically patch and fix the issue [4–6].

For nearly twelve hours, teams were scored based on how capably their systems protected hosts, scanned the network for vulnerabilities and maintained the correct function of software. The wining CRS was "Mayhem" by ForAllSecure a fully autonomous system for finding and fixing computer security vulnerabilities. The machine also earned itself a prestigious "Black Badge" trophy at DEF CON (an honor given to unbeaten players and the first non-human to receive the honor), as well as a spot in the Smithsonian Institution. It also competed in DEF CON's annual CTF event against some of the world's best hackers—another first [7]. The winning team also gets the chance to enter its system into the real Def Con CTF competition to see how it performs against the best human players of the offensive coding game [8].

The competition generated patched software and IDS signatures generated by the competition machines that were released into the public domain. It also allowed practitioners to learn and test their cyber skills again the machines [9].

IDS Intrusion Detection Systems refer to a wide range of systems from anti-virus software to hierarchical systems that monitor the traffic of networks and Host systems. They can generate signature-based IDS (SIDS) that refer to the detection of attacks by looking for specific patterns, such as byte sequences in network traffic, or known malicious instruction sequences used by malware [10]. Another is Statistical anomaly-based IDS (AIDS) that seek to detect unknown attacks that do not follow specific patterns. This uses machine-learning to generate models of trustworthy activity and compare new behavior against these models. While subject to false positives it can all view what Analyst firm Gartner term user and entity behavior Analytics (UEBA) for human and network malicious behavior detection [11]. A third example cyber-attack detection approach looks at the specific protocols used in a system comparing deviations in protocol states observed in events with predetermined profiles of trusted definitions of protocol benign activity (SPAD) [12].

The Tempo of OODA Loops

One of the issues you have got in a military sense is that you can be too quick in responding to cyber attack that a lot of cyber defensive weapons are very fragile. When they are figuratively exposed to the air they start to crumble because people quickly see how they work and then can protect themselves against them. If you have a big arsenal of cyber weapons and then one of your adversary's upsets you a bit and there is an escalation, if you have a superfast system it will adapt and will try to out maneuver you. If in the first attack you throw absolutely everything you have got at them within a microsecond, now you have nothing else. There is a lesson from military planning that looks at what is called OODA loops and the procedure: observe, orient, decide and act [13]. OODA was a method developed in combat operations that evolved a decision making cycle that you go through whether you are a fighter pilot or a general with situational awareness. You observe, then you orient, decide and then act, similar to the Plan-check-Do-Act concept of the Deming cycle from quality management systems in business but aimed at responsive action in military situation [14].

For a fighter pilot, you observer, you find out where everybody is in your environment, you orient yourself to that and decide for yourself what you are next going to do, you do it and then you go round the loop again. If you can get inside your opponent's OODA loop then you can out maneuver them because you are thinking and responding faster than their OODA loop. This is one of the big issues for the Military, you want to be inside your enemy's OODA but ideally you want to position yourself just inside it, not a million times faster than it for the reason explained earlier [15]. This suggest a good level of situational awareness such that it can be responsive to planned and unplanned events.

Try Throwing Some Treacle in!

A lot of the things we see have the OODA loop characteristic in cyber security and the speed of response that is appropriate and proportionate. Some affects require humans to realize the effect has actually happened. If you take down somebody's communications system, you need them to realize that they cannot communicate because that is part of the affect. There is a certain tempo to the attack and response. You can have when you architect systems, too much speed, one of the response things for systems in general, be it energy management systems, enterprise security management or city shopping malls, is just *try throwing some treacle in!* because you do not always need things to be moving so quickly. If you can slow down the attack, sludge stuff up it allows humans and also automated defense systems more time in which to react and do things. So for example, cut down the bandwidth, increase the propagation delays often you find you can do that without affecting business critically and it is giving you a greater resilience. It is the equivalent of putting the two lines of fences around a military compound and you know it will take attackers a certain amount of time to breach the first and then get across the moat to the second, and that tells you then how frequently you have to patrol.

Attacking at 1.2 Terabytes Per Second

Distributed Denial of service (DDOS) attacks can get up to a terabyte per second traffic to a corporate website service at the time of writing is the current world record, and is overwhelming fast. This was seen in the Mirai botnet attack on 21 October 2016 disrupting internet service in Europe and US. The attack was focused on the company Dny that controls much of the internet's domain name system (DNS) infrastructure brings down sites including Twitter, PayPal, Spotify the Guardian, Netflix, Reddit, CNN and many others in Europe and US. The Mirai attack was unusual in that it used many computers and devices of the internet of things including digital cameras and Digital Video Cameras to launch an attack estimated to involve 100,000 malicious endpoints and achieved an attack strength of 1.2 Tbps [16].

The velocity of this is to overwhelm but it can also be used by machine intelligence to make way for stealth attack of the future. The example of the $1 billion stolen from several Russian and European banks in 2015. The Russian anti-virus software firm Kaspersky Lab described this as a series of attacks through phishing schemes and other methods including infiltrating ATMs to release money for the criminals to collect or altering customer bank accounts from $1000 to $10,000 to create money to steal [17]. These were below the radar of most DNS monitoring and is an example of a stealth attack across a wide range of targets.

Beyond the biggest data breach in history of potentially three billion user accounts stolen from Yahoo! in 2013 but not announced publicly till late 2016 [18]; the rise of ransomware attacks represent a particular virulent form of machine attack using malware to covertly install on a victims device such as mobile, computer or wearable to extort money. Examples of this type of attack include the NHS Health service in UK attack shutting down patient record systems for 48 hours in several hospitals [19] to what DarkNet, a UK Hacker group, estimated was 33,000 publicly available MongDb databases that were hacked in 2016 by ransomware demanding payment in bitcoins from 0.2 bitcoins (US$184) to 1 bitcoin (US$921) [20].

Digital Judo and Boiled Frogs

I call it Digital Judo, attacked done against adaptive systems. There is a very nice example of a person called the "Spamking" in 2007 who was caught twice by Microsoft for spamming everyone on Hotmail [21], the second time he did it was a work of genius. He had an adaptive spam filter that watched what everybody on Hotmail was doing with an email. So if they all received this email and they were all putting it into the junk folder then the thing would learn adaptively that was junk. So he set up a million fake accounts, sent out his spam, it was moved by the spam filter into the junk and his fake accounts all moved it back again so the adaptive system learnt that so many users are saying it is not junk and not marked as junk and allowed to remain. Another thing you can do is what is called a "boiled frog" attack where you just raise the temperature of threshold to attack in system. You know the system is just trying to learn, so you keep below the threshold where it is going to trigger an alert but the thing adapts and learns the moves the threshold to a point where you can complete your attack and it will not notice [22].

There are ways you can attack systems that adapt that are qualitatively different from ways that are more conventional. In Karate you can beat up a sack of potatoes because you can throw a limb out very quickly, but you cannot use Judo or Aikido on it because you require a living person to react against you, you are going to use their reactions and their muscles against them. It is a similar thing that you have got a system that does not adapt then you cannot use these techniques. Thankfully people are putting more adaptation into their systems.

Shooting Fish in a Barrel and the Future of Intelligent Machine Cyber Attacks

With machine learning and adaptive systems has the world moved on? Now you have this new class of advanced cyber enabled hackers that can use machine intelligence as part of their weaponry. This is increasing new ways to attack and defend with increasing levels of sophistication.

Organized criminals and sophisticated attackers can often use commercial-off-the-shelf widely available malware because we not patching put systems. We may be still relying on anti-virus where all the organized crime gangs are using counter-antivirus services to check their malware and avoid the latest antivirus before they release it. It is like shooting fish in a barrel in attacking systems. One of the aims of cyber essentials, a UK government standard in training course, is to raise the level of cyber security awareness and hygiene so the sophisticated attackers can no longer look like relatively unsophisticated attackers. If the environment is such that you cannot use those kinds of easy tools and you really want to get to a certain target then you are going to have to start showing your hand that you are for example, a nation state who have full resources for cyber security attacks.

It terms of where we are going with cyberattacks, you can certainly buy kits now, develop bot nets to send out and collect the results and make ransomware money that could be several thousands of millions in money. It is commoditized and if you can deskill the ability to find vulnerabilities, exploit them, identify targets of interest and go after them, then this will be more prevalent in the future.

Cyberattacks at Scale and Resilience Against Shocks

But it is the "at scale" that is the thing. One of the things we can see from the field of ecological research in biology and natural sciences, is that if you want general resilience against shocks, you need diversity, you have a diverse collection of ecological niches. We have an awful lot of *monoculture,* great big organizations where is exactly the same version of windows on all their machines, all of their plants are using exactly the same programable logic controllers. A bit more diversity would help us, so we can learn from different disciplines here.

This seems similar to the issue of hyperscaling for the benefit of using cloud computing that exploits the feature of many common servers to increase scale and power of computing. This is driven by the economics of common scalable systems driving more growth and demand and the rise of a few very large data centers and hyper scale providers. There seems to be a paradox here in that this scaling is driven by economics to give access to may while it may be a threat to security through common centralization. We need to think intelligently in how we can protect and fragment our personal data for example so we do not have things all in one basket.

How Do You Plan for This and Lessons of Blockchain?

As a CFO how do you plan for the distribution of authority for financial decisions, it feels similar? Rather than one person at the top who decides the decisions, you have a community making different decisions in different ways and you are allowing that to happen. So the question is when does it need to be centralized and when can you diversity decision making without it ending up fragmenting the organization in a bad way. Actually, fragmentation can be very helpful in a lot of ways, you just need make sure it is not disruptive fragmentation.

Blockchain could be another target for cyber attacked given it fits that kind of distributed architecture and decision making process. Could this conversely be a cyberattack target given its economic transaction role?

It depends how it works, collusion is a big problem behind the scenes. A lot of the time when they talk about distributed ledger or block chain they do not actually need it. Because they are talking about using it within a trusted community so you do not need all the expensive overhead of proof of work and mining and other things. If you look at how the Linux kernel was developed it used something called a Git repository. This is a distributed database and it uses cryptographic hashes to make sure nobody can manipulate the shared understanding of what has been previously committed. A lot of time people talk about blockchain but they could do everything they want to do but with a Git repro. It is understanding that blockchain is a collection of different components all glued together and you need to understand what the different components do and which ones you need.

You can improve security operations by having monitoring with machine learning, but you can go after the attacker as well, who is trying to make you believe everything is fine or that something has changed and you need to alter the system. So you think you have situational awareness? Do you need global situational awareness? Can you have local control with no overall global status awareness? It is possible you can still have the protection you need.

Is that Really a Smart Home?

With the 4th industrial revolution we will have the connect home, connected lights, connected garage, connected living room device. Do you want a smart control hub system if this could be a risk for cyber security too? Equally do you want those smart appliances to track your movements, listen to your voice and "see" your images and activities in your own living space?

There is a trade-off in the need to know why you want to centralize this type of information and to give this level of personal data access. What are the benefits that outweigh the risks of doing it. So you could have a central control system for all your systems in your house but if these could be used for nefarious reasons. For example my smart lights could be switched remotely on or off or the heating energy system could be overloaded as a gateway to some other system, for example, triggering the home security doors to open in a false heating or fire alert that then might enable someone to gain entry to something that might be of value to steal. It is an equation of cost, risk and value and does it really matter at the end of the day.

Machine learning and algorithms are starting to be used in cyber-attacks. Ransomware could be described as intelligent software that can activate itself or be activated remotely and to start to have a controlling effect on the outcome of victims. From the protect side it is important to have a completely different mindset to protect business in the twenty-first-century. There needs to be more investment in more than just an awareness of machine learning and AI. Both machine learning in advanced analytics and deep neural nets that could be described as A.I. in business is starting to influence how cyber security needs to consider its impact and consequences.

The Rise of Narrative Engineering—Human Behavior, Cultural Change and Rhetoric Is the New Cyber Security Skills

The prevention strategy and the attack canvas is getting more complex. The skills in the average organization is simple not there in order to respond to new levels of cyber-attack sophistication. The level of skills that cyber security practitioners now need are changing. Cyber essentials is one thing but the reality is that they have no skill in the area that they need which is the area of human behavior and being able to affect cultural change. If you look at most cyber security professionals, they realize they need to spend more as an organization to set up firewalls because they are completely focused on the technical and they will go to the board and put forward a logical case and they will not get the money. The reason they did not get the money is because they did not use "rhetoric". They had no pathos of empathy in order to understand how to communicate persuasively when we come up with a new technical security policy we need stronger password because people need to, but no one thought that people are just going to stick them on their monitor. The skills we need are essential technical skills but we also need cultural skills that are equally essential. When we are talking about AI and the way in which it can change an organization it is very much seen as a battle of narratives. Narrative engineering I think is something that is going to become increasingly important.

Managing the narratives will be critical, it is managing the cognitive space, just look at fake news and all the data and words on social media and the media in general today. There is an increasing realization we do not really have the tools to counter this. This is countering influence campaigns and conducting them on our own terms and agendas is a battle of narratives and we need within organizations and society to win this battle.

It is focusing on the social engineering of cyber security when most people focus on the in-depth knowledge of operating systems yet someone can pick up the phone to convince people to give them information or the wider implications of government or terrorist group social media manipulation.

We need cultural change in the way we deal with cyber security in organizations and the change needs to be around creating well governed spaces.

The Case of the Connected Car Cyber Attack

For example an automotive manufacturer, as an attacker I might be one of several people, I might be a terrorist, I might be an organized crime gang, I might be a competitor, I might be foreign intelligence service. When I look at what I can do, I could hack into the production line so I can change it so you get more defects, you get more recalls, it lowers the reputation of your brand. You think that it is just poor quality control, you do not even realize you are under a cyber-attack. Other things I could do might be to take all of your intellectual property and build a product that look very similar to a western car for example. Armed with a detailed understanding of your vehicle I can infect service center computers that every car that goes in for a service gets malware on it that can be triggered at any point. It could include ransomware so it encrypts part of the system so you can not drive the car or you lose some performance, it will not go above 30 miles an hour and on your head up display comes a bit coin address for you to be able to pay and release it. It is adaptive, and it is smart, and what happens is the systems are talking back to through command and control and when the price is too high and not enough people are paying, you drop the price a bit. So you are dynamically alternating how much the ransom is. It is still there and it keeps coming back and lots of people get used to paying amounts by bit coin. That is what can happen to any organization and that is only really scratching the surface.

Are Cyber Security Professionals Involved in Products and Process Design?

The point is you can have those highly trained cyber security professionals but how will they help when you have faulty issues on your production line? That is not a cyberattack because you do not know it is a cyberattack. How are they going to help when you are designing your systems to try and make sure they are more cyber secure? Take the example of Johnson and Johnson, they have an insulin pump that was recently shown to be remotely hackable that a hacker could exploit to overdose diabetic patients with insulin, though it describes the risk as low. The company communicated this in letters sent on Monday to doctors and about 114,000 patients who use the device in the United States and Canada [23].

The question is at what point in the product design, process design, producing that insulin pump did the cyber security professional step in? Nowhere, they were not invited in, and the cyber security professionals can bleat all they like about you need to bring us in rather than at the end, but actually what we need to do is make it mainstream, Security-by-design.

Security-by-Design

So somebody who is designing a car needs to understand enough about cyber security, we will get there because it surrounds everyone, you can not grow up without an understand of this. The awareness level will increase but what we need to do is to catalyze the change to a point where we have it built-in.

The awareness for designing security into systems is increasing, companies like ARM holdings, a UK international computing chip designer and others are saying that in the case of the Internet of Things IoT devices are increasing the attack surface and targets for malicious cyber activity. Mike Muller, the CTO of ARM Holdings has said that protection against hackers works best when it is multi-layered, so ARM is extending our security technology into hardware subsystems and trusted software [24]. Systems can start to have built-in security features with tool kits and services to help companies use secure technology by design built it is still only part of the way that needs the skills and awareness on the other side by professionals in all areas of business who can have the mind set to think about cyber security is all stage of business activity.

Creative Deviousness

You need that *creative deviousness*, if you are looking at some trusted platform chip that is doing some cryptography, You need to approach the problem by looking for side tunnel attacks, so when it is doing some form of calculation, does it give a different heat signature, or is it noisy in an electromagnetic sense so I can tell quiet what it is doing. It is a mindset of creative deviousness.

The Case of Traffic Light Systems

There was the case where we were talking to people who were designing traffic light systems and they were very pleased that their electronic controls meant you could not have at a cross roads two green lights at the same time. But they were led lights so we explained that if we were an attacker we would turn one on then the other and the second so quickly so they would both look as if they were on at the same time. How do we teach that? But this is what we need to get into people's minds, they need to have a little hacker insider them thinking how would I subvert a business system? this is key.

Algorithms, a New Kind of Cyberattack Vector

So whether we will need machine learning and artificial intelligence to auto-mate zero day attack detection and response is starting to become a reality but the psychological approach and mind set is also equally critical.

There is a need for better situational awareness to understand what is going on. One part of this is in understand what is going on inside the algorithm itself as in the case of the recent work by the Royal Society on Machine learning and one of the recommendations is for improved visibility of what the algorithms are doing [25]. The need is to see through the opac-ity of machine automation logic to be able to understand and trace back where errors caused by automation or deviancy and criminal activity caused directly or overtly by machine intelligence computation or rules built in by humans. The issues of corruption and the very ethics of decisions made by automation and algorithms are expanding the impact of cyber security risk and due diligence. Visibility and the ability to get through obfuscation in understand where is the problem, or how some system came to make an automated decision is another type of new cyberattack vector is important.

In developing algorithms involve often a large amount of corporate investment in training data and developing the deep learning network. WebMD for example offers machine algorithm advice through its APIs who have incurred the expense to develop algorithm to diagnose medical issues. You can pay a subscription, put your information in, and it will tell you the results and diagnosis. But in other scenarios not related to WebMD, some researchers recently showed that in some cases with just the API access it does not take very many probes with test data to able to work out all of the weights on the hidden layers on a deep learning network, so you can actually steal and reproduce the algorithm [26].

If you have a business and you have spent ages developing the algorithm that is your intellectual property, it is sitting behind a web front end and somebody can come and just send a few bits of test data and steel what you have got, more than that, work out what the test data was that you trained it on.

Samy Kamkar is a legend, in 2013 shortly after amazon announced it would deliver by drone he released his own drone that would fly up and would use a weakness in the Wi-Fi comms to corral all the amazon drone together so it would form it's own drone army arm and fly them away under its own control [27].

Summary

The development of personal, economic and civil security and privacy is a pressing issue of the 4th Industrial revolution and our time. This is not just in terms of its new attack surfaces and risks of the connected assets and devices with see in the internet of things. It is also the social and psychological impact that spread from fake news to terrorist and surveillance threats and responses. This is a continuously evolving area of technological cat-and-mouse that will pervade every aspect of life as the physical world and the virtual world are interconnected and more deeply entwined.

This requires individuals, organizations and governments to work in unprecedented ways to enable the multi-layers of protection and response to the new attack vectors that will emerge. This is a important development that is manifest in its consequences for the 4th Industrial Revolution.

Notes and References

1. Address Resolution Protocol (arp). http://www.erg.abdn.ac.uk/users/gorry/course/inet-pages/arp.html.
2. Chapter: Configuring SPAN and RSPAN, Cisco Catalyst 4500 Series Switch Software Configuration Guide, 12.2(53)SG. http://www.cisco.com/c/en/us/td/docs/switches/lan/catalyst4500/12-2/53SG/configuration/config/span.html.
3. DARPA Grand Challenge. http://archive.darpa.mil/cybergrandchallenge/.
4. Cyber Reasoning System CRS. http://www.raytheoncyber.com/capabilities/reasoning/ http://www.raytheoncyber.com/rtnwcm/groups/public/documents/content/cyber-reasoning-info-pdf.pdf.
5. Cyber Reasoning systems CRS. https://www.helpnetsecurity.com/2016/08/22/cyber-reasoning-system/.
6. Cyber reasoning systems automating cyber warfare. https://medium.com/@joey_rideout/cyber-reasoning-systems-automating-cyber-warfare-3329f339edeb#.xv7hryf19.
7. Mayhem wins Darpa. https://forallsecure.com/blog/2016/08/06/mayhem-wins-darpa-cgc/ https://forallsecure.com/.
8. 'Mayhem' program wins grand hacking challenge, 5 Aug 2016. http://www.bbc.co.uk/news/technology-36980307.
9. Defcon 24. https://www.defcon.org/html/defcon-24/dc-24-cgc.html.
10. Intrusion detection system IDS. https://en.wikipedia.org/wiki/Intrusion_detection_system.
11. Gartner report: Market Guide for User and Entity Behavior Analytics. September 2015.

12. Michael E. Whitman; Herbert J. Mattord. (2009). Principles of Information Security. Cengage Learning EMEA. ISBN 978-1-4239-0177-8.
13. OODA Loop. https://en.wikipedia.org/wiki/OODA_loop.
14. PDSA Cycle Deming Institute. https://deming.org/management-system/pdsacycle.
15. Inside the OODA loop. http://www.artofmanliness.com/2014/09/15/ooda-loop/.
16. DDoS attack that disrupted internet was largest of its kind in history, experts say 26 Oct 2016 The Guardian. https://www.theguardian.com/technology/2016/oct/26/ddos-attack-dyn-mirai-botnet.
17. Hackers steal up to $1 billion from banks, DW.COM 16 Feb 2015. http://www.dw.com/en/hackers-steal-up-to-1-billion-from-banks/a-18260327.
18. Ransomeware threat on the rise as 40 businesses attacked 3 Aug 2016. https://www.theguardian.com/technology/2016/aug/03/ransomware-threat-on-the-rise-as-40-of-businesses-attacked.
19. Biggest NHS trust hit by ransomware attack 16 Jan 2017. http://www.serverlink.co.uk/home/2017/01/16/biggest-nhs-trust-hit-by-ransomware-attack/.
20. Mongodb ransack 33000 databases hacked Jan 2017. http://www.darknet.org.uk/2017/01/mongodb-ransack-33000-databases-hacked/.
21. US Authorities arrest internet span king June 1 2007. https://www.scmagazineuk.com/us-authorities-arrest-internet-spam-king/article/562484/.
22. E. Chan-Tin, V.Heorhiadi, N.Hopper, Y.Kim, The Frog-Boiling Attack: Limitations of Secure Network Coordinate Systems. ACM Transactions on Information and System Security (TISSEC) Volume 14 Issue 3, November 2011 Article No. 27. http://dl.acm.org/citation.cfm?id=2043627.
23. J&J warns diabetic patients: Insulin pump vulnerable to hacking Oct 2016. http://uk.reuters.com/article/us-johnson-johnson-cyber-insulin-pumps-e-idUK-KCN12411L.
24. Making secure chips for IoT devices, January 2917, http://openmobilealliance.org/making-secure-chips-for-iot-devices/.
25. AI public services: biases, accountability and transparency (III), 8 March 2017 Eleonora Reform. http://www.reform.uk/reformer/ai-public-services-biases-accountability-and-transparency-iii/.
26. Stealing an AI algorithm and its underlying data is a "high-school level exercise", Sept 26 2016. https://qz.com/786219/stealing-an-ai-algorithm-and-its-underlying-data-is-a-high-school-level-exercise/.
27. Skyjack hacker drones could steal your amazon parcels right out of the air, 4 December 2013. http://www.pocket-lint.com/news/125598-skyjack-hacker-drones-could-steal-your-amazon-parcels-right-out-of-the-air.

9

Impact of Ethics, Machines and Society on Intelligent Systems

Introduction

The most important thing is you can't talk about artificial intelligence without talking about intelligence. One of the big mistakes people make is that they are making AI into specific things like deep learning or Arnold Schwarzenegger terminator movie, but the point is that any word tends to be used in lots of different ways when defining definitions. So I use local definitions, for me the definition I use usually for intelligence is "doing the right things at the right time", very simple, and then Artificial Intelligence is just "an artifact we have constructed getting that to do the right things at the right time".

From a computer science perspective, the problem of intelligence I see is actually a problem of search. There are a set of possible things you can do in a situation but how do you know the right thing to do? Part of that is not just searching between a set of things you can do, but also constructing what you think the consequences could be.

Consider the old chess computer programs, how many moves ahead do they look and that determines how well they play?

There are rules that can be used to plan out the response to the game situation. It is a kind of "framing problem" of knowing what information is available and how far the chess player can think ahead.

When you are talking about the framing problem you are basically talking about is all the combinatorial possible things. To consider all the possible things you could possibly do is inconceivable for a human, even for

© The Author(s) 2018
M. Skilton and F. Hovsepian, *The 4th Industrial Revolution*,
https://doi.org/10.1007/978-3-319-62479-2_9

chess. In a 35 move game of chess there are around 10^{120} options, more than there are atoms in the universe and the game GO is even bigger with 2.08×10^{170} moves with each end point with up to 361 legal moves. Yet these are trivial compared to biology that deals with biological complexity of the human brain with 100 billion neurons and 100 Trillion connections.

Reducing the Search Space

What framing does is the same as we see in human culture and language, is to find ways to reducing the search space. Humans do a lot of this by social learning, so there are gestures that you just never make. The Human brain is very good at filtering out information and focusing on a specific action of attention on the task right down the commuter adjust action of how to grasp an object. People think of negative constraints as a negative thing but you can recast that as "focus", it is basically that your culture has put in front of you things that are most likely to be useful. We talk about "thinking out of the box" what you are basically talking about is making a bigger search, leaping into another area.

Cognitive Horizon

Cognitive horizon is an idea that may be related to this which is an effect of "lensing" but related to what is the "knowable" from the perspective of what a human can understand.

This concept is similar to a view by Patrick Winston's Ph.D., Ford Professor of Artificial Intelligence and Computer Science at MIT [1], in "you can only learn something that you almost know" [2] which suggested that in order to learn something, you need to already have enough background knowledge about the subject in question that the teaching will make sense, and that you can integrate it to your existing structures of knowledge [3].

This is related closely to such topics as the *illusion of transparency* generated by hindsight bias and human brain reinterpretation of situations; and *self-anchoring* from the inability of the human brain to visualize other minds [4]. This phenomenon is mentioned in Steve Wozniak's autobiography, iWoz [5]. He notes that the Apple I's concept of combining a video terminal and a computer in one case appeared to be a significant change, but in his mind it was a simple decision. He had previously developed a MITS Altair-like microcomputer [6], but found it limited by its unfriendly switches-and-lights interface. He had also developed a video terminal, which was good for communicating with powerful computers from a distance. Combining the two was just the next logical step [7–9].

So you are not going to suddenly learn Chinese right now, it is why you have to keep trying when learning something new or improving proficiency. In teaching something to students you have to scaffold them up using concepts and training data and other techniques to build learning.

From the computer science perspective, machine and natural intelligence are more-or-less isomorphic corresponding or similar in form and relations. In terms of search they are identical so basically, in a subject area there are different subsets of things we can search over but in terms of making computation work, focusing on the fact that there is just intelligence and intelligent comes down to these various sets of search problems, it involves simultaneously:

- The search for what chain of things to do?
- But also what kind of things are there?
- And what kind of contexts are actually important?

So you are learning a lot different things at the same time but still each of those can be single searches. If you are trying to figure out what kinds of context are they, you can figure that as a clustering problem of associated information. You are trying to search for what is the best cluster, and how many clusters are there?

Chess players have actually done one better by using computers to search this space. It is not only training themselves with them but they are also using them in exploring to pick out patterns that they exploit. The use of Deep neural networks have rapidly evolved to the extent that by 2015 Deep Learning Machine teaching itself Chess in 72 Hours, and later playing at International Master Level. This achievement was a world first with a machine that learnt to play chess by evaluating the board rather than using brute force to work out every possible move [10].

This can be used elsewhere to discover patterns. Another example was in recruitment to process employees with various levels of education. They had used machine algorithms, thrown a whole bunch of data at them and come up with these categories. An example in 2016 was a company, HiringSolved announcing the beta launch of RAI, "the first artificial intelligence assistant for recruiting." The goal of RAI was sold as a way to free up recruiters from the tedium of sourcing candidates [11, 12]. The system uses pattern recognition to profile candidates and while can be used for promoting recruitment diversity and removal of human bias it can also raise many questions about how such criteria and training data is developed.

Top Down and Bottom up Thinking

The research field in AI has argued against the perceived bottom up approach of machine learning mechanistic approach and the lack of top done outcome driven thinking. There is still a debate but when you see some people producing quite good software as in the case of driverless cars, you can't really say there is no top down thinking at all. Sometimes they are just not talking about it; I think one of the really fun things is the European Union requiring explainability of some kind. For me they cannot use deep learning. There are ways you can use to describe what deep learning does probabilistically but it just means they need to stop saying "we don't know" I don't know to what extent is just deception, they are just saying this to get off the hook or it is not having a broad enough education and not realizing that they need to know the broader issues involved.

This is all part of the framing question of what is intelligence.

It is interesting when considering the level of intelligence in plants and animal compared to humans. You say things are not really "intelligent" unless they are like a human but does that not mean that instead of the using the term intelligence, just say "like a human". So I think it is much more useful in getting people to understand the real processes involved.

Skills in Coding AI

A key issue is the skills needed to program machine learning. A company may develop and release a library of machine learning to help programmers develop skills to learn how to be better programmers in AI. Coding is as much an art as a science. Most programmers may not have all the skills to learn to be great programmers. By crowd sourcing and making things open source it is possible to help upskill many average to good programmers.

It is a bit like Bill Joy, a prodigious programming talent and the kind of code he produced and the entire team would have struggled but he did it all on his own. Joy's prowess as a computer programmer is legendary, with an oft-told anecdote that he wrote the vi editor, the screen text editor for the Unix operating system, in a weekend. Joy denies this assertion [13].

It is like football or art or anything else, some people are just amazing programmers, and they are sought out, but they also have to figure out what to do with the other 30,000 programmers that are hired and try to help them, because they are still way above average programmers so they need to figure out how they can be a useful as can be and contributing.

They don't want you to have to know the math and do all this stuff, they just want you to be able to recognize when you call this particular tool just like in any other programming pattern.

Ethics of Access to Education to Participate in and Benefit from Machine Learning

This does relate to ethical questions about access to education and knowledge to understand machine learning and to be part of it in society. That is at the bottom level, at the very top level with management you have issues like how will this change the world?

Right now with the collapse of space brought on by the internet, I don't think it is just AI, it is more about communication and technology, they you have all the money and power that is connected with the internet and this technological transformation in the 4th industrial revolution.

The question is how to equitably distribute that? I think there are going to be some huge levels of transnational wealth redistribution, there has to be or there is going to be potential intergovernmental disagreements and local problems which is also a sort of transnational redistribution.

The challenge for many people is trying to understand something they don't understand.

Objective and Subjective Well-being

One of the things that keeps people out of access to economic wealth and health, making them less receptive to different people is the human access to education and wealth. It seems jobs are less stable now, what is going on with the quality of life when you have all these services that can be automated through artificial intelligence? One of the things in society is how to define ways to divide wealth and access to health and resources. We don't even know to divide, we are not denominating a lot of our transactions and money anymore when these are moving into the digital economy. This makes it hard to generate revenue appropriately from this perspective. It is hard to say what kind of business that google or Facebook for example are doing from a transnational perspective in this regard. These are not just objective measures of wellbeing from an income and health perspective but also from a subjective wellbeing in terms of quality of life, happiness and a life worth living.

These are areas that relates to objective and subjective wellbeing and several international and government bodies are still trying to figure out what is value and how to measure it. This includes the OECD study on Guidelines on Measuring Subjective Well-being and societal progress for diversity and fairness of wealth and health distribution [14]. Other research is at the core level of the meaning and levels of happiness and fulfilment of meaningful human lives [15].

These matters impact on in matters of automation and artificial intelligence both in terms of loss of employment and personal human self-worth defined by employment. But it also impacts on the bigger questions of productivity and societal well-being in what humans will do as the increase in automation changes work and social interaction. Conversely, as artificial intelligence seeks to mimic and reflect emotion and understanding of human values, it also means being able to measure and define what is wellbeing and the value of a good life.

Eudaimonia Happiness: An Alternative to Hedonic Happiness

Research into wellbeing has questioned hedonic happiness that is based on increased pleasure and decreased pain leads to grater happiness for more advanced concepts of a life worth living. Eudaimonia happiness looks at happiness as based on welfare and human flourishing through virtuous experience and human good. Eudaimonia stresses that not all desires are worth pursuing as, even though some of them may yield pleasure, they would not produce wellness.

Underpinning psychological wellbeing is based on ideas of self-actualization of personal growth, self-acceptance, autonomy, environmental mastery, positive relationships and a meaningful purpose in life [16].

When basic human needs are met and a number of these factors when satisfied lead to well-being [17].

This area can be subjective too. It affects your health and interestingly it affects your health from what *you think is going on*. So if you perceive yourself as sliding down then you will be less healthy, if you perceive yourself as socially dominant than you will be more healthy. When you have good access to good information that can make you healthier, it can help you make better decisions about clothes to put on during the day, there are all kinds of information.

As machines become more prevalent in society these questions in terms of the human ethical impact and on these issues will become more pressing.

Modularity and OOD

Machines with use modularity as a way to design multi-component systems efficiently. This is an important field in robotics where there are significant developed in planning hierarchies for a robot.

A planning hierarchy in robotics is useful in decision automation from movement to actions based on sensors and response priorities [18].

Rodney Brookes, Roboticist, was getting people to emphasize modularity, minimal representations, decentralized planning. The design was to aim to arbitrate so the modules can still be self-contained while at the same time it allows you exploit other modules if you want, a principle found in Object Oriented Design OOD.

Any autonomous system has to be able manage a set of priorities and that it is proactive about pursing those priorities. This can prove difficult when considering programming for concurrency for example.

To make this easier I get them to think about how do you set those priorities and how they change in response to the environment and just the handle of that, because in natural environments lot of things happen. Most Specialized robots today of course only operate in defined constrained and known environments.

People just think that AI is just something that programs itself, but actually it listens to its environment and the idea of how the cybernetic feedback and action cycle is being applied. These are important issues in the design of machine learning and planning representations that need to become learnable action patterns.

Early on we found we could not program everything as predefined. Every piece that was in there was highly salient so you couldn't just machine learn away from that without dissipating objectives taking place.

This was akin to the work by Carl Hewitt, the Computer Scientist who created planner programming for automated planning and planning theory in actor models. Carl developed an actor model for computation for scalable robust systems. An Actor is an entity that can receive and send messages as well as create new actors. The Actor Model can be used as a framework for modeling, understanding, and reasoning about, a wide range of concurrent systems [19]. This precedes much earlier work on an universal modular actor formalism developed by Hewitt and team in 1973 that proposes a modular Actor architecture and definitional method for artificial intelligence [20].

I am not talking about the actor models in the multi-agent systems and simultaneous systems; or each module being an actor. I am really talking about setting the priorities of the system as a whole, so setting up its priorities for each of the components of a machine system. It is about that "focus" and combinatorics. Each of the components should make an ordinary programing problem as much as possible because that is what programmers are good at. So you try to simplify the modularity of the components as much as possible while at the same time let be as powerful as possible.

The people who do automated planning they have to make components simple because otherwise the planners can't plan around them. In the case of a web camera, mobile phone or robot we can have a module for face recognition. This can be a component of a larger system that is made up of many component modules with an aim to achieve a overall outcome.

Superintelligence or a Humane Future

One extreme of machine automation has been the discussion around the emergence of general artificial intelligence and what has been described as the rise of superintelligence made famous by notable speakers including and Elon Musk, Stephen Hawking and Nick Bostrum.

A central issue of superintelligence by Nick Bostrum's 2014 book argues that if machine brains surpass human brains in general intelligence, then this new superintelligence could replace humans as the dominant lifeform on Earth. Sufficiently intelligent machines could improve their own capabilities faster than human computer scientists, and the outcome could be an existential catastrophe for humans [21].

However my view is that it assumes that every intelligence wants to take over the world. The counter view from Bostrum is that a causality similar to Darwinian natural selection could mean that the competing resources may drive the superior intelligence to dominate the inferior intelligence to extinction.

What they are really worried about is that some how magically that if you have some human capacity you wouldn't necessarily turn into an ape and ape like mothers. It makes no sense.

They think about it but they just assume that is what it means to be intelligent, that as you get more intelligent you get more like us because we are the most intelligent thing that there is. It is just wrong. We are talking like Lamark and Lamarkism [22].

So we anthropomorphize and infer things. Lamarck was an older version of evolution before Darwin. The idea in Lamarkism was that basically the things that were evolving the longest were human so that everything was starting as little bubbles coming out of the gas of swamps and all of the different plants and animals where at different stages of along the chain of evolution that lead you to humans as god's apex of evolution.

This is what I mean by Lamarck and in the context of artificial intelligence is that it is growing and coming towards us, and that is wrong, that is Lamarck.

"We already have lots of intelligent entities walking the planet, not all of them want to take over the world". It needs to be caveated with what proportion of people have more competitive attitudes rather than just collaborative or just asocial.

In Europe you tend to cultural stereotypes of getting more people who are group oriented, they are trying to think about maximizing the common good. They punish people who they felt don't contribute to the group.

Then there are competitive people who are willing to pay a penalty in order to make you pay a bigger penalty. You get that more in countries with more people and income, the poorer countries and more competitive strategies.

People think that humans have this general intelligence and so lets worry about this artificial general intelligence. Because its like human intelligence but only better. But humans don't have general intelligence. We do have neurons that are in connections with different functions performed on different parts of the brain. Different parts of the brain have totally different connectivity, and different structures.

Our brain is modularized too and that is part of the reason why we have focus. And we can remember huge number of photographs and you can say whether you have seen it before or not but you don't. But you don't memorize a phone book. So there is clearly specialized that we can and can't do.

In researching this book machine learning expert specialists view superintelligence and artificial general intelligence with some skepticism, seeing this in the timeframe of 50 years–250 or 300 years in the future. But the matters discussed are useful is shedding light on an important societal debate around the consequences of machines that can potentially think and learn to interact and profoundly change social and human experience in 4th industrial revolution.

Super Human Performance

What is happen now is not superintelligence. There is human intelligence and then there is anthropomorphizing artificial intelligence. Then there is specialized machine learning or AI which is like the Infineon Rubik cube solver who can solve the cube in 0.67 of a second [23].

But that's not the same as generalized experience, it can only do one thing super humanly fast.

It is super human performance, which is specialist advanced machine intelligence that can work way much faster that any human could ever do. You cannot run the 100 meters with ten Husain Bolts in 1 second!

There are things happening now that are fundamentally going to change the competitive landscape of jobs by machines that no human could do.

This has been true since they invented tools for thousands of years, I think the main thing that is changing is the rate of change. Calculators can already do arithmetic faster than any human. The rate of change is increasing in gaining these capacities which are clearly super human in ways we did not expect.

Yes the google saving energy is good, I heard examples in the 1990s of back propagation saving energy so its not new but because its google it gets publicity.

But this is an escalation of specialist machine intelligence surely that in previous decades was not possible.

That is the thing about specialism, the more combinatory ideas of where you can apply things and solving different kinds of problems.

I really think that the big problems are social, one of the areas I research is trying to find out what it is to be human? what are ethics about? What aesthetics are about? Assuming we can do all this sort of things, what is it we want to do?

A lot of people are already confronting this.

Living like its 1915 the Great Depression and Impact of Technology

If you wanted to live at the standard of living of people from 1915, you only have to work 17 weeks a year in 2017. I have actually known people like that. I knew a guy who grew Christmas trees and he literally only worked two months a year. He had a Cabin in Michigan, he had friends, he loved his life, he was married but hey separated because his wife couldn't stand it. But he still was happy and had a life.

You can make that kind of decision and some people just don't.

I really think what we need now is a revolution in governance because we have to deal with this. Every time we get this new technology, we get this mess of wealth and inequality, then you get the social disruption and ultimately you get a new type of government. We need to do this with as least damage and pain as possible.

But how much do we really need this adjustment?, how much does it affect most people's lives really? A lot of people just like working for each other, they already are selling peas, painting walls; my Great Grandfather was a painter, that's the kind of thing we could be doing by we aren't.

Have you read, The road to Wigan Pier By George Orwell published in 1937? It is a series of essays that really gives you a picture of what its is like to be living at that time. It is a searing account of the author's observations of bleak living conditions of working-class life in the industrial heartlands of Yorkshire and Lancashire in the 1930s before World War II. It talks about the poor living and work conditions and grinding poverty before delivering a long meditation on creating a fairer society.

One of the things he talks about is what a game changer that "we can buy clothes off a rack". So up until about 1920, if you think about this, for thousands of years until about 1920, how you dressed really signaled a lot about how much money you had, it was a social queue. You could not have clean cloths every week because cloths took forever to assemble.

A lot of the time that people where making these cloths was just for their own family. My mother did this, I grew up wearing clothes that I wore until I was older and outgrew them.

With the rise of machine production including automated weaving and production of clothings, there was a shift in the quality of life. George Orwell spoke about these changes and is illustrative of the kind of industrial revolution transformation that technology brought in that era, brought starkly to life in The road to Wigan Pier.

The 4th Industrial Revolution Change is Different

The 4th Industrial Revolution highlights changes that are fusing technology, social, biology and environmental issues. Climate change for example is an existential risk. In other areas the use of bioengineering medical advances for disease treatments to automated self-driving cars are changing the basis and impact beyond human mechanical efficiencies to new ways to change how resources and energy are consumed to living processes and food management.

The dimensions of these issues are moving from the human scale of automation to impacts on whole transport and cities to global concerns that could. While some may generate greater good of health and wellbeing, others are clearly existential threats from over consumption of resources to carbon and other pollutants that affect everyone. These are wicked problems in that today's technology and social organizations may not be capable of solving these challenges. If the rate of change is also increasing then how can these be resolved will require radical solutions and reimagination of how technology and the awareness to be aware, sense, measure the true situation and respond may require machine intelligence and AI.

We have big problems, the sustainable population, how to maintain individual and population security. I had this on my personal webpage since the 90s but now everyone is talking about it. And another is why would you build Artificial Intelligence if there is the smallest chance it might take over the world? which I don't actually think it will. But even if there was the smallest chance the point is we have these other things that are bigger threats, we know are coming, and we have to handle. The thing about human beings is that they are capable of such bad things. There has definitely been some really bad things such as human trafficking and Syria and throughout the history of humankind. But by a march we are also unbelievably successful and we are incredibly pro-social and we create change at a huge scale. It is inconceivable but we are changing the biomass of the entire planet by our own action and the animals we eat.

I think Nick Bostrom is right logically about the super intelligence, but it is wrong to think that that alone can give motive for artificial Intelligence. What actually is being described is a perfect description of human culture since we had writing about 2000 years ago. You just get this unbelievable increase in the number of human population and then this leads to domination. We are just talking about the same thing.

These are clearly not trivial problems, but if we have unlimited energy we will be ok or if we hold global warming to some level. The fundamental thing is that we cannot have the average population increase anymore. I hope we will all stay healthy. That is a huge change, everyone knows people who have large families, that is a huge shift if you are talking about how to keep the population stable or even declining so that we have more space to maintain biodiversity. This is incredible.

Transparency and Accountability for Liability in AI and the Legal Status of Robots

We were talking about the fact that people can use deception on each other and that they can exploit the fact that people are obsessed with this concept of AI and they can do that to get funding from Billionaire tech leader for their university institute. They can also do that to try to get out of regulations and regulatory obligations.

There was this idea that you make robots into legal person's and then you tax them and the proletariat working class people will love it because it they would consider it as actually my job that is being cut.

The European parliament legal affairs committee in 2016 developed draft legislation ideas that considered the status of robots and AI as "electronic persons" and voluntary code of ethical conduct for owners in the regulate who would be accountable for the social, environmental and human health impacts of robotics and ensure that they operate in accordance with legal, safety and ethical standards [24]. This would also make changes to the taxation and social systems for robotics to underpin changings from automation and the basis of taxation generation [25].

But actually the point was they wanted to turn them into electronic persons who make their own money and hold their own liability and that is just nuts. It is basically wrong.

You have created an artifact and you are entirely responsible for that. So understanding the notion of good justice and obligations, there is already an issue here because companies are legal entities they are covered by bankruptcy which makes sense for legal persons or entities, for actual persons. But for a company that allows them create shell companies and then to displace liabilities, that is already a problem. If you can create basically a shell company that does really have any people in it then the notions of corporate ethical legality goes put the window. There is no recourse and justice to penalize that. You raise a Tax code, I will write a robot code to evade it is not like people where you actually count them. So we can build ways to evade tax codes and the same goes for liabilities such as the shell companies.

Less extreme than that is algorithms so people claiming that there they have no liability or transparency because the solution is in the "system". This is not true, you can explain exactly why the system did what it did. It doesn't mean you can say which part the program did it; we don't care about that, any more if you kill someone and say which neuron it was. You can understand how the system is trained. We can ask when was the system version released?, What was the process you used by which you decided it was valid? Those are the kind of things that install explanation. There are lots of different kinds of explanation and it is important to get people to understand that it is not only an obligation and not to allow engineers this wiggle room to try to get out this.

In order to do this there also needs to be some visibility in the way to see what these things are doing. It is not just the outcome obligations but it is also being able to trace and see what is going on and is there an issue.

It depends of what level of explanation you require and what is wanted. You can still make very transparent what the protocol was by which the system was trained, and by which version it was released and given that authority. But also in trade-offs, it is exactly like environmental protection. Sometimes if you make the effort to go out and make a more explainable system, a more transparent system, you actually end up with a better system because design is benefited by transparency as well.

AI and Ethics Policy Design

If you are trying to understand the impact and changes of AI you are actually talking about ethics as well. Ethics is the means by which society with be held together into the larger social ecosystem.

The principles and that is why it is actually a continuum, it is part of ethics across the social framework.

There are different types of ethics. We have ethics that we don't even think about, we don't even know, from social norms to areas we never go into such as personal space and racial terms. Then we have things that we learn through religion or social communitization. But then we have things that are constantly modifying such as decisions around crime and punishment to decisions around education, economic taxation and distribution of decision making.

IEEE have a global international initiative for ethical considerations in Artificial Intelligence and Autonomous Systems [26]. It is currently exploring the topic for new standards and solutions, certifications and codes of conduct, and consensus building for ethical implementation of intelligent technologies.

A first document has been published in open forum on ethically aligned design. This defines Ethically Aligned Design EAD as a vision for prioritizing human Wellbeing with artificial intelligence and autonomous systems represents the collective input of over one hundred global thought leaders from academia, science, government and corporate sectors in the fields of Artificial Intelligence, ethics, philosophy, and policy.

Concepts in the first report and explored by the IEEE imitative include

- General principles
- Embedding values into autonomous intelligent systems (AIS)
- Methodologies to Guide Ethical Research and Design
- Safety and Beneficence of Artificial General Intelligence (AGI) and Artificial Superintelligence (ASI)
- Personal Data and Individual Access Control
- Reframing Autonomous Weapons Systems
- Economics/Humanitarian Issues
- Law

The scope of recent publications in this field investigated by the IEEE global Ethics in AI and AS (Autonomous Systems) initiative include code of ethics for human-robot interactions to prevent abuse, physical and mental through the use of artificial agents on other humans; the impact of racism and cultural consequences enacted through automata; personal privacy impact online; to protection and safeguards for vulnerable population, disabilities and mental care.

Moral decision making is a central part that is often debated with autonomous cars but can apply to any situation where human life may be threaten directly or indirectly from the proximity and action of autonomous intelligent systems (AIS). This includes the enforcement, moral emotions, dignity, trust and deception scenarios that may occur with the use and presence of AIS based systems.

A similar expansive investigation described in a report by Stanford University September 2016 entitled "The hundred year study on Artificial Intelligence and life in 2030", is a long term investigation into the field of

Artificial Intelligence (AI) and its influences on people, their communities, and society. It considers the science, engineering, and deployment of AI-enabled computing systems [27].

The Stanford report states that Society is now at a crucial juncture in determining how to deploy AI-based technologies in ways that promote rather than hinder democratic values such as freedom, equality, and transparency.

In the world of business systems and business strategy that is putting together a kind of cogent approach such as in innovation to standards development in industry. It is about practical changes in how we need to understand these new technologies and new business models and consequences.

Summary

A dystopian vision could be that one of the real fears is a polarization of different ideas challenged by the impact of AI on society. For example, the promotion of preferential treatment of one group over another or why companies are looking for the one in a million great programmers. Others seeking good education access for everyone, good nutrition, open borders and all the liberal ideals. If it got to the point where we could just program things to influence and control sections of society just from AI then that would be disaster.

I don't see that as long term stable though, you need to have a reasonably large society, maybe not 9 billion people, but you need diversity which requires liberalism, It is actually something that biology calls the fundamental things of evolution. The amount of diversity determines the rate of change and I think that is part of why people are afraid of immigration for example because change is hard. If you don't have diversity you atrophy but if you do too little diversity you become fragile, you can not adapt. The universe does not hold still. You need diversity, you need more agility.

It could be the homogenizing effect of machine learning or the mass 1-0-1 for individual personalization. There are many things to play for and many aspects of legislation and governance still being explored and written.

Machine automation and Artificial Intelligence will change decision making in many ways from how work and human productivity will work to replaces or assisted to fundamentally new industries and experiences. How the transparency, privacy and ethical questions will be resolved will continue as necessary changes as this artificial intelligence becomes entangled with our own experiences, life choices and very biological and environmental wellbeing.

What just a few decades ago would have been fantastical dreams and pure science fiction are either already with us or on the cognitive horizon of the current and next living generation lifetime.

What will the future hold for the next decades and our children? Artificial Intelligence is that Pandora's box that has already opened and will never be the same as we enter a new post-industrial revolution that will redefine and be critical to the very survival of an increasing resource constrained and interconnected world.

Notes and References

1. Patrick Winston, MIT http://people.csail.mit.edu/phw/.
2. Winston, Patrick Henry, "Learning Structural Descriptions from Examples," in The Psychology of Computer Vision, edited by Patrick H. Winston, McGraw-Hill Book Company, New York, 1975. Based on a Ph.D. theses, MIT, Cambridge, MA, 1970.
3. https://plus.google.com/+KajSotala/posts/hTLCqxM2tSF.
4. http://lesswrong.com/lw/kg/expecting_short_inferential_distances/.
5. http://www.iwoz.org/.
6. http://wiki.c2.com/?YouCantLearnSomethingUntilYouAlreadyAlmostKnowIt.
7. Roberts, Ed (November 1971). "Electronic desk calculator you can build". Popular Electronics. Vol. 35 no. 5. pp. 27–32.
8. http://www.woz.org/category/tags/zaltair.
9. Wozniak, Steve; Smith, Gina (2006). iWoz: Computer Geek to Cult Icon: How I Invented the Personal Computer, Co-Founded Apple, and Had Fun Doing It. W. W. Norton & Company. ISBN 0-393-06143-4.
10. Deep Learning Machine Teaches Itself Chess in 72 Hours, Plays at International Master Level Sept 14 2015 https://www.technologyreview.com/s/541276/deep-learning-machine-teaches-itself-chess-in-72-hours-plays-at-international-master/.
11. https://hiringsolved.com/blog/rai-artificial-intelligence-for-recruiting/.
12. Machine Learning and Artificial intelligence - Science Matters, January 2017.
13. "Bill Joy's greatest gift to man – the vi editor", Ashlee Vance, The Register, September 11, 2003.
14. OECD Guidelines on Measuring Subjective Well-being March 20 2013 http://www.oecd.org/statistics/oecd-guidelines-on-measuring-subjective-well-being-9789264191655-en.htm.
15. What is Subjective Well-Being? Understanding and Measuring Subjective Well-Being, http://positivepsychology.org.uk/subjective-well-being/.

16. Ryff's model of psychological well-being. Carol Ryff's Model of Psychological Well-being: The Six Criteria of Well-Being http://livingmeanings.com/six-criteria-well-ryffs-multidimensional-model/.
17. What is Eudaimonia? The Concept of Eudaimonic Well-Being and Happiness, Positive Psychology UK http://positivepsychology.org.uk/the-concept-of-eudaimonic-well-being/.
18. R. Knepper, S.S. Srinivasa, M.T. Mason, Hierarchical Planning Architectures for Mobile Manipulation Tasks in Indoor Environments http://people.csail.mit.edu/rak/www/sites/default/files/pubs/KneSriMas10a.pdf.
19. Actor Model of Computation: Scalable Robust Information Systems. Carl Hewitt Aug 9 2010 https://arxiv.org/abs/1008.1459.
20. A Universal Modular Actor Formalism for Artificial Intelligence, Carl Hewitt, Peter Bishop, Richard Steiger, AI Proceeding IJCAI'73 Proceedings of the 3rd international joint conference on Artificial intelligence Pages 235–245 1973 http://dl.acm.org/citation.cfm?id=1624804.
21. Nick Bostrom. Superintelligence: Paths, Dangers, Strategies, OUP Oxford (3 July 2014).
22. Evolution Theories Before Darwin, Famous Scientists. https://www.famousscientists.org/evolution-theories-before-darwin/.
23. New Record! Robot Solves Rubik's Cube in Less Than a Second. Living Science, Nov 2016 http://www.livescience.com/56828-robot-sets-rubiks-cube-world-record.html.
24. Robots: Legal Affairs Committee calls for EU-wide rules EU Parliament News http://www.europarl.europa.eu/news/en/news-room/20170110IPR57613/robots-legal-affairs-committee-calls-for-eu-wide-rules.
25. Draft Report – with recommendations to the Commission on Civil Law Rules on Robotics (2015/2103(INL)). Committee of Legal Affairs. 31.5.2016 http://www.europarl.europa.eu/sides/getDoc.do?pubRef=-//EP//NONSGML%2BCOMPARL%2BPE-582.443%2B01%2BDOC%2BPDF%2BV0//EN.
26. Ethnically Aligned Design IEEE report 1 https://standards.ieee.org/develop/indconn/ec/autonomous_systems.html.
27. One Hundred Year Study on Artificial Intelligence (AI100), Stanford University https://ai100.stanford.edu/2016-report.

10

Impact of Population, Water, Energy and Climate Change on Intelligent Systems

Introduction

I attended the International petroleum week conference in London in last January 2017. It's the first international conference with oil companies I have seen where they have been taking climate change seriously. They had previously been paying lip service to it, but now almost as a kind of existential threat in realizing business-as-usual is the one thing they wouldn't face. The energy resource and price discussion is now "lower for longer" in terms of the oil price, and even the discussion of "lower forever". We are in an "age of fossil fuel abundance", and what is in scarcity of supply in the future is now the opportunity to combust fossil fuels because of the concern about carbon.

The most immediate consequences are changes in two driving forces, one is "post Paris" and the sense that policy makers and politicians finally, despite Donald Trump, are taking climate change seriously. The other is the impact of unconventional oil and gas which has created this sense of abundance rather than scarcity, coupled with the realization that there are lots of conventional hydrocarbons available even in a world of 50 US Dollars a barrel. What they confront is a situation where there is going to be a lower price and there are longer term and medium term concerns about demand. The result is the immediate focus on cost and driving down operating cost to survive in a world of 50 US Dollars a barrel. This is primarily a concern for international oil companies because they do not have access to the low cost, low hanging fruit of the oil fields of the middle east. They tend to be left with the more expensive, technologically challenging, off shore issues.

© The Author(s) 2018
M. Skilton and F. Hovsepian, *The 4th Industrial Revolution*,
https://doi.org/10.1007/978-3-319-62479-2_10

It looks like this has finally become part of their risk management process and have been flagged up on a risk targets as needing to be addressed. This has been described within a larger context of what is called the global energy trilemma seeking to combine security of energy supply, affordability while protection the environment sustainably [1, 2].

When will Global Oil Demand Peak?

The cost per barrel is one of the key performance indicators, the way that it was not before. In the past it was all about replacing reserves production ratio, and in a world of 100 US Dollars a barrel, which incidentally is not that long ago, they were really trying to gain access to regional reserves regardless of cost. I think there has been a realization in international oil companies that they have to think about how they can make money and be profitable in a world where we have 50 or 60 US Dollars a barrel? Which historically is high but it is not high enough for the kind of end of "easy oil" scenarios that the international oil companies face. In fact digitization is part of the process for driving down cost but equally so is standardization where they are trying to stop the oil field service companies constantly coming up with bespoke solutions that cost more. And this notion of co-operition that in a national setting it pays to cooperate with your competitors to drive down costs so that you all benefit, even though at one level you are in competition. There are lots of things happening realizing that if you think of this traditionally, it is just another business cycle and we go through phases of up and down. But then there is this notion that it is the end of the resource super-cycle and for example what we see in China is a moving away from a materials-energy intensive economic model of development in China which fueled the super-cycle over the last fifteen, twenty years. This is a cyclical process but at the end there is a short-term story that is saying that because of the massive reductions in investment being made now there will be a tighten of the mater in the early twenty twenties because demand will continue to grow. There may be a period of relief in the early 2020's with high prices that may turn out to be a false signal in that the sense that now, what makes it different is that there is this structural destruction of demand between now and 2050 and beyond. That must be an inevitable consequence of climate change policy. The debate is all about when will global oil demand peak? The company Royal Dutch Shell have talked about the peaking happening in the 2020s others 2030s, 2040s, but the point is the conversation has now changed. Not to "will it?" to "when will it?". If you look at the various scenarios and exercises that are going on currently on an annual basis, BP for example in their 20–30 forecast admitted for the first time that someone's assets are going to get stranded. There has also been a big debate around the speed of uptake of electric cars. Some of the things you are looking at elsewhere in the 4th Industrial Revolution are part of the existential threats to the business model of fossil fuel industries because they will have the impact of reducing demand. It is not just electric car, it is also the growing efficiency of the internal combustion engine, and also car sharing. There will be fewer cars of the road and those car consuming less oil or no oil has an impact on the demand for oil.

Accelerating Demand Destruction

What is interesting is that the various scenarios show that while there is a decline in the transportation sector for oil which represents about 20% of global demand, there is also a prediction for growing demand in petrochemicals. Oil is a feed stock and natural gas is a feed stock which may be aligned with the notion of the 4th Industrial Revolution and the kind of products that are being produced, and that we tend to forget that hydrocarbons are also a raw material for industrial production. BP have a story line that says the two can essentially cancel each other out the loss of demand in transportation maybe countered by the growth in demand for petrochemicals, but that remains to be seen. Certainly the International Energy Agency (IEA) [3] narrative at the moment is what I call "mind the gap" because by 2050 we are not going to want anywhere near the amount of fossil fuels that we use today, but in the 2020s we are still going to need a lot and the consequence of saying we must stop investing and divesting in fossil fuels is that we will face a crunch in the 2020s. You can therefore have the scenario of the short-term crunch that may actually accelerate demand destruction because higher prices for fossil fuels may drive people away, and may make electric cars for example more attractive. The problem is low fossil fuel prices have an impact on the cost of renewables and alternative energy.

The other thing to understand from a very practical issue is that the oil and gas industry is a long-term business with large upfront capital costs, so the decision that are made in the 2020s are still paying off in the 2050s and certainly in the 2040s. You cannot future proof the fields you are developing. It requires having to think very hard about the world of 2040 and 2050 it terms of what will be the price? What will be the level of demand? Where we are making sufficient money on our investments?

Learning How to Move to New Low Carbon Economy Technologies

A theme we have observed in the 4th Industrial revolution has been the setting up of sites to establish new ways of working. This is from exemplar hospital to trial new patient care digital systems; candidate smart cities to develop showcase technology to the digital energy grid to pilot whole energy and cross vector technology to combine power, gas and try out new forms of energy. The reason they are doing this is to try to learn how to integrate these new technologies together.

It is not straight forward. If you look at the gas networks in the national grid in the UK, and the incumbents seeking to protect their assets. The actual reason they may want to see hydrogen as a fuel on the agenda is because hydrogen sustains the demand for natural gas. It also enables to repurpose at the local scale the gas distribution network. That industry has been going through a process for many years, replacing the metal pipes with plastic pipes because cannot use hydrogen in metal pipes. The route to hydrogen, the H21 initiative for example [4] is about sustaining demand. We have done some work at the UK Energy Research Center (UKERC) [5] looking at the future role of gas in the UK and there is a future that is compatible with our climate change targets, by in which gas is used as a raw material to produce hydrogen but you need to also have carbon capture and storage (CCS) [6] for this to work. So there are key enabling technologies without which it will not work. There you can take a step back because the UK government scrapped its funding for CCS a couple of years ago. This has consequences because the production process for hydrogen involves stream reforming or partial oxidation from methane that also produces large amounts of carbon dioxide [7]. If you cannot remove that this will not work. There is also a energy penalty, it is costly. None of these things are cheaper than the incumbents (Table 10.1).

I think this whole idea of what the future energy system looks like and the energy geography particularly in how it fits together is important.

We do have this process of rescaling going on today where we are moving away from a system which has got relatively small number of centralized points of generation when it comes to electricity. There is only ten or eleven points of access into the national transmission system in the UK now for Gas. If you think about what wind turbines have done to the grid you have thousands of points of generation which previously you did not have. What we are rescaling, regionalizing is that you end up with a patchwork. You may

Table 10.1 Hydrogen production: Steam-Methane reforming and partial oxidation

Hydrogen production
Steam-Methane reforming
Steam-methane reforming reaction
$CH_4 + H_2O$ (+ heat) $\rightarrow CO + 3H_2$
Water-gas shift reaction
$CO + H_2O \rightarrow CO_2 + H_2$ (+ small amount of heat)
Partial oxidation
Partial oxidation of methane reaction
$CH_4 + \frac{1}{2}O_2 \rightarrow CO + 2H_2$ (+ heat)
Water-gas shift reaction
$CO + H_2O \rightarrow CO_2 + H_2$ (+ small amount of heat)

have a national transmission system for methane natural gas, which is actually supporting in some areas the existing system but in others it is facilitating hydrogen because the regional economy is hydrogen based.

You have got to factor in all these other things and to ask what are the key facilitating technologies? What are the likely black swans (disruptive events that are difficult to predict)? Cheap energy electricity storage can completely change the world. The recent example of Tesla and its Powerwall battery are just the beginning. Tesla are having problems with their Powerwall's at the moment. The company discontinued its larger 10-kilowatt-hour Powerwall but kept the smaller 6.4 kWh in production. The larger Powerwall was intended for protection during power failures, uses nickel-cobalt chemistry, and is good for about 500 cycles. The smaller Powerwall is intended for solar power time-shifting, uses nickel-manganese, and can be cycled 5000 times. The numbers just didn't add up, 10 kWh Powerwall cost installers $3500, and to that you added the price of a power inverter, transfer switch, and a significant amount of wiring. The average American home uses about 30 kWh of energy daily, making this an eight-hour battery when the utility company power fails. Even scaling back to just the essentials—no air conditioning, no electric stove, maybe no electric hair dryer—you'd get maybe two days of runtime. Alternatives such as natural gas or propane generator could provide 7–22 kWh and work for days and overall total costs where 60% cheaper than a 10 kWh battery backup generator [8].

We will perhaps look back in fifteen years that this was like a "Sony Betamax", that was not the answer! I have this thing the size of a book on the wall that got all this storage. If that happens, then all bets are off about what happens to the oil companies for example. Suddenly all that capacity can be stored. They have to worry about potentially threats out there to their demand. We all know the storage issue is critical, and if we solve storage then everything changes. It also changes the situation in terms of electric vehicles and the cost of storage and the range of the vehicle, all those things are coming along rapidly.

The Shape of Future Energy Systems in the 4th Industrial Revolution

In the 4th Industrial revolution there are a number of cross-cutting concerns of which this whole area of climate change is clearly one of them. In the field of energy and resources it is difficult to see where to focus on, do countries and geographies invest on a range of energies or develop a few key technologies? There are significant changes in the sources of energy and resources in the coming twenty thirty years. Digitization and artificial intelligence will play a key role in this. Artificial intelligence is now being used to optimize for example the energy consumption and management in data centers. Data centers are also huge consumers of energy and they are a relatively new consumer of energy.

A lot of these technologies have impacts on energy demand. But one of the things that is also happening is that people are thinking more in terms of becoming energy service companies, particularly down stream and in the mid stream. For example, the engineering companies GE and Siemens are looking at this perspective. We consume energy services, we do not consume the primary energy, we do not even know for a light bulb the electricity providing that light can come from any given number of sources. Two weeks ago we have a whole 24 hour day where there was no coal fire generation throughout the UK. representing the first coal-free day since the 1880s and the early industrial revolution [9]. By 2025 the government is saying there will be no coal fire in the UK but it looks like it will be gone well before that date. The potential spanner is Brexit but the market will push this, not what the government says.

Things are happening more quickly than expected. This is true also in the energy sphere around these questions of energy services and renewables and the rescaling of the energy system. Al of this is part of the 4th industrial revolution. In green growth in a low carbon future are part of the 4th industrial revolution story. If you align green growth, low carbon transition as a key element to the 4th industrial revolution because one of the important issues the 4th industrial revolution must address is climate change.

Food-Energy-Water-Climate Paradox

Looking at the Food-Energy-Water-Climate paradox that was been developed by the it seems that water supply could be the big problem issue by 2030 with several regions around the world. It is this convergence of how energy and resources are interdependent as well.

The energy system is of course very water intensive. Unconventional gas generation, such as shale, tends to be the one people target, but actually all forms of energy production use a lot of water.

1. Global Energy demand increase 50% by 2030 (International Energy Agency IEA) [10].
2. Global Water demand increase 30% by 2030 (United Nations World Water Assessment Program, UN Educational, Scientific, and cultural Organization UNESCO WWDR4 Report [11] and Global Food Policy Report 2016, International Food Policy Research Institute IFPRI [12].
3. Global Food demand increase 50% by 2030 (Food and Agriculture Organizations of the United Nations FAO) [13, 14].

From a business perspective what needs to be done to plan for this impact? Today it appears to be over the horizon but all of this is connected.

But we are beginning to look at production and consumption. We are starting now to be worried about the amount of carbon related to our consumption pattern. This is a whole move away from a world where we saying how much carbon is produced in my country, to saying lets look at the carbon consequences of consumption of my country. This is because we know what we have done in developing countries is off shored a lot of our carbon and energy intensive products, they are traveling in some cases thousands of miles coming from China and elsewhere. As a result when we look at our territorial production and say "oh look our carbon emissions have gone down" but in reality, in consumption terms, they have gone up. At a planetary level they continue to rise. This same notion of looking not at the carbon intensive but the water intensity of production is part of the total debate.

If you go to the supermarket today, you are expecting throughout the year to be able to buy certain products such as strawberries and greens.

But they are being produced elsewhere in the world in a fashion that is not only energy and carbon intensive but also water intensive. So we are beginning to understand the consequences of "embedded water" in the goods we consume.

Part of this is about coming to terms with the ecological consequences of globalization. Which has meant that we have these global production systems where far flung places have increased their energy and water consumption to supply us with asparagus from Peru in the depths of winter. Do we really need it? Does it taste as good?

This then feeds into the food security issue, not our food security. You could say our food security is generating insecurity in the places where this food is being produced. In the economies where this is being produced, for example Kenya, it is impacting because a lot of production of food there is not for the local economy. A lot of the water and energy being consumed is not for the benefit of the local economy.

I would say one of the ways of looking at this is through the whole process of globalization and the extended supply chains that we now have that feed the advanced world. As the middleclass grows globally, that process intensifies. For example, the impact of meat consumption in China has global impact because the Chinese are buying up large parts of Latin America. This is the same in terms of looking at energy trilemma [2], globalization is the missing link. What tends to happen is we have taken globalization for granted. It is just the way the world is. But we don't think about the critical consequences of that. In fact much of the 4th Industrial revolution is not just a rescaling but potentially a re-localization. It is an understanding that the consequences of our extended supply chain are not ecologically sustainable. They are not good for many of these nations that have export economies.

OECD are working on research into well-being [15] and in particular subjective well-being and the lack of measures to track how this is changing. The problem with human attention span and spatial awareness is that you cannot see this impact until it affects the supply chain or government. The objective pursuit of material wealth of the earlier industrial revolutions is now impacting climate, resources and jobs and changing the quality of life. Longer term with the projection of population growth project in the order of 8 or 9 billion by 2050 this is only going to impact further. Nearer term the work such as the well-being research by the OECD are seeking was to measure this change and impact on well-being over time and how we are going to redress this issue. This is the shift from objective to subjective well-being that will become increasingly critical with both climate change and artificial intelligence impacting jobs and its potential to address these change as well.

Climate change is the context in which this is happening. As the climate changes the stresses on the planetary and local scale systems are even greater. If you think globalization is ecologically unsustainable today, as the world warms it becomes even less sustainable. This is because areas of food production shifts and the availability of water changes. I think Global warming is really a misnomer, it is really climate change, because in large parts of the world it will not necessarily alter things immediately. Warming will be happening but it will be the expression of that through the change in climate will be some what different. We are certain that the areas of food production will shift and areas of water stress will increase. The military for example are interested in planning scenarios for areas of future conflict as they see climate change as a threat escalator. In world of changing climate and global warming, conflict over water in the middle east becomes far more significant that worrying about oil. Availability of food, problems of supplying basic nutrition to parts of the world potentially increases the level of inequality, so the world becomes far more inequitable than it is already. We know that as we have a world where there are more extreme climate events and more natural hazards, the least well off are the ones who are least capable of dealing with them. But we also know from climate modeling that those parts of the world most likely to be affected are the least well off parts of the world. We can sit in our comfortable middle class homes in the UK, US, Europe or elsewhere and feel relatively isolated, but one of the things I say to students is "you need to understand the consequences of your consumption" when they say "what can we do about it?" I say "You live in a taken for granted globalized world", "Just look what you consume?". Try to align the 4th industrial revolution with some sense of sustainability because it needs to be a world that ultimately more sustainable than the world today.

Population Paradox

The growth of human population and the increasing demand for food, energy, water and its impact on climate and well-being of the environment. There is only one planet and infinite resources that must met this increasing demand. Yet there are paradoxes within this of both aging and increased longevity yet falling population in some advanced economies of Europe, Japan and America while growth in Africa and Asian regions. This presents complex challenges of attributing responsibilities and causes to regions and countries that have different levels of wealth, population energy and food demands. Predictions of population changes have a wide margin, the lowest UN population projections indicate only the possibility of a fall to 5.5 billion by 2100, the highest is 14 billion and medium 9 billion [16].

Studies on the total planet resources and the rate of consumption that can replaced currently forecasts we are consuming 1.6 "earths" resources and we "overshot" in 2016 on August 8, six days earlier than the previous year, as estimated by the Global Footprint Network [17]. The GFN estimates that human consumption first began to exceed the Earth's capacity in the early 1970s, the issue is this situation cannot be sustainable in the long-run [18].

We are Fast Reaching the Limits to Planetary Resource Growth

If we want to protect the physical world we love we have to consider the policies and behavior in the physical and virtual connected worlds that could impact both worlds. Climate change are truly new challenges, we have to think globally to be able to make the living locally sustainable, that is a paradox.

It is a selective process, an asymmetrical process in the sense that information will not be globalized. Even if there are food riots and water shortages, we will know about them 24-7. In a sense the world monitors itself in a way that it never used to. This morning I saw a report about space satellites that can now count the number of albatrosses on a rock in remote islands in the middle of the Pacific Ocean [19].

There is a level of global surveillance about what is going on which means as things start to happen we potentially could detect this in real time. There are already many examples of extreme weather events, that causality is not clear, but how many more do you need before action will be taken? We see changes in the timing of spring season already, all sorts of things telling us that the climate is changing.

Of course, the climate change deniers will say "there are always changes" but again it comes back to the pace and consequence.

From the 4th industrial revolution perspective if you think back to the 1st industrial revolution it laid the seeds for a totally ecologically unsustainable system.

It is about limits to growth, in some ways it is not a question of timing, it is not the climate change models where wrong, it was the timing wasn't right for the population to see the causality for themselves.

We have got to the point where the current planetary system is fast reaching its limits to growth.

The only way forward is a 4th industrial revolution but it has to address these ecological challenges.

Part of this is the low-carbon-energy transition but it is also coming to terms with things like the energy-food-water mix through which we are satisfying our demands and consumption in ways which are completely sustainable moving forward.

If we have 8 or 9 billion people on the planet by 2050 matters greatly, more mouths to feed, more people consuming energy. We know from geography that the population growth is in the parts of the world that are most affected. India will soon pass China in terms of the most populous state, but actually if you look at the population projections, sub Saharan Africa is the area where there will be the most rapid population growth between now and 2050, which is the part of the world least able to cope.

But we are not planning for things that are even in the short term, in my view 2050 is not long term.

It comes back to my point about investment cycles and 2050. Companies are making decisions now about infrastructure, even if you look at 2035, 2040 which is the endpoint for many projections and scenarios at the moment, that is not that far away.

We have significant challenges ahead if you see the disconnect between what the climate change scenarios are telling us what we need to do, even if you take the IEA 450 scenario for world energy demand outlook versus where the Paris agreement takes us.

- The IEA 450 Scenario assumes that different groups of countries adopt binding economy-wide emissions targets in successive steps, reflecting their different stages of economic development and their respective responsibility for past emissions [20, 21].
- The Paris Agreement's central aim is to strengthen the global response to the threat of climate change by keeping a global temperature rise this century well below 2°C above pre-industrial levels and to pursue efforts to limit the temperature increase even further to 1.5°C [22].

Climate Change

Climate change is the paradox of forecasting greenhouse gas emissions impact and social and political impacts. The Intergovernmental Panel on Climate Change (IPCC) reports provide guidance into greenhouse gas (GHG) emissions that include Carbon Dioxide, Methane, Nitrous Oxide, Tropospheric ozone and chlorofluorocarbons, Halons and other Carbon and Sulfur compounds and global temperature change. Carbon Dioxide is by far the highest impact of GHG at 60% of radiative effect Wm^2 (Watts per Meter Squared) and Methane 20% [23]. Since the Industry Revolution from the year 1750 atmospheric concentrations of Carbon Dioxide have increased by 40% [24]. Projections from analysis of trapped gases in glacial waters going back 800,000 years paleoclimate record reveal the current climatic warming is occurring much more rapidly than past warming events. The data also suggest that global temperature is warmer now than it has been in the past 1000 years, and possibly longer. As the Earth moved out of ice ages over the past million years, the global temperature rose a total of 4–7°C over about 5000 years. In the past century alone, the temperature has climbed 0.7°C, roughly ten times faster than the average rate of ice-age-recovery warming. Two-thirds of the warming has occurred since 1975, at a rate of roughly 0.15–0.20°C per decade [25]. The rate at which surface temperatures go up is not proportional to the rate of CO_2 emissions, but to the total amount of atmospheric CO_2 added since the start of the industrial revolution [26].

IPCC AR5 2013 Report Projections forward to 2100 for global temperature rise from natural and anthropogenic activity of environmental pollution and pollutants originating from human activity. These scenarios forecast a mean temperature rise of between two and 6°C by the year 2100 and an average of 3–4°C [27, 28]. In 2016 global temperature peaked at 1.38°C above levels experienced in the 19th century, close to the 1.5°C limit agreed in the COP21 UN climate change conference in Paris in December 2015 [29]. July 2016 was the warmest month since modern record keeping began in 1880, with each month since October 2015 setting a new high mark for heat [30].

The scenario of a four degree increase in global temperature as higher case scenario outcome would result in most regions in the world seeing up to 70% reduction in water availability through loss of natural run off processes including around 50% reduction in glaciers. A similar impact of 40% fall in maize and wheat crop yields and 30% fall in rice yields. Marine ecosystems would be impact by ocean acidification from increases sea temperatures reducing stocks for fisheries and consequential impact on employment and coastal communities. The 60% probability of the Greenland ice sheet melting could contribute in the long term to a seven meter global increase in sea level. Estimates of sea level rises of half to one meter would significantly impact populations of 150 million in Asia, Africa, Caribbean and Pacific island regions [31].

Mind the Gap

The United Nations Environment UNEP produces an annual report called the "emissions gap" [32] which looks at the difference between where we are and where we need to go. Of course the emissions gap is growing and the later we leave it the steeper the cliff. The 2016 UNEP report already said that there was only three years to save the 1.5°C climate rise target by 2030 and that the long-term objectives of the Paris Agreement require even stronger actions than previously identified, calling for accelerated efforts pre-2020, as well as increasing the ambition of the Nationally Determined Contributions.

This is one of Lord Stern's arguments in the 2006 UK Government report on the economics of climate change and that early action is one of the most cost effective things that can be done [33]. Its doesn't help we have the likes of Donald Trump in the White House at the moment. But moving on, what is interesting is that China's response to Trump is not to let us off the hook because those in the White House have decided not to believe in climate change. Examples like China now wish to occupy the moral high ground and are doing that because their number one concern is actually urban air population as a co-benefit is the reduction of carbon emissions. They have got to clear up the air with one third of all deaths in China linked to toxic smog [34] and around 2.2 million deaths in India and China from air pollution in 2015 [35]. They also understand the water side of this energy equation.

There will come a point where it is a bit like rearranging the deck chairs on the Titanic, the inevitability of climate change and global warming of more than 2°C. Many feel that the 2°C target is not achievable.

Investing in the Right Infrastructure

Making the right investment decisions on infrastructure is important. Yet some infrastructure projects such as the UK H2 Railway line between London and Manchester just to over people around for employment but may not address other options and technologies [36]. Arguably the problem is not the need to move people but one of capacity and too many people traveling already and not enough transport capacity. This creates a demand for transport but needs to consider other infrastructure and technological options. For example this is strongly related to the other infrastructure challenge of a national and local telecommunications network that is capable of supporting remote working. Investments to provide both urban and rural coverage as well as the move to faster more immersive networks such as 5G will potentially enable new forms of virtual and augmented reality working negating the need for physical movement [37]. Another is the US TransCanada Keystone XL pipeline recently approved and the arguments over it's lack of ability to create long term jobs, lower prices of oil or create the right energy dependency mix in the long term in the first place [38].

I was on holiday in Iceland last year and were on top of a Volcano on a travel excursion and we got a 4G signal yet in other areas of UK in the countryside we just cannot get a mobile signal. So the issue is really about where do you put your priorities?

Building physical infrastructure to move people is actually a very old fashioned solution, that is the earlier industrial revolution. What we need are solutions for the 4th industrial revolution that can cut out the physical movement. 3D printing does the same thing, you can design and make it locally, so maybe these are another aspect of the changing relationship between places. Physically moving from one place to another to carry out functions is something that we will be doing less and less.

The Destruction of the Friction of Distance

If people can work one day a week at home, people could be encouraged to do so. You might be in a situation where you are in an office space that treats people with "hot desking" and less desks available and smaller rooms it becomes increasingly uncomfortable. So they may encourage working from home, we then pay for the Wi-Fi and the electricity, heating and light. The company reduced its costs with less office space so there are equity issues about what is going on. If every home and office has to have Wi-Fi to be able to carry out your work you need to also ensure its suitable for the type of work being done. How do you ensure quite zones for work? or alternatively how to maximize face to face contact for collaboration and decision making? When does benefit-in-kind cross over to a necessity for doing your job becomes blurred as the technology enables cross-over between work and home spaces?

Its changes the relationship between people's relationship with places and the friction of distance. One of the stories from the industrial revolution through today is the destruction of the friction of distance.

So we end up in many instances of people living in a world which is upon a pin head. Because we can have conversations with people across the world at next to no cost, besides you need Wi-Fi and networks and a computer to do it. In an information economy still has underlying materials intensity.

The materials-intensive economy has been changing and globalizing but not in the same way and it is not the sense that in a 100 US Dollar barrel world you have a high friction of distance because the cost of meeting is higher. In a 50 US Dollar barrel world you can get for example a price war of gasoline at the shopping malls, people do respond to that. Putting a price on the availability of energy will change behaviors.

I think artificial intelligence will play a key role in this as people don't like being told what to do or don't have the visibility or control across the supply chain and ecosystem to optimize its outcomes. An example of this is Google DeepMind demonstrating a reduction in Data Center cooling costs of 40% using machine learning [39]. In other instances, AI could be used to change when people use appliances in the home to reduce their energy consumption from when to put the kettle on or run the washing machine cycle. The question is how this is done through influence working passively behind the scenes or active control of use and behavior. It sounds a little Orwellian in some control behind the machine and everyday life, but something has to change, either through market changes, consumer behavior changes or policies or a combination of these. With social media and other connected ways of smart devices and places, there is a broader change made possible in the nature and optimization of the ecosystem in the 4th Industrial Revolution.

Aligning the Right Incentives in the Capacity to be "Smart"

We don't seem to get the things aligned, if you take the case of the simplification of energy tariffs at the policy level. With for example in our tariffs you don't have a system sufficiently flexible and not "smart". Even the most basic washing machine today have a timer on it so you can which it on in the middle of the night but here may be no benefit because they are not paying less for that off-peak period. You need a tariff system that aligns with you ability of your appliances to be smart. It takes you out of the decisions because if you want to dry your clothes now the decision to do it three hours later because the machine learning system controls this. If you have a system where you have a smart meter in the home and it also knows what tariff system you are on, it can develop machine learning algorithms to advise and control appliances and your behavior better. The capacity for appliances to be smart only works if the regulations and pricing mechanisms that it is connected to are equally smart and flexible.

I agree policy and regulation is one thing but we should not necessarily over anthropomorphize the situation. In the 4th Industrial Revolution there can be such complexity in the system that humanity, humans cannot know all the factors to optimize these smart appliances and consumption behaviors. I believe integration of automation and AI in a way that it is optimizing for the benefit of the policy implementation. In the previous 1st, 2nd and 3rd Industrial Revolutions it was a trade and transaction thing. In the 4th Industrial revolution it needs intelligent systems which means machine learning and Artificial Intelligence with sufficient computing power and internetworking. It cannot be done without it. There are other levels of ecosystem dependencies going on now where if we want smart homes, smart cities and so on, this is the way to go. That is what we need to encourage because we cannot solve it by ourselves.

The Future of the Kettle and Solar Panels

The kettle is an incredible inefficient way of heating water. This device and our behavior is constantly reheating the same water and only a small amount of it we actually drink. Yet we fill the kettle up just to make a cup of tea, rather than just have enough water in the kettle for the purpose of making just a cup of tea. Some homes have these hot water on-demand appliances that might be more energy efficient. People used to worry about is it more efficient to have a kettle on a gas hob or an electric hob because of the number of energy conversion transformations that had taken place? The kettle is an interesting metaphor for the wider issues.

Germany had one town where they implemented new sources of energy such as solar panels that contributed a significant amount to their energy use through renewable energy [40]. Similarly in Denmark and these are countries that do not have a lot of sun light [41].

In the European context we put the solar power panels in the north where the sun doesn't shine and the wind turbines where the wind doesn't blow because it is a national decision. The situation is we are not getting together and looking at the whole map of Europe and the solar radiation levels and the wind patterns to work out where would be the optimum place to put these things. It is massively affected by current tariffs.

The Need for Whole Systems Thinking

The approach here is the need for "whole systems thinking" becomes paramount. It is both open systems and closed systems loops for effective feedback and control systems design.

Our electricity grid is becoming interconnected at a European scale and there has not been a closed national system for quite a while. This is one of the problems of Brexit in that one of the ways we seek to back up intermittency of power supply is through interconnection between countries. There are several plans to interconnected the UK with Norway and Iceland as well as continental Europe, but what will happen to these with Brexit is unclear. So you have a more interconnected European grid, the problem is, for example, do have weather patterns where the wind doesn't blow anywhere in north western Europe, so you need to be able at some point to backup. What is happening is we are moving away from a centralized system that provides 24-7 consistent access to secure energy, to a system with more and more intermittency that you have to back up that intermittency by using as much of the old system for the days when you need it. But you have to pay for the gas turbines to be there even when they are not in use for that capacity to be available. So the load on that capacity can be very low but you still have to have a business model that pays for its availability. We have this problem in the UK at the moment because the industry will not build new gas turbines because the load is not high enough. We have a problem as we shut down our nuclear power stations and coal fire power stations but need more capacity. We will use it less but still have to have it, so moving to low carbon system needs a viable plan of transition. With the rise for example of electric vehicles (EVs) this just adds to the demand and complexity.

If you go back over the last 15–20 years there have been different government projections of EVs, one it will double the amount of electricity consumed at a national scale. We dicarbon through electricity doesn't seem to be the party line at the moment. We are not envisaging the huge increases in electricity because we are also making very bold assumptions about increases in efficiency. This is were being smarter becomes more important, it is about getting the same level of service from far less energy input and also managing it and there by better management, promoting demand reduction. So we are moving into a system where decoupling of internet growth and energy consumption is well on the way, we are needing to move to a situation where we accelerate that. We are producing goods and services with less and less energy and that energy is generating less and less carbon. This is what we have got to do. Ultimately if you think back to Nicolas Sterns comment about "climate change is market failure" that essentially we are not paying the true costs associated with fossil fuel, the future costs of energy are going to have to be high [24]. Because if you internalize those costs you do that by having the necessary high carbon price to drive all the other innovations. You have to pay more for your energy service because what you have been paying before has no been covering the real cost to the environment.

It does not help if you have governments who say we are going to cap the rise in energy prices. It is very complicated because the cost per unit of solar is coming down, but you need the whole system thinking, but who is paying the cost of intermittency? That is not is a question I think that has been answered satisfactorily. In Germany, for example, they are building new coal fired power stations to back up their wind and solar farms, and they will not meet their carbon reduction targets.

Summary

The impact of the 4th Industrial Revolution will have many general considerations that are not just the concern of one industry, country or individual. The new technologies that fuse physical, digital and biological domains will have the power to create and change how society will address the very real changes and threats of the new era.

We have seen the internet will not only enable new kinds of communities and networking, but bring new forms of computing and resources at a scale never seen before. Combining this with the intelligence of machine learning and the actuation of robotics and automation in and across industries changes how locations and experience will become intertwined between the physical and virtual worlds.

Cyber security and personal privacy will radically change, and has already changed in many social networks and perceptions of governance and government. We live in a connected common of networks and associations that need to be cognizant of the great advances and also the things we value and need to protect.

The new machine intelligence will change how decisions are made and who is accountable and the liability and consequences of this new technology driven era. Even if artificial intelligence becomes transparent and intrinsic to how work, social engagement function in the society of the future, it has profound issues over the rising inequity and diversity that this might bring. Added to this is the 21st central changes of the population, water supply, energy demands and climate change will become the leading debate and issues of this new era and the role of artificial intelligence in addressing this.

Notes and References

1. World Energy Trilemma, World Energy Council, https://www.worldenergy.org/work-programme/strategic-insight/assessment-of-energy-climate-change-policy/.
2. Michael Bradshaw, Global Energy Dilemmas: Energy Security, Globalization, and Climate Change, Polity Press; 1 edition 1 Nov. 2013 https://www.amazon.co.uk/Global-Energy-Dilemmas-Security-Globalization/dp/0745650643/ref=sr_1_fkmr0_1?ie=UTF8&qid=1493983081&sr=8-1-fkmr0&keywords=energy+trilemma++michael+bradshaw.
3. International Energy Agency https://www.iea.org/.
4. H21 initiative: Interview with Kiwa Gastec on if scheme will go the distance, Gas World. July 18 2016 https://www.gasworld.com/h21-initiative-will-it-go-the-distance/2010726.article.
5. The UK Energy Research Centre http://www.ukerc.ac.uk/.
6. Cardin Capture and storage association CCSa http://www.ccsassociation.org/what-is-ccs/.
7. Hydrogen production: Natural gas reforming, Energy.gov. Office of Energy Efficiency & Renewable Energy https://energy.gov/eere/fuelcells/hydrogen-production-natural-gas-reforming.

8. Tesla kills off its 10-kWh Powerwall: The chemistry wasn't there. March 30 2016 https://www.extremetech.com/extreme/225692-tesla-kills-off-its-10-kwh-powerwall-the-chemistry-wasnt-there.

9. First coal-free day in Britain since 1880s, 22 April 2017, bbc.com http://www.bbc.co.uk/news/uk-39675418.

10. World Energy Outlook, 2015, International Energy Agency IEA https://www.iea.org/Textbase/npsum/WEO2015SUM.pdf.

11. Global Water resources under increasing pressure. United Nations World Water Assessment Program WWDR4 Report, UN Educational, Scientific, and cultural Organization UNESCO http://www.unesco.org/fileadmin/MULTIMEDIA/HQ/SC/pdf/WWDR4%20Background%20Briefing%20Note_ENG.pdf.

12. Global Food Policy Report 2016 IFPRI http://ebrary.ifpri.org/utils/getfile/collection/p15738coll2/id/130207/filename/130418.pdf.

13. World Agriculture towards 2030/2050, 2012 Report: Food and Agriculture Organizations of the United Nations (FAO) http://www.fao.org/docrep/016/ap106e/ap106e.pdf.

14. How to Feed the World in 2050, October 2009 Report: Food and Agriculture Organizations of the United Nations (FAO) http://www.fao.org/fileadmin/templates/wsfs/docs/expert_paper/How_to_Feed_the_World_in_2050.pdf.

15. Measuring Well-being and Progress: Well-being Research, OECD http://www.oecd.org/statistics/measuring-well-being-and-progress.htm.

16. UN World Population Forecast to 2300, United Nations Department of Economic and Social Affairs/Population Division 2004 http://www.un.org/esa/population/publications/longrange2/WorldPop2300final.pdf.

17. The overshoot day website http://www.overshootday.org/.

18. Humans have already used up 2015s supply of Earth's resources – analysis 12 August 2015, The Guardian. https://www.theguardian.com/environment/2015/aug/12/humans-have-already-used-up-2015s-supply-of-earths-resources-analysis.

19. Albatross numbers on remote islands are being counted via space, 4 May 2017, The Independent. http://www.independent.co.uk/news/science/albatross-space-numbers-count-space-satellites-chatham-islands-birds-northern-royal-digital-globe-a7716806.html.

20. International Energy Agency World Energy Outlook, 2°C Scenario (2DS) 4°C Scenario (4DS) and 6°C Scenario (6DS) https://www.iea.org/publications/scenariosandprojections/.

21. International Energy Agency IEA 450 World Energy Demand Outlook https://www.iea.org/media/weowebsite/energymodel/Methodology_450_Scenario.pdf.

22. The Paris Climate Change Agreement 2015 United Nations http://unfccc.int/paris_agreement/items/9485.php.

23. "Climate Change Indicators in the United States". National Oceanic and Atmospheric Administration NOAA United States. 2012. Figure 4. The Annual Greenhouse Gas Index AGGI, 1979–2011.

24. Carbon Dioxide Information Center CDIAC. Recent Greenhouse Gas Concentrations DOI:10.3334/CDIAC/atg.032 updated April 2016 http://cdiac.ornl.gov/pns/current_ghg.html.

25. NASA Earth Observatory Paleoclimatology study of past climates http://earthobservatory.nasa.gov/Features/GlobalWarming/page3.php.

26. Does CO2 always correlate with temperature (and if not, why not?) Skeptical Science https://www.skepticalscience.com/co2-temperature-correlation.htm.

27. IPCC Climate Change 2007: Synthesis Report. Anthropogenic Activity. http://www.ipcc.ch/pdf/assessment-report/ar4/syr/ar4_syr.pdf.

28. Intergovernmental Panel on Climate Change (IPCC) Climate Change 2013 Report (AR5) http://www.ipcc.ch/report/ar5/wg1/.

29. Conference of Parties 21st Conference on Climate Change COP21, December 2015, Paris, France http://unfccc.int/meetings/paris_nov_2015/meeting/8926.php.

30. July was hottest month on record for the globe. National Oceanic and Atmospheric Administration, US Department of Commerce. NOAA August 17 2016 http://www.noaa.gov/news/july-was-hottest-month-on-record-for-globe.

31. Impact pf Global Temperature rise of 4 Degrees Celsius, 7 Degrees Fahrenheit http://www.metoffice.gov.uk/climate-guide/climate-change/impacts/four-degree-rise Data produced from 2007 Intergovernmental Panel on Climate Change (IPCC) published its 4th Assessment Report (AR4) http://www.metoffice.gov.uk/climate-guide/climate-change/impacts/four-degree-rise/map.

32. The Emissions Gap Report 2016 - A UNEP Synthesis Report, United Nations Environment http://wedocs.unep.org/bitstream/handle/20.500.11822/10016/emission_gap_report_2016.pdf.

33. Stern Report: The economics of Climate change, UK Government 2006 http://www.wwf.se/source.php/1169157/Stern%20Report_Exec%20Summary.pdf.

34. State of Global Air, 2017 A SPECIAL REPORT ON GLOBAL EXPOSURE TO AIR POLLUTION AND ITS DISEASE BURDEN. A collaboration between the Institute for Health Metrics IHE and Evaluation's Global Burden of Disease Project and the Health Effects Institute IHME. https://www.stateofglobalair.org/sites/default/files/SOGA2017_report.pdf.

35. Around 2.2 million deaths in India and China from air pollution: Study 14 February 2017 http://www.cnbc.com/2017/02/14/around-22-million-deaths-in-india-and-china-from-air-pollution-study.html.

36. What do we know about HS2? 15 November 2015 http://www.bbc.co.uk/news/uk-16473296.

37. UK 5G network https://5g.co.uk/guides/what-is-5g/.

38. Keystone XL pipeline: Why is it so disputed? 24 January 2017 BBC http://www.bbc.co.uk/news/world-us-canada-30103078.

39. DeepMind AI Reduces Google Data Centre Cooling Bill by 40% 20 July 2016 https://deepmind.com/blog/deepmind-ai-reduces-google-data-centre-cooling-bill-40/.

40. This German village generates 500% more energy than it needs 4 May 2017 inhabitat http://inhabitat.com/german-village-produces-500-of-its-energy-from-renewable-sources/.

41. 5 Countries Leading the Way Toward 100% Renewable Energy, Ecowatch 9 January 2015 http://www.ecowatch.com/5-countries-leading-the-way-toward-100-renewable-energy-1881999459.html.

Part IV

The Impact of Artificial Intelligence on Business

11

Example Case Studies of Impact of Artificial Intelligence on Jobs and Productivity

Introduction

"If there is a chance to improve and upscale the quality and efficiency of systems and operations, why wouldn't everyone take the opportunity?" was raised by a Nikhil Kulkami, a recent graduate. He is very much the next generation that will have much to say in how the workplace and society will change. This is the scope of where we are planning to head, especially with the drive to implement more intelligent solutions for the infrastructures available in today's society; this drive is being achieved through integrating artificial intelligence (AI), which is the goal of allowing 'computer systems to exhibit intelligence in some manner' [1]. Artificial intelligence has progressed from the development standpoint in computer science to being fully used to extract, analyse and predict vast amounts of data in varying industries. The integration of technologies like AI is helping improve the operation and efficiency of several infrastructures, as well as reducing their financial costs.

The next section in this document highlights real examples of industries which have implemented artificial intelligence in their daily processes. We provide a summary table for quick reference of the types of Artificial Intelligence and the pragmatic impact of these in managing planned and unplanned outcomes. We then provide a list of practitioner case studies that describe how artificial intelligence is being used today.

© The Author(s) 2018
M. Skilton and F. Hovsepian, *The 4th Industrial Revolution*,
https://doi.org/10.1007/978-3-319-62479-2_11

Example Use Cases in Artificial Intelligence

The follow examples of practitioner development of 4th industrial intelligent systems are described in three areas

- Industry Context
  - How the particular situation in an example industry can be augmented, or replaced by machine intelligence, and combined with machine sensors, objects and human interaction. Several examples of use cases are not simply applicable to one vertical industry, but may often be applied to a wide variety of industries. Examples include identity management, surveillance and marketing human behavior.
- Systems used
  - The types of machine learning and other 4th industrial technologies are combined to enable an intelligent system
- Outcomes
  - The results of the intelligent system impact on the particular context.

While the specific training data and algorithm logics may be for that industry case, it is illustrative of the potential areas of application systems intelligence and new technologies that might be used to solve or enable new outcomes. The following framework is intended to provide a practical guide of potential areas/domains, where the emerging field of artificial intelligence combines with other nascent technologies to solve a given problem, or undertake a task that was previously untenable. This we believe is indicative of the 4th industrial revolution. (see Fig. 11.1).

Practitioner Classifications of Artificial Intelligence Use Cases in Business

The following table provides a summary of examples of how machine learning is already being used to develop intelligent systems responses. The table has been split into broadly two types of intelligence, one driven by known planned events and the other by unplanned events that may be known or unknown.

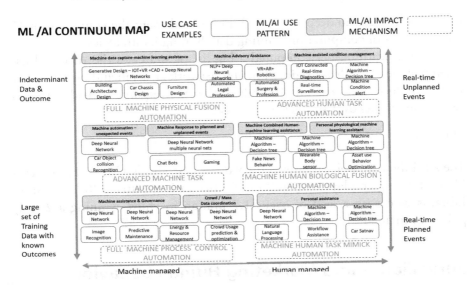

Fig. 11.1 Practitioner classifications of emerging Intelligence Systems use cases

Gaming Industry

Deep Neural Network Predicting Unplanned Deceptive Human Behavior Patterns

Industry Context

A deep learning neural net called Libratus, developed by Carnegie Mellon University has been used to play Poker. The game includes statistical prediction but also interestingly, a behavioural element, where human players may bluff their behavior as part of the game strategy. This behavior was included in the neural network analysis of Libratus and successfully used to predict human behavior in both play and deception or bluffing.

Libratus's algorithms are not specific to poker, or even just to games. The AI has not been taught any strategies and instead has to work out its own way to play based on the information it's given—in this case, the rules of poker. This means that Libratus could be applied to any situation that requires a response based on imperfect information.

Systems used

Using Multi-scenario deep learning, Libratus had spent the equivalent of 15 million hours of computation training data honing its strategies.

The deep learning net computed a big list of strategies the AI could use when play began. It has a series of neural network layers including "endgame solver", it took into account "mistakes" the AI's opponents made. The AI also looked for its own strategic weaknesses.

Outcomes

The AI, Libratus, took on four of the world's best Heads-Up No-Limit Texas Hold 'Em poker players at a Pennsylvania casino. After 120,000 hands, Libratus won with a lead of over $1.7 million in chips, winning a 20-day poker tournament. [2]

Surveillance and Marketing Human Behavior

Surveillance Tracking Planning and Unplanned Behavior

Industry Context

Surveillance technology is used to film movements and human behavior. This is used to detect anomalous behavior using the machine learning analysis.

The AI uses this metadata to build up a picture of how companies, departments and individual employees normally function, and flag anomalies in people's behavior in real time. The idea is that it could detect when someone might pose a security risk by stepping outside of their usual behavioral patterns.

Systems used

Data regular supply of employee metadata, including everything from the files you access and how often you look at them to when you use a key card at a company door.

AI uses this metadata to build up a picture of how companies, departments and individual employees normally function, and flag anomalies in people's behavior in real time.

Deep learning neural net is trained to analyze human behavior. Company https://www.statustoday.com/. Used to identify threats, improve productivity and communication and understand employee.

Outcomes

System could flag if an employee starts copying large numbers of files they don't normally view, for example. Are they just going about their job, or could they be stealing confidential information?

Catch employee actions that could accidentally cause a security breach, like responding to a phishing email or opening an attachment laden with malware. AI can be used to track employee productivity however there are also concerns over privacy rights of employees.

"If people know they're being monitored, they can change their behavior to game the system," Phil Legg at the University of the West of England says flagging unusual behavior will never catch every security risk. [3]

Security and Identity Management

Physiological Pattern Recognition of Human Movement for Identity Management

Industry context

VAuth device, developed at the University of Michigan in Ann Arbor, uses an accelerometer hidden in a pair of glasses or earphones or worn around the neck. The accelerometer measures vibrations created as the wearer speaks. An algorithm then compares those vibrations with the audio signal received by the digital assistant. If the vibrations and the audio match, then the voice command is received as normal. If not, the assistant is blocked from responding.

Systems used

IoT tracking and Machine Learning algorithm to record accelerometer movements of owner voice speech physiology compared to potential theft or mimicry.

VAuth was tested with 18 people saying 30 different commands. It was able to match speech vibrations with audio signals 97% of the time, and did not act on commands issued by someone other than the device owner.

Outcomes

Voice assistants can be activated by white noise containing hidden voice commands unintelligible to humans.

Authenticating a user's commands would prevent this problem and could also protect against methods of "hacking" a voice-controlled device.

Combining this technology with biometric voice identification, says Sorber, could be the best way to secure many wireless devices. "The more mobile and untethered our computing environment gets, the harder it is to really do a great job of securing things,"

Google's "trusted voice" feature unlocks the phone only after matching the voice command against a biometric profile of its owner's voice. However, there are ways around this by impersonating or playing recordings of the owner's voice to the device. [4]

Knowledge Advice and Guidance

Virtual Assistant—Chat Bot to Answer Human Subject Queries

Industry context

NTT Resonant is a chat bot, which operates the Goo web portal and search engine, created a system called Oshi-el to answer people's relationship questions, like a virtual agony aunt.

Systems used

Deep neural net Trained their algorithm using almost 190,000 questions and 770,000 answers from the company's Oshiete goo forum.

Focus on this genre of query as "non-factoid" questions are difficult for AI to address.

Outcomes

Based on this data, they came up with a generic structure for answers that includes a sentence showing sympathy, a suggested solution to the problem, an additional comment and a note of encouragement.

The Oshi-el AI then selects and combines appropriate sentences to use from a database based on the words used in the question. To combat the ambiguous nature of certain words—"relationship", for example, could refer to a romantic situation or a business partnership—they use the category or title of each question to give the AI more context.

Answers tend to appear scripted such as "I can see this is a difficult time for you. I understand your feelings," says Oshi-el in response to a 30-year-old woman who finds herself stuck in a love triangle (the response has been translated from the original Japanese). The approach is limited, to be able to write a more comprehensive answer, an AI would need to actually "understand" the question [in the context of AI], so an AI can only grasp the very shallow surface of things. [5]

Healthcare

Medical Condition Assistant—Skin Cancer Cell Recognition

Industry context

In the UK, there are at least 100,000 diagnoses of skin cancer per year, of which 2500 people will die. Skin cancer is actually very treatable, but only if it's caught early and the signs are spotted by the eye of a trained dermatologist with a dermatoscope (a handheld microscope that offers low-level magnification). The five-year survival rate, if spotted at the earliest state, is around 97%—but that drops to 14% if detected late.

Systems used

Deep learning net with image recognition.

Stanford's algorithm was fed 129,450 training images of 2032 different skin diseases (broken into 735 groups to account for diseases with a small number of images). After learning what cancers typically look like, the software was tested against the clinicians in three areas: keratinocyte carcinoma classification, melanoma classification and melanoma classification using dermoscopy.

Computer scientists, dermatologists, and engineers at Stanford University taught the software to identify deadly and common types of skin cancers using a database of images. The results were compared to those from 21 expert clinicians and the algorithm was able to match their performance across 130,000 tests.

Outcomes

Stanford researchers use deep learning and image recognition to spot the warning signs of skin cancer with 91% accuracy [6].

Medical Condition Assistant—Wearable Continuous Wellbeing Monitoring

Industry context

Wearable tech can now detect when you're about to fall ill, simply by tracking your vital signs.

Stanford University research group used smart watch data could record unusually high heart rates, and sometimes higher skin temperatures, up to three days before the volunteers had symptoms of a cold or other infection.

"Once these wearables collect enough data to know what your normal baseline readings are, they can get very good at sensing when something's amiss," says Snyder. "We think that if your heart rate and skin temperature are elevated for about 2 hours, there's a strong chance you're getting sick."

Continuous tracking of your vital signs is more informative than having a doctor measure them once a year and comparing them with population averages, Snyder says. "Heart rate, for example, varies a lot so population averages don't tell you much," he says.

Systems used

A new wave of wearable sensors allows frequent and continuous measurements of body functions (physiology), including heart rate, skin temperature, blood oxygen levels, and physical activity. We investigated the ability of wearable sensors to follow physiological changes that occur over the course of a day, during illness and other activities. Data from these sensors revealed personalized differences in daily patterns of activities.

Outcomes

Snyder's team is now hoping to build algorithms that will enable smart-watches to notify wearers when they might be falling ill. "I'm predicting that your smartwatch will be able to alert you before you get sick, or confirm that you're sick if you're feeling a bit off," he says. "If your watch says you're getting something, you'll know to go lie down instead of going out drinking and dancing."

Questions raised over phycological impact of feedback on users may not prevent illness. Overall, these results indicate that the information provided by wearable sensors is physiologically meaningful and actionable. Wearable sensors are likely to play an important role in managing health. [7]

Knowledge Management Assistance in Medical Services

Industry context

IBM Watson has accumulated recognition in its ability to deliver precise and factual information through its algorithms such as natural language processing, hypothesis generation and dynamic learning [8]. Traditional computing systems rely heavily on structured data, whereas Watson's access to unstructured data means that it'll be able to differentiate between different kinds of information' [9]. Asking a query to Watson results in the AI segregating the question into different keywords, where it'll form a hypothesis and conducts several tests before providing an answer.

Systems Used

Deep neural nets, natural language processing

Outcomes

IBM Watson has now extended its services to the medical sector, where it has been providing its assistance in areas such as oncology, genomics, drug discovery and several other fields [10]. What makes Watson useful in this situation is that it is able to assist doctors & medical researchers with providing effective and immediate treatment for patients. As depicted in [11]. A patient with a severe heart condition runs a very active lifestyle, which can have an adverse effect on their health; to avoid this, doctors provide a query to IBM Watson, where the AI will analyse the patient's medical and family histories and compare it with other patients within the Watson cloud. Through this analysis, the AI will be able to formulate an immediate treatment for the patient's condition, ensuring that they can retain an active lifestyle without being susceptible to the condition [11]. Watson is a fundamental asset for the medical industry, in that treatment can be devised immediately and doctors are continuously informed about the patient's condition through the Watson cloud.

Asset Condition Monitoring Maintenance

Building Condition Monitoring and Maintenance Control

Industry context

Software firm CGnal, based in Milan, Italy, analyzed a year's worth of data from the heating and ventilation units in an Italian hospital. Sensors are now commonly built into heating, ventilation and air conditioning units, and the team had records such as temperature, humidity and electricity use, relating to appliances in operating theatres and first aid rooms as well as corridors.

Systems used

CGnal used a deep neural network and trained the machine learning algorithm on data from the first half of 2015, looking for differences in the readings of similar appliances. They then tested it on data from the second half of the year—could it predict faults before they happened?
  Historical asset actual performance data.
  Connection to existing telemetry [remote sensing] datasets.
  Comparisons to real-time current asset performance.
  Remotely control asset usage and state.
  Condition geolocation context optimization.

Outcomes

The system predicted 76 out of 124 real faults, including 41 out of 44 where an appliance's temperature rose above tolerable levels, with a false positive rate of 5%. [12]

Surveillance and Security Counter Measures

Monitoring Social Networks for Fake News

Industry context

While the percentage of misinformation is relatively small, we have much more work ahead on our roadmap. Normally we wouldn't share specifics about our work in progress, but given the importance of these issues and the amount of interest in this topic, I want to outline some of the projects we already have underway:

- Stronger detection. The most important thing we can do is improve our ability to classify misinformation. This means better technical systems to detect what people will flag as false before they do it themselves.
- Easy reporting. Making it much easier for people to report stories as fake will help us catch more misinformation faster.
- Third party verification. There are many respected fact checking organizations and, while we have reached out to some, we plan to learn from many more.
- Warnings. We are exploring labeling stories that have been flagged as false by third parties or our community, and showing warnings when people read or share them.
- Related articles quality. We are raising the bar for stories that appear in related articles under links in News Feed.
- Disrupting fake news economics. A lot of misinformation is driven by financially motivated spam. We're looking into disrupting the economics with ads policies like the one we announced earlier this week, and better ad farm detection.
- Listening. We will continue to work with journalists and others in the news industry to get their input, in particular, to better understand their fact checking systems and learn from them.

Systems used

Machine learning text pattern recognition
Sources pattern recognition—economic spamming and bot automation
Human social media likes, shares behavior pattern recognition

Human 3rd party verification services

Governance Algorithm policy management—acceptable usage on page and link through pages

Outcomes

Facebook is launching an educational tool as part of measures it is taking to counter fake news.

For three days, an ad will appear at the top of users' news feeds linking to advice on "how to spot fake news" and report it.

The campaign, which will be promoted in 14 countries, is "designed to help people become more discerning readers", the social media firm said.

But experts questioned whether the measure would have any real impact.

"Until Facebook stops rewarding the architects of fake news with huge traffic, this problem will just get worse," Tom Felle, a lecturer in digital journalism at City University told the BBC.

From Friday, users who click on Facebook's ad will be redirected to its help centre, where they will see a list of 10 tips for identifying false stories. [13, 14]

Automobile Engineering

Racing Car Generative Design

Industry Context

The Hack Rod team desired to develop an optimal chassis for their new racing car. They rigger up a chassis of an existing car (and the racing car driver) with hundreds of sensors, thereby creating a "digital central nervous system" for the car and driver that would eventually provide readings on the physical forces affecting both the car and the driver.

Systems used

Engineering design software (Autodesk Dreamcatcher), network of sensors, machine learning techniques.

Outcomes

They periodically captured the readings from on the race car sensors, and once complete, the data was fed into the Autodesk Dreamcatcher software, which was subsequently used to generate a new chassis design.

Once a final design for the chassis had been selected, the design is handed off to the Autodesk Design Graph that encapsulates a machine learning search capability that makes recommendations for the parts list for the selected design, such as nuts, bolts, and other components to match the design requirements.

According to Bob Pete, the author of the article [15]

Generative design is creating complex engineering results that were previously not able to be manufactured. The rapid progress in the advanced manufacturing space is now allowing for this complexity to be produced.

Furniture Design

The Elbo Chair

Industry Context

The purpose of this project was to define the constraints (requirements) for a chair, such as it should be 18 inches off the floor and capable of supporting a person weighing 300 pounds.

Typically, such requirements would be handed over to the designer who would mull it over for a while and decide how it should look, the materials to be used and manner in which it should be constructed. Nevertheless, the emerging field of generative design changes all that, now the process involves handing over large amounts of data to the software, in this case Autodesk.

Systems used

Engineering design software (Autodesk Dreamcatcher), machine learning techniques.

Outcomes

A modern Danish mid-century modern style chair.

The chair was created by Arthur Harsuvanakit and Brittany Presten of Autodesk's generative design lab—nevertheless, they did not design it, because they collaborated with Dreamcatcher, Autodesk's generative design CAD system. They fed the software a digital 3-D model of a chair and the Lambda Chair from design studio Berkeley Mills.

The software churned out hundreds of designs, optimizing as it went. It shaved dead weight and adjusted joint placement to improve load-bearing abilities, creating thinner, more intricate structures. "It just gets bonier as the iterations go higher," Harsuvanakit says. "It's cool to let it go too far—some of it looks like bug skeletons to me." [16]

Aeronautical Engineering Design

Partition that Separates the Crew's Section from the Rest of the Cabin

Industry context

The partitions used to separate the cabin crew's workstation from the rest of the cabin is a major engineering conundrum, especially to the aircraft manufacturers, who desire these partitions to be as small and light as humanly possible.

To make the task a little more challenging, because the cabin crew sit on foldout chairs affixed to that partition, and therefore the partition must support this weight.

Systems used

Engineering design software (Autodesk Dreamcatcher), machine learning techniques and 3D Printing

Outcomes

Cheaper, stronger, aircraft partitions.

European aircraft manufacturer Airbus collaborated with Autodesk to rethink the design of these partitions. Its new partition was 3-D printed using some wild new algorithms based on slime mold and bone growth. The new partition weighs in at just 66 pounds significantly lighter than Airbus's original partitions that weighed 143 pounds apiece.

"Our goal was to reduce the weight by 30 percent, and we altogether achieved weight reduction by 55 percent," says Bastian Schaefer, innovation manager at Airbus. "And we're right at the beginning." [17]

Moreover, because the designs created by the generative design software are so complex, classical manufacturing techniques were out of the question when it came to actually building the part. This is a wonderful example of where a computer-generated design has to be created by using software to 3D print the part—the fusion of the two technologies is critical to generative design's success.

Benjamin says the design principles are similar to those used by the Autodesk Within Medical program, which uses generative algorithms to create implants for reconstructive surgeries.

Building Architecture Design

Building Design and Aesthetics

Industry context

The design of building structures using machine learning algorithm to compute blended ideas from nature and construction mathematics to create new architecture designed with new physical and aesthetic characteristics not possible by human physical design skills alone. The result is termed generative components.

Systems used

Engineering design software (Autodesk Dreamcatcher), machine learning techniques.

Outcomes

Design of buildings previously thought unimaginable.

Generative design is very much in the spirit of machine learning, the best description of this comes from Lars Hesselgren, who once said,

Generative design is not about designing a building, it's about designing the system that designs a building. [18]

Lars Hesselgren is the director of research at PLP Architects [19].

Well-known examples of generative design being used in the world of architecture is the Beijing National Stadium and the Beijing National Aquatics Centre – better known as the Bird's Nest and the Water Cube, respectively were designed with the help of generative design.

We built version 34 because it was better. But version 1 would have worked fine. Generative design allowed us to get better results in a fraction of the time.

Said J Parrish, the former director of ArupSport, who provided engineering and design services for both of Beijing's major Olympic venues. Parrish also helped pioneer the rapid prototyping face of generative design.

Other leading architects and engineers who use software based on generative design (or the Bentley's version of it, namely, GenerativeComponents®) include Arup, Buro Happold, Foster + Partners, Grimshaw Architects, HOK, Kohn Pedersen Fox, Morphosis, and SHoP Architects. [20]

Automated Transport

Self-Driving Automobile

Industry Context

The Connected car is a great example of an ecosystem of lots of different types of machine learning, neural nets, image recognition, actuators, sensors, and robotics all in one platform.

It has many systems and subsystems that are a kind of modularity of components that provide different functions that are managed with different priorities to control the vehicle.

It illustrates how these different types of machine intelligence can be applied to different problems and opportunities and to combined this into an overall working system of systems to ultimately achieve assisted driving to full driverless cars.

Systems Used

Artificial intelligence has been around for a very long time. The basic techniques have developed but also there has been a lot of technological innovations. For example, the ability to have auto-scaling cloud based computing power means that anybody, large or small, could spin up a vast number of CPU instances and run a very big machine learning algorithm on large datasets, then shut it all down again and do it for hardly any cost. Five years ago if you tried to do that you would have to buy an awful lot of tin and stick it in a data center, this just would not have been feasibility from a practical perspective. Many more people have now got access to the kind of computing power you need to actually show progress in some of these AI techniques. Another aspect is the increasing ease with which it is possible to exploit GPUs and massive parallel processing of those cores, which were previously just in the realms of computer games and computer graphics that have now been added to cloud platforms as a computing resource at scale.

Solving the "in-th-car" problem is simply much more difficult than initially thought. The type of problems that appear in self-driving cars, are dissimilar to popular examples we have encountered thus far. We may be able to use deep learning to play GO and Chess with lots of possible variations of the game but the boundaries and rules are known and will not be going outside. If you are given an unexpected route in a game are minor in comparison to a car where there are other road users that may not obey the law, pedestrians may walk out in front of you and other possible events. The kind of intelligence that is needed in self-driving cars is going to be an ensemble approach. This will need lots of different AI techniques and algorithms, no single one of them is going to be sufficient for an autonomous vehicle, we are not at a point where you can simply train a giant neural net to drive a car. It is going to be many different kinds of AI working together to keep in check each other to make some of this work. There is massive onboard sensor ability and processing ability, many vehicles, such as the ones from Tesla need to install a level of hardware on their as standard that would be capable of the software for autonomous vehicle, even more than they do now, to potentially drive from A to B all the way. It is autonomous vehicle ready in that they do not have software that is sufficiently advanced, they can deliver that software over the air (OTA) and enable those cars to be self-driving later on, at least that is the theory.

Outcomes

Artificial intelligence is certainly becoming one of the most invested in technologies. There are many mergers and acquisitions especially within the automotive domain. Ford announced in February 2017 that it was investing 1 Billion US dollars in "Argo AI" within the next five years, which is a startup formed in December of 2016 primarily focused on developing software for autonomous vehicle technology. Argo AI will become a subsidiary of Ford and will have its own board of directors and operate as an independent unit. The Argo AI initiative is considered to be part of Ford's self-driving car project, and the plan appears to be the mass production of an autonomous vehicle ready for car sharing in 2021. There is much change in the automotive industry, and vehicle manufacturers need to move quickly to adopt connected car technologies, as highlighted in a recent BearingPoint consulting thought leadership review of industry impact [21].

Crowd Sourcing Intelligence

Industry context

There is a lot of processing in the car, but then you have got smart cities and integration so the car sensors become extended. It can make use of information that "street furniture" can provide and that give things that are specific events such as the traffic light is about to go red. Or it can look at a range of data such as a high volume of traffic ahead and identify an alternative less busy road so it can optimize its route overall. Mark Burnett at Bearing point said

> I think this ecosystem is a very important concept, its also important to recognize that this menagerie of different types of AI data processing in the car it can extend to the cloud and there will also be this crowd sourcing. If a car in front has already put on the brakes, that probably should be relayed to other vehicle to vehicle communications or vehicle to edge communications so the concept of edge and fog computing become important.

There are also cars that are connected with telematics of some sort, mostly they are connected to a particular cloud based platform for telematics services. When you need fast response and the communication maybe between vehicles is available, it makes much more sense to use this edge based computing that could be processing actually in the telecoms mast or near by or one or two tiers back, and the data may never need to go back to the cloud or traditional client-server model, it may be just some routing from local cache crowd sourced information.

Systems Used

Crowd sourcing, IoT sensor networks, smart road signs, cloud computing and edge network computing.

Outcomes

Crowd sourced collaborative vehicles all helping each other.

Tesla update 6.0 was an example similar to this in learning from a car's driving characteristics to record the GPS location and then adjust the pneumatic suspension and "remember" next time the car passing that same route to improve the driving experience. This data can be shared to other vehicles. Tesla update 8.1 provided integration with autopilot functions. [22, 23]

Energy and Utility Ecosystem Management

Artificial Intelligence Balance Between Supply & Demand

Industry Context

National Grid and Google DeepMind are intending to form a collaboration, due to the electricity network being constantly challenged with increasing demand, as National Grid spent around 'tens of billions of pounds' just to produce 330 TWh of energy in 2014. National Grid is hoping to integrate renewable energy to help support the increasing demand, but the intermittency from sources like wind and solar make it an increasing challenge for the network.

Systems Used

What DeepMind wishes to achieve with its AI system is to utilize *machine learning* techniques to help predict trends in demand & supply, and be able to reduce around 10% of the country's energy consumption without needing to add new infrastructure. The AI-company is also looking to assist National Grid in maximizing their use of renewable sources, ensuring that environmental impact can also be reduced [24].

Outcomes

'Ingesting data, predicting trends and suggesting solutions is perfectly suited to DeepMind's neural network expertise'; having an AI system for National Grid will be useful in the sense that it may be able to identify a greater number of solutions than its human grid operators. While this may be a potential relationship, National Grid is still in negotiations with DeepMind to see what type of service the AI-focused group can provide. The end goal for National Grid is to bring improvements to their performance, as well as maximize renewable energy usage and help consumers on their savings [25].

Intelligent Energy Assistant

Industry Context

Having the best service for electricity and gas ensures that consumers are able to receive better rewards and savings; however, the task of searching an energy provider is both tedious and time consuming. To help resolve this issue, MyWave Ltd have designed an intelligent assistant known as Myia, who searches and compares the energy market for better deals through an online questionnaire. Within the questionnaire, the customer will be required to provide their personal details and the details of the retailers they're currently associated with. While this may seem like a simple scenario, Myia seeks to continuously inform the consumer if a better service has been found. Another interesting aspect of Myia is that the consumer will not have to go through the same questions, as the AI will remember your set responses [26].

Systems Used

The main mechanism that Myia uses to suggest its solutions is machine learning, which'll be used to continuously analyze and predict trends in the market and recommend newly found solutions to the consumer base. Myia also monitors your energy bill, so if a change is detected, it will recommend a better service provider.

Outcomes

By launching the intelligent assistant in New Zealand, customers now have saved 10–15% on their energy bills, with hopes to provide the same service in other industries like insurance and retail [27].

Intelligent Robots Assessing the Health of Water Pipes

Industry Context

Water utilities in San Francisco are now receiving assistance in their assessment of water pipelines by sending an intelligent robot through inspected pipes. HiBot, the company behind this initiative, is looking to rectify the mistakes the water municipalities make in their replacement projects, as it is often the case of 'getting rid of perfectly functional pipes, while waiting too long on those primed to rupture' [28].

The company also believes that over 40% of the existing network can be saved and that a $400 million saving can be achieved as the utilities are estimated to spend around $1 trillion in just replacement.

Systems Used

The way HiBot operates is to send miniature robots into the pipelines, with a RFT sensor (Remote Field testing) & a camera fitted to the device.

The robot will analyze the pipe and validate the previous rating provided by the utility, based on its own analysis. The AI houses a significant amount of historical data, where it uses the machine learning algorithms to help predict pipe failures within the network, by incorporating a wide variety of factors such as soil characteristics, age and leakage histories.

Outcomes

The company believes the system can accurately predict future failures at 80–90% rate, ensuring more accurate models of failures can be provided [29].

Summary

From a general practitioner point of view is it is clear that artificial intelligence is still evolving, and that new theories and models to create training data to be able to pursue meaningful and useful machine intelligence. Whether self-driving cars will be truly computer only, or whether it will need human assistance is certainly open to debate. It is grounded in the notion that defining artificial intelligence from imitation of human tasks to more complex human and non-human tasks will be driven by the quality of models of computation. Clearly, specialized machine intelligence has made huge strides in the recent decades. While historically the expectation of artificial intelligence has been repeatedly exaggerated, it is the evolution of computing languages and systems models with sensors and data that will continue to address challenges in defining AI and approaches to using AI effectively.

Notes and References

1. W. Teahan J, Artifical Intelligence - Agents & Environments, Bookboon, 2010.
2. AI just won a poker tournament against professional players, 31 Jan 2017, New Scientist https://www.newscientist.com/article/2119815-ai-just-won-a-poker-tournament-against-professional-players/.
3. AI tracks your every move and tells your boss if you're slacking 30 Jan 2017, New Scientist https://www.newscientist.com/article/2119734-ai-tracks-your-every-move-and-tells-your-boss-if-youre-slacking/.
4. Voice-checking device stops hackers hijacking your Siri or Alexa, 30 Jan 2017, New Scientist https://www.newscientist.com/article/2119766-voice-checking-device-stops-hackers-hijacking-your-siri-or-alexa/.
5. AI agony aunt gives love advise online, 26 Jan 2017, New Scientist https://www.newscientist.com/article/2119347-ai-agony-aunt-learns-to-dole-out-relationship-advice-online/.
6. Stanford's new AI can recognize the warning signs of skin cancer as effectively as human dermatologists http://www.alphr.com/science/1005233/stanford-s-new-ai-can-recognise-the-warning-signs-of-skin-cancer-as-effectively-as.
7. Digital Health: Tracking Physiomes and Activity Using Wearable Biosensors Reveals Useful Health-Related Information, PLOS Biology Journal Li et al Jan 12 2017 http://journals.plos.org/plosbiology/article?id=10.1371/journal.pbio.2001402.
8. D. Burrus, "What can Watson do for your company?," WIRED, 2017. [Online]. Available: https://www.wired.com/insights/2015/02/what-can-watson-do-for-your-company/. [Accessed 17 April 2017].
9. IBM Watson, "IBM Watson: How it Works," Youtube, 7 October 2014. [Online]. Available: https://www.youtube.com/watch?v=_Xcmh1LQB9I&t=131s. [Accessed 17 April 2017].
10. IBM Watson, "IBM Watson on Health," IBM, 2017. [Online]. Available: https://www.ibm.com/watson/health [Accessed 24 April 2017].
11. IBM Watson Think Academy, "How it Works: IBM Watson Health," Youtube, 20 May 2015. [Online]. Available: https://www.youtube.com/watch?v=ZPXCF5e1_HI. [Accessed 17 April 2017].
12. Smart buildings predict when critical systems are about to fail, 21 Jan 2017 New Scientist https://www.newscientist.com/article/2118499-smart-buildings-predict-when-critical-systems-are-about-to-fail/.

13. Managing Fake News on social media, Mark Zuckerberg, Facebook founder, 19 Nov 2016 https://www.facebook.com/zuck/posts/10103269806149061.

14. Facebook to tackle fake news with educational campaign, April, 2017 BBC http://www.bbc.co.uk/news/technology-39517033.

15. Where VR Meets the Road: How GPUs Power 'Hack Rod', World's First AI-Generated Car, https://blogs.nvidia.com/blog/2016/07/26/hack-rod-car-ai/.

16. So. Algorithms Are Designing Chairs Now, https://www.wired.com/2016/10/elbo-chair-autodesk-algorithm/.

17. Airbus' Newest Design Is Based on Bones and Slime Mold https://www.wired.com/2015/12/airbuss-newest-design-is-based-on-slime-mold-and-bones/.

18. Generative Design Is Changing the Face of Architecture, http://www.cadalyst.com/cad/building-design/generative-design-is-changing-face-architecture-12948.

19. http://www.plparchitecture.com/lars-hesselgren.html.

20. GenerativeComponents® Advanced design software for architects and engineers, https://www.bentley.com/~/asset/14/3827.ashx.

21. OEMs and connected-cars: time to seize the connected future. BearingPoint 2017 https://www.bearingpoint.com/en-gb/our-success/thought-leadership/oems-and-connected-cars-time-to-seize-the-connected-future/.

22. https://www.tesla.com/blog/software-v60.

23. https://www.tesla.com/en_GB/software.

24. S. Anthony, "DeepMind in Talks with National Grid to reduce UK energy use by 10%," Ars Technica UK, 14 March 2017. [Online]. Available: https://arstechnica.co.uk/information-technology/2017/03/deepmind-national-grid-machine-learning/?comments=1. [Accessed 11 April 2017].

25. S. S, "Google's Deepmind wants to cut 10% off the entire UK's energy bill," Business Insider UK, 13 March 2017. [Online]. Available: http://uk.businessinsider.com/google-deepmind-wants-to-cut-ten-percent-off-entire-uk-energy-bill-using-artificial-intelligence-2017-3. [Accessed 20 April 2017].

26. MyWave Ltd, "FAQs - MyWave abd Myia," MyWave, [Online]. Available: https://myia.ai/FAQs.html. [Accessed 12 April 2017].

27. O. Smith, "Meet Myia: AI that's got the energy giants flustered," The Memo, 29 September 2016. [Online]. Available: https://www.thememo.com/2016/09/29/meet-myia-ai-thats-got-the-energy-giants-flustered/. [Accessed 29 September 2016].

28. D. Terdiman, "How Robots And AI Could Save American Water Utilities Half A Trillion Dollars," Fast Company, 24 April 2017. [Online]. Available: https://www.fastcompany.com/3068423/how-robots-and-ai-could-save-american-water-utilities-half-a-trillion-dolla. [Accessed 18 April 2017].

29. HiBot, "HiBot: Home Page," HiBot, USA, 2017. [Online]. Available: http://www.hibot-usa.com/. [Accessed 18 April 2017].

12

Conclusion

In earlier chapters we have introduced various technologies that fuse together and emerge as the 4th Industrial Revolution, it is very important to take a holistic stance on this issue and consider the impact these technologies have when used in combination rather than as individuals.

One of the core technologies driving the 4th industrial revolution is machine learning, the current incarnation of which became highly noticeable around 2000, according to the executive chairman of Alphabet, Dr. Eric Schmidt who recently stated [1]:

> I being prejudiced by my years in the AI-Winter, when I first saw the involving vision and speech, and we used it in our ads, I said oh-you-know, it won't scale it won't really generalize because these are mathematical that are simple improvements in good engineering - and I've been proven completely wrong

This comment should not be taken lightly, given that Eric Schmidt is one of the top technology executives today who not only has a Ph.D. in Computer Science, but also a very successful career history in executive management.

Nevertheless, it is true that AI has a patchy history, it began in early 1940s with lots of predictions and promises that were often optimistic and underestimated the complex and difficult nature of the problems on hand. However, the current multilayer neural network models have adopted a different approach to the ones classically used in computer science and AI. This time the motivation and impetus came from the realm of cognitive and neural science. The idea here is that we do not program these kinds of machines

© The Author(s) 2018
M. Skilton and F. Hovsepian, *The 4th Industrial Revolution*,
https://doi.org/10.1007/978-3-319-62479-2_12

by telling them what to do each step of the way, but rather we instruct the machine how to lean to solve problems for itself.

This approach is made possible by the convergence of increasing computing power, big data and machine learning, which are reshaping the world in which we live. We are beginning to see machine intelligence being embedded into many devices and even aspects of our own lives, and as this technology evolves it will become the defining technology of the 4th Industrial Revolution, much as steam was for the 1st, electricity for the 2nd, and the microprocessor for the 3rd Industrial Revolutions.

This new generation of AI is therefore quite different compared with anything else we have seen before, in many respects one can say that we have finally began to build the dream that Alan Turing had when he talked of the "Child Machine", that we could teach rather than program. We must therefore begin to think more in terms of cognition and neuroscience, rather than in terms of algorithms that one could consider as representations of ideas that came out of first order logic.

We must now consider ways that will allow us to determine which are the more capable machines given that we are no longer dealing with classical computers, but rather a new breed of cognitively enhanced machines. For example, when you use Google speech or Google photos, in many cases you are using neural networks that are 11 or 12 layers deep.

Alan Kay [2] captured the essence of the changes that we are facing, when he said "… of course the future isn't about data at all, it's about meaning". Meaning is a concept that rightly belongs to the world of cognition, and is a much harder concept to grapple with when compared to those we are accustomed to seeing within the world of computation. In keeping with these thoughts, we would like to introduce a concept called the Cognitive Horizon.

Cognitive Horizon

In order to set the scene for the remainder of this chapter we shall now introduce a concept first introduced by Rodriguez, et al. [3], who describe it as:

> Angler is a collaborative tool that aims to be a mental prosthetic for enhancing problem solving and decision analysis. It is grounded in methods such as Scenario Based Planning, or SBP, that deal with cognitive biases and uncertainty by extracting assumptions held by a group, and expanding the range of deductions created by those assumptions, *the cognitive horizon.*

and also define it on their website [4].

> The *cognitive horizon* of a person or a group can be loosely defined as the transitive closure of possible deductions starting from an initial set of assumptions. This horizon can be narrowed by competing or contradicting hypotheses.

While Rodriguez et al. are focused on human collaboration, cognitive bias, and problem solving we believe that an extended version of this concept works well for artificial entities such as intelligent agents, where the Cognitive Horizon is used to capture the cognitive limitations of such a system.

> <u>Definition:</u> The ***Cognitive Horizon*** of a system (be it an individual or group of individuals, natural or artificial) is the transitive closure of all possible deductions starting from an initial set of statements that are assumed true.

The cognitive horizon therefore, is the sum total of all knowledge that a system can potentially possess at any instant in time—namely, facts together with the result of all reasoning performed on the set of all such statements. In a formal setting, this would be the collection of all theories known by such an entity.

For example, suppose we create a system (let us call it "System-one") whose only assumptions are the basics of arithmetic (formally, the axioms of arithmetic), then the only deductions this system is able to infer will be statements about arithmetic—and the transitive closure of this system are all the true statements regarding arithmetic. Now consider a second system ("System-two") whose initial statements include not just those of arithmetic, but also all those related to Euclidean geometry. This second system is not only able to infer new statements about arithmetic, but also new statements about geometry, and its transitive closure is the collection of all true statements of arithmetic together with all the true statements of geometry. Moreover, the Cognitive Horizon of System-two is much bigger than the Cognitive Horizon of System-one, because it includes all the true statements that System-one is able to generate.

One important point to note is that by adding a new set of assumptions to the system, it not only increases its cognitive horizon by the transitive closure of the new axioms, which opens a new window of possibility to where the system is able to use combinations of the base assumptions. One can paraphrase this by saying, the whole is greater than the sum of its parts.

In this framework, *innovations* may be thought of as discovering new truths from known theories, whereas *inventions* are new theories, new facts

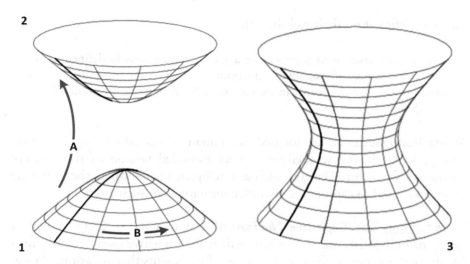

Fig. 12.1 Cognitive Horizon

that were not known before, nor could they have been deduced from other known theories - they often involve a leap in imagination producing a new theory.

We can see this more easily using Fig. 12.1, for the case on the left the cognitive horizon is represented by the surface labeled '1'. *Innovations* in this case is represented by the blue arrow labeled 'B', which represents a shift in context for the particular perspective or idea. Notice that the arrow only moves a point from one region of the surface to another, and is unable to move a given point to the surface labeled '2', furthermore, all such movements (for example the one indicated by the red line) stay on this surface and represent another innovation.

The purple arrow labeled 'A', which extends the cognitive horizon to a completely new surface hereto unknown to the intelligent system, represents an *invention*—a paradigm-shift rather than a shift in context.

In the beginning innovations may take place on either surface, after some time the system begins to assimilate the new concepts and is able to transgress between the two surfaces, eventually the surface on the right (labeled as '3') emerges. New innovations (represented by the red line) are able to take ideas and shift them to a different context, which now includes regions of what used to be a disconnected surface and only amenable via an invention.

One can now begin to partially order various cognitively enhanced systems by considering their associated cognitive horizons, which not only measures what the system's cognitive capabilities are today, but also what it may be capable of tomorrow—in relation to another such system. As a simple example, a system that is only capable of performing arithmetic as well as geometry has a bigger cognitive horizon compared to one that is only capable of performing arithmetic tasks.

A very nice example of how an inventor grapples with the new ideas, and finally is able to cross the chasm to a disconnected cognitive horizon is given by Carver Mead who describes his experience of discovering new techniques and technologies, Mead [5].

One can extend the cognitive horizon, in a different dimension by not simply considering true facts that are either base assumptions or inferences made from them, but by also allowing statements that are *justified true beliefs*, which some philosophers call 'knowledge'. Carver Mead [6] talks about beliefs, imagination and the possible, which human beings have the innate ability to create and manipulate, and which provides them with the capability to transgress the chasm that exists between disconnected cognitive horizons.

Innovation Matrix

Obviously many AI projects are either innovative or invention in nature, and therefore it would be useful to have some kind of framework for deciding the kind of problem one is attempting to solve, and therefore the kind of resources that might be need to achieve those goals.

For example, as Alan Kay explains [7]:

Innovation is taking an idea into the marketplace, invention is what happened at XEROX Parc

We used some of the concepts discussed by Alan Kay to form the following definition:

To invent is to create something entirely new, something that did not exist before, whereas to innovate is to take an existing concept and make it better, or to take an existing concept into the marketplace.

There is a big difference between a random brainstorm and a concerted effort, and therefore we can capture the various kinds of innovation by using

Table 12.1 4 different types of innovation

Problem definition	Well defined	Breakthrough innovation (Mavericks, Skunk works Open innovation)	Sustaining innovation (Roadmapping, R&D Labs, Engineering, Acqusitions)
	Not well defined	Basic research (Research divisions, Academic partnerships, Conferences)	Disruptive innovation (VC Model, Innovation labs, Launchpads)
		Not well defined	Well defined
		Domain definition	

the following four categories that appears in an article by Greg Satell [8] (Table 12.1).

This categorization is explained by Satell as follows:

- **Basic research** rarely leads directly to new products or services, many corporations invest serious money into it.

  This is typically the kind of work that is undertaken by those working within a university or commercial R&D facility. The problems are often unclear and ill-defined, and it is not clear what kind of outcome is expected from these kinds of projects, because primarily the point of such projects is to discover how things work.

- **Sustaining innovation** is probably the most common in the corporate world and is often referred to as engineering rather than science. Like basic research, much of this is done by internal R&D labs.

  This is Apple Corporation's sweet-spot, it is the kind of innovation that Apple excels at, namely projects where there is a clearly defined problem and a reasonably good understanding of how to solve it.

- **Disruptive innovation** is particularly tricky because you don't know it until you see it and sometimes its value isn't immediately clear. That's why venture capital firms expect the vast majority of their investments to fail.

  Clayton Christensen introduced the concept of disruptive innovation in his classic book The Innovator's Dilemma. These tend to be new approaches to old products and services.

- **Breakthrough Innovation** Often, a particular field has trouble moving forward because they need a new approach. That's why breakthroughs often come from newcomers.

Thomas Kuhn called this 'revolutionary science' because it involves a *paradigm shift*. In this case, the problem is well defined, but the path to the solution is unclear, usually because those involved in the domain have hit a wall.

We like to think of *"**Breakthrough Innovation**"* as *"**Invention**"*, primarily because there appears to be a qualitative difference between an invention (paradigm shift) and an innovation (shift in context)—as described in the previous section on cognitive horizons.

Therefore, we can use an Innovation Matrix, to classify various organizations. For example, Apple would be considered an example of an organization within the Sustaining Innovation category. Google would be classified the category of Disruptive Innovation, whereas "parc" (formerly known as XEROX Parc) would be classified in the Basic Research category. While this somewhat of a coarse classification, it nevertheless helps in determining the nature of the project under consideration and the kind of resources (and associated timelines) that may be necessary to achieve a successful conclusion for the project.

One must not underestimate the effort, funding and people that may easily be consumed by an AI project for a very long time. For example, neural networks were a concept that began in the 1940s, then later revisited by the likes of Marvin Minsky and Seymour Papert in the 1960s. Geoffrey Hinton and in team worked through the so-called AI winter during the 1980s and we are now just beginning to see the fruits of the culminated efforts starting in the early 2000s.

Notwithstanding, it is important to mention that many of the systems today have already been industry proved, and despite the common hype that typically surrounds AI many of these systems are not only in use today, but have been part of our society for the last couple of decades. For example, we have been using neural network technologies to perform automatic recognition of handwritten checks on behalf of banks all over the world [9].

Four Leadership Principles and the Issue of Ethics and Jobs

In a recent article, Klaus Schwab [10] begin his article with the following profound thought:

> Every day we see the emergence of new technologies. And every day we see a widening gap between progress and society's ability to cope with its consequences. Whether it is an impending shift in the nature of work as technology changes production systems, or the ethical implications of reengineering what it means to be human, the changes we see around us threaten to overwhelm us if we cannot collaborate to understand and direct them.

and he proposes four principles that he believes should guide our policy and practice as we progress further into this revolution:

1. focus on systems rather than technologies, because the important considerations will be on the wide-reaching changes to business, society and politics rather than technologies for their own sake.
2. empower our societies to master technologies and act to counter a fatalistic and deterministic view of progress. Otherwise, there is no room for optimism and positive transformation, and society's agency is nullified.
3. we need to prioritize futures by design rather than default. Collaboration between all stakeholders must play a central role in how we integrate these transformative technologies. Otherwise, our future will be delivered by default.
4. focus on key values as a feature of new technologies, rather than as a bug. Technologies used in a way that increase disparity, poverty, discrimination and environmental damage work against the future we seek. For the investment in these technologies to be justifiable, they must bring us a better world, not one of increased insecurity and dislocation.

and in conclusion Schwab states:

> The Fourth Industrial Revolution and the systemic changes it will usher in emphasize more than ever the critical need for collaborative engagement around increasingly complex and fast-moving issues.

With regard to jobs, there are many predictions, including one by Peter Diamandis [11]:

> … in the next ten years 40% of today's fortune 500 companies will no longer exist

And in a different article, he states [12]:

In 2013, Dr. Carl Benedikt Frey of the Oxford Martin School estimated that 47% of jobs in the US are "at risk" of being automated in the next 20 years.

The figure was recently verified by McKinsey & Company, who suggests 45% of jobs today will be automated with exponential technologies, such as machine learning, artificial intelligence, robotics and 3D printing.

The concept is called technological unemployment, and most careers, from factory workers and farmers to doctors and lawyers, are likely to be impacted. The impact will likely be even more severe in the developing world.

Most leaders within the AI community, including the leading Artificial Intelligence scientist and director of research at Google, who literally wrote the book on Artificial Intelligence, is also worried about the elimination of many jobs. In a recent interview, he stated:

> "I don't buy into the killer robot [theory]," he told CNBC this week. The real worry is how to prepare for the mass elimination of jobs that is surely coming, he said. "I certainly see that there will be disruptions in employment … we've already seen a lot of change, that's going to continue," Norvig said in an interview, before a lecture on machine learning at the Stevens Institute of Technology. [13]

Schwab [14] once again highlights the far-reaching implications of current disruptions to business models and for jobs, and recommends a concerted effort by all the stakeholders. Moreover, he provides a description for the drivers of change for this disruption:

> According to many industry observers, we are today on the cusp of a Fourth Industrial Revolution. Developments in previously disjointed fields such as artificial intelligence and machine learning, robotics, nanotechnology, 3D printing and genetics and biotechnology are all building on and amplifying one another. Smart systems—homes, factories, farms, grids or entire cities— will help tackle problems ranging from supply chain management to climate change.

Many complex questions have emerged over the last few years, regarding our society of human beings, such as questions regarding ethics and well-being of the society when considered as a whole rather than the well-being of an individual member of that society. It is clear that much debate is needed before we, as human beings, decide on the collective form our society will take in the near future.

AI and Machine Learning Driving Inventions in Hardware

There are a number of contenders in this space, however, the two main ones are Quantum Computing and Neuromorphic Computing—both of which we have described in Chap. 2. Neuromorphic computing is a new and novel universal model for computation that is closely aligned with the natural structure of a neural network. Moreover, it is an event-driven distributed architecture that results in very low power consumption, which added to its ability to scale easily makes this a desirable processing component for many researchers within the AI field.

> Neuromorphic computing is anticipated to gain momentum owing to the increasing demand for artificial intelligence. Artificial intelligence is extensively used in nonlinear controls & robotics, language processing, translation & chatterbots, and computer vision & image processing, among others. [15]

There are a number of organizations working on products specifically aimed at implementing and deploying neural network models that were mentioned in the section on Neuromorphic Computing in Chap. 2.

The main alternative hardware architectures include:

- Google's TPU
- Various flavors of chips from Nvidia [16] and [17], whose CEO recently announced that Nvidia will be spending most of its $2.5B R&D budget on developing hardware for AI applications.

This is quite different compared to the 3rd Industrial Revolution, where hardware was the focus for the industry, and software was developed at a later stage, making it particularly difficult task because some of the features that may have been omitted meant that the resulting software was both fragile and failed to scale properly.

Final Comment

It is prudent to re-emphasize that the drivers for the 4th Industrial Revolution are not individual technologies, but the fusion of a number of advanced technologies together with novel problem solving mindsets and approaches, which are likely to have a significant impact on businesses and society.

For example, generative design combined with machine intelligence techniques by themselves will generate novel design, nevertheless, these designs are far too complex to manufacture using conventional techniques—and therefore the additive manufacturing techniques (such as 3D printing) play a critical role in creating the final product.

The 4th Industrial Revolution is now underway and we can expect to see many changes as new technologies mature and reach the marketplace; the ever increasing fusion of maturing technologies will enable humanity to solve problems that were considered impossible just a decade prior.

We have already mentioned a handful of examples where some organizations are using artificial intelligence techniques to solve problems for their particular business sector, ranging from health, education to legal and cyber security. Perceptive organizations are already investing in proof of concept studies to determine whether there are any opportunities to utilize not just AI technologies, but all the other technologies that are within the 4th Industrial Revolution umbrella. These technologies are likely to provide new market opportunities, as well as provide a competitive advantage within the sector in which the business operates.

The classical notions of data and numerical processing within the traditional enterprise architectures are still relevant to the organization today (Fig. 12.2), nevertheless, with time we are going to see many more advanced technologies reaching maturity and being deployed by various organizations and businesses across the globe. Many of these technologies are quite different to those we have become accustomed to, they require a different set of skills and a new mind-set to develop new solutions for problems that we could not solve with today's technology. It would be unwise for any individual, or organization, to retain the belief that even those within the technology sector can easily assimilate the newer technologies.

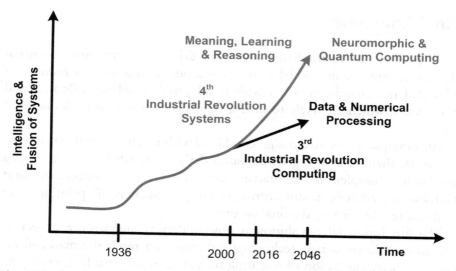

Fig. 12.2 Prediction for the divergent paths of the last two revolutions

This comment is pertinent in the case of software, where the paradigms have changed over the years from procedural to object-oriented and now the ever-increasing adoption of the reactive paradigm. Despite the efforts from major vendors and providers, who offer APIs and examples of how these newer systems may be utilized, they are often useful for those who already understand the underlying technology and who grasp a new way of thinking.

We live in what is possibly the most exciting period in human history, where the spectrum of opportunities are only constrained by our ability to image what may be possible given the technologies we have described, and those that are still within an R&D lab somewhere in the world.

One final remark that we would like to leave with the reader, who is currently looking at AI and asking themselves: how can I do what I already do except do it better, cheaper and faster? That is not the question you should be asking, the question you should be asking is: what can I do today that is fundamentally different to what I have been doing up until now?

Notes and References

1. The Great A.I. Awakening: A Conversation with Eric Schmidt, https://youtu.be/-UViiNq-dxk.
2. "Founder School Session: The Future Doesn't Have to Be Incremental", https://youtu.be/gTAghAJcO1o?t=2m47s.
3. Rodriguez, A., Boyce, T., Lowrance, J. and Yeh, E. (2005), Angler: collaboratively expanding your cognitive horizon, in International Conference on Intelligence Analysis Proceedings, Published by MITRE https://www.researchgate.net/publication/245408779_Angler_collaboratively_expanding_your_cognitive_horizon.
4. http://www.ai.sri.com/~angler/.
5. "How Things Really Work, a lecture by Gordon Bell and Carver Mead" https://youtu.be/zBpWkTETwD8?t=19m22s.
6. "How Things Really Work, a lecture by Gordon Bell and Carver Mead" https://youtu.be/zBpWkTETwD8?t=25m58s.
7. Alan Kay, 2013: Interview https://youtu.be/NY6XqmMm4YA?t=21m47s.
8. "4 Types of Innovation (and how to approach them)" http://www.digitaltonto.com/2012/4-types-of-innovation-and-how-to-approach-them/.
9. http://www.a2ia.com/en.
10. Four leadership principles for the Fourth Industrial Revolution, https://www.weforum.org/agenda/2016/10/four-leadership-principles-for-the-fourth-industrial-revolution/.
11. Peter Diamandis and Abundance In the Exponential Era | XMFG | Singularity University https://youtu.be/i6Gl_wQxi80.
12. If Robots and AI Steal Our Jobs, a Universal Basic Income Could Help, https://singularityhub.com/2016/12/13/if-robots-steal-our-jobs-a-universal-basic-income-could-help/.
13. Here's how one of Google's top scientists thinks people should prepare for machine learning, http://www.cnbc.com/2017/04/29/googles-peter-norvig-how-to-prepare-for-ai-job-losses.html.
14. The Future of Jobs Employment, Skills and Workforce Strategy for the Fourth Industrial Revolution http://www3.weforum.org/docs/Media/WEF_Future_of_Jobs_embargoed.pdf.
15. "Neuromorphic Computing Industry Insights" http://www.grandviewresearch.com/industry-analysis/neuromorphic-computing-market.
16. Nvidia CEO: Software Is Eating the World, but AI Is Going to Eat Software, https://www.technologyreview.com/s/607831/nvidia-ceo-software-is-eating-the-world-but-ai-is-going-to-eat-software/.
17. Why NVIDIA Is Building Its Own TPU, https://www.forbes.com/sites/moorinsights/2017/05/15/why-nvidia-is-building-its-own-tpu/#5503f5e347f4.

Appendix

Here is a list of languages and frameworks commonly used in machine learning.

Languages

See Table A.1.

It is common practice to prototype concepts in a language such as Python, then port the solution over to Java or C++ for deployment. Another recent development is the availability of cloud-based Machine-Learning-as-a-Service platforms that include:

- Amazon Machine Learning
- DataRobot
- Google Prediction
- IBM Watson, and
- Microsoft Azure Machine Learning.

© The Editor(s) (if applicable) and The Author(s) 2018
M. Skilton and F. Hovsepian, *The 4th Industrial Revolution*,
https://doi.org/10.1007/978-3-319-62479-2

Table A.1 Machine learning languages

Language	Comment
Python	Python is a general-purpose programming (and scripting) language, that has gained popularity over the recent years for building machine learning solutions, however, unlike R and MATLAB, the machine learning idioms are not part of the language itself, but available through libraries • *MunPy*, ideal for working with array structures, typically used in combination with SciPy • *Pandas*, for working with small datasets • *sqlite3*, interface for SQLite databases, commonly used for annotating and querying • *SymPy*, for undertaking symbolic mathematical tasks • *matplot* and *seaborn*, for *ploting* • *Django* and *Flask*, for developing web front-ends • *PyQt*, for creating desktop front-ends Although specialized machine learning libraries are available: • *scikit-learn*, which is a convenient API for basic machine learning tasks • *Theano*, for implementing machine learning algorithms that can distribute across many cores (such as the ones available in modern GPUs) • *TensorFlow*, for doing any kind of heavy-lifting The biggest advantage Python has over other comparable languages in this list, is that Python can be used to build complex end-to-end solutions
MATLAB/Octave	MATLAB is very popular within the research community, primarily because of its ability to handle complex mathematical expressions, symbolic computation and an extensive collection of toolboxes that offer support for different fields, ranging from computational biology to deep learning algorithms Octave is a free alternative, it has a less mature IDE and significantly fewer toolboxes
R	R is a purpose-built language intended for statistical computing, which provides easy access to a collection of machine learning algorithms through the CRAN repository

(continued)

Table A.1 (continued)

Language	Comment
Java/Scala	Many practicing software engineers are familiar with Java, and therefore it is common to find it being used due to its platform independence using JVMs
C/C++	In the case of embedded smart systems, that require the integration of devices and sensors, it often becomes necessary to use a language that is intended for developing low-level software, where computational efficiency and the efficient use of memory are critical. Machine learning libraries are available for this family of languages, however, they are quite specialized in nature • *Recommender*, is a C library for product recommendations/suggestions using collaborative filtering • *OpenCV*, is an excellent toolkit for developing any kind of machine vision software. It has C++/C, Python, Java, C# and MATLAB interfaces and supports Windows, Linux, Android and Mac OS/X • *CUDA*, contains a very fast C++/CUDA implementation of convolutional (Deep Learning) algorithms • *Kaldi*, is an open source toolkit for speech recognition using C++ (Apache 2.0 license)
Julia	*Julia* is a very new language that tries to combine the flexibility of high-level languages, such as MATLAB and Python, while maintaining the speed of a low-level language such as C
Go	Go is an open-standard language created by Google, and initially intended to implement Google's infrastructure, nevertheless, it is early days yet and we could easily see many projects using Go to implement machine learning solutions where historically they may have used Java/C++ • *Go Learn*, is an actively maintained, open-source (MIT License) machine learning package for Go
.NET	C#.Net if often utilized to build Computer Vision and general-purpose machine learning software on the Microsoft platform • *Emgu CV*, cross platform wrapper of OpenCV which can be compiled in Mono to run on Windows, Linux, Mac OS X, iOS and Android

(continued)

Table A.1　(continued)

Language	Comment
Family of Functional languages	There are a number of functional languages that are used within the realm of machine learning, including the second oldest programming language in existence today, namely, LISP **Common Lisp**: • *Mgl*, Neural networks (including Boltzmann Machines, Feed-forward and Recurrent Neural Networks), Gaussian Processes • *mgl-gpr*, for building solutions that may require Evolutionary algorithms • *cl-libsvm*, wrapper for Support Vector Machines **Clojure**: • *Clojure-openNLP*, is used for Natural Language Processing **Haskell**: • *LambdaNet*, is a purely functional neural network library implemented in Haskell, and useful for building rapid prototypes of neural networks in Haskell (open-source MIT License)

Frameworks

See Table A.2.

Table A.2　Machine learning frameworks

Software (license type)	Operating systems	Interface (language used to implement)	Comments/URL
Apache Singa (Apache 2.0)	Linux, Mac OS X, MS Windows	Python, C++, Java (C++)	Singa is focused on distributed deep learning, by partitioning the model and data, it can parallelize the training http://singa.incubator.apache.org/en/index.html

(continued)

Table A.2   (continued)

Software (license type)	Operating systems	Interface (language used to implement)	Comments/URL
Apache Spark/Mlib (Apache 2.0)	Standalone Deploy Mode (deploy Spark on a private cluster) Amazon EC2 Apache Mesos Hadoop YARN	Java, Scala, Python, R (Scala)	Mlib is a distributed machine learning framework that sits on top of Spark Core, which is almost 10x faster than disk-based implementations used by Apache Mahout and 100x faster than MapReduce. This is primarily due to the distributed memory-based Spark architecture that provides an interface for programming entire clusters with implicit data parallelism and fault-tolerance
Caffe (BSD License)	Linux, Mac OS X, MS Windows	Python, MATLAB (C++)	Deep learning framework geared towards image classification http://haffe.berkeleyvision.org
Deeplearning4j (Apache 2.0)	Linux, Mac OS X, Android, MS Windows	Java, Scala, Clojure, Python (Java)	Deeplearning4j allows for fast prototyping for non-researchers, and aims to be customizable at scale https://deeplearning4j.org
Encog (Apache 2.0)	Linux, Mac OSX, MS Windows	Java, C#, GPU/CUDA, C/C++ (Java, C++)	Encog is a machine learning framework that supports a variety of algorithms that support various kinds of neural networks http://www.heatonresearch.com/encog https://github.com/encog
H2O (Apache 2.0)	Linux, Mac OS X, MS Windows	Java, Scala, Python, R (Java)	H2O scales statistics, machine learning and math over Big Data https://www.h2o.ai

(continued)

Table A.2 (continued)

Software (license type)	Operating systems	Interface (language used to implement)	Comments/URL
Keras (MIT License)	Linux, Mac OS X, MS Windows	Python (Python)	A Theano based deep learning library for Theano and TensorFlow https://keras.io
Microsoft Cognitive Toolkit (MIT License)	MS Windows, Linux (OSX via Docker)	Python, C++, BrainScript (C++)	Previously known as CNTK, it is an open-source toolkit with a variety of use cases (projects) https://www.microsoft.com/en-us/research/product/cognitive-toolkit/
MATLAB (Proprietary)	Linux, Mac OS X, MS Windows	C++, Java, C#, Python (C++, Java)	Programming language developed by MathWorks, primarily intended for numerical computation, but has extensive symbolic computing abilities with extensive support for machine learning https://www.mathworks.com/
MXNet (Apache 2.0)	Linux, Mac OS X, AWS, iOS, Android, MS Windows	C++, Python, Matlab, Go, Scala, Julia, JavaScript, R (C++)	Allows you to define, train and deploy deep neural networks https://mxnet.io
Neural Designer (Proprietary)	Linux, Mac OS X, MS Windows	Graphical user Interface (C++)	Software tool for data analytics based on neural networks http://neuraldesigner.com
Nengo (Custom)	Linux, Mac OS X, MS Windows	Python, Java, OpenCL, (Java)	Free for personal use, but licensing required for commercial purposes. Runs on neuromorphic hardware - SpinNaker http://nengo.ca
OpenNN (GNU LGPL)	Cross-platform	C++ (C++)	OpenNN (not to be confused with OpenAI) is a C++ library that implements neural networks http://www.opennn.net

(continued)

Table A.2   (continued)

Software (license type)	Operating systems	Interface (language used to implement)	Comments/URL
RNNLIB (GNU GPLv3)	Linux, Mac OSX	C++ (C++, Python)	It is a recurrent neural network library for sequence learning problems https://sourceforge.net/projects/rnnl
TensorFlow (Apache 2.0)	Linux, Mac OS X, MS Windows	Python, C++, Java, Go, Haskell (C++)	Open source library for computation using data flow graphs for scalable machine learning, originally developed by the Google Brain team at Google.Runs on many kinds of CPUs, GPUs and the new TPU from Google https://www.tensorflow.org/
Theano (BSD License)	Cross-platform	Python (Python)	A Python framework for fast computation of mathematical expressions http://deeplearning.net/software/theano
Torch (BSD License)	Linux, Mac OS X, Android, iOS MS Windows	C via LuaJIT (C, Lua)	A utility framework for C++/OpenCL (has an underlying C/CUDA implementation) with wide support for machine learning algorithms http://torch.ch
Weka 3 (GNU GPL3)	Linux, Mac OS X, MS Windows	C#, Groovy, Java, Python (with limitations) (Java)	A collection of machine learning algorithms mainly focused on data mining kinds of tasks http://www.cs.waikato.ac.nz/ml/weka
Wolfram Mathematica (Proprietary)	MS Windows, Mac OS X, Linux	Java, C++, OpenCL, CUDA (C++)	A full mathematical symbolic computation software, that includes support for machine learning algorithms http://www.wolfram.com/mathematica

Index

© The Editor(s) (if applicable) and The Author(s) 2018
M. Skilton and F. Hovsepian, *The 4th Industrial Revolution*,
https://doi.org/10.1007/978-3-319-62479-2